Standard Practical Plumbing

STANDARD
PRACTICAL
PLUMBING

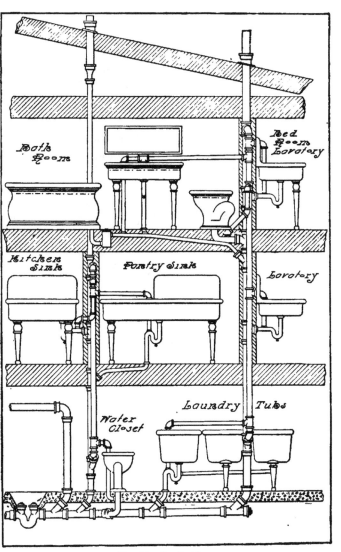

Plumbing for Residence.

STANDARD
PRACTICAL
PLUMBING

AN EXHAUSTIVE TREATISE ON ALL BRANCHES OF

PLUMBING CONSTRUCTION

INCLUDING

DRAINAGE AND VENTING, VENTILATION, HOT AND
COLD WATER SUPPLY AND CIRCULATION

THE WORK SHOWS THE LATEST AND BEST PLUMBING
PRACTICE, SPECIAL ATTENTION BEING GIVEN TO THE
SKILLED WORK OF THE PLUMBER, AND TO THE THEORY
UNDERLYING PLUMBING DEVICES AND OPERATIONS

By R. M. STARBUCK

Author of "Practical Wrinkles for the Plumber,"
"Modern Plumbing Illustrated"

A SPECIAL FEATURE: 347 ORIGINAL ILLUSTRATIONS, EACH
ONE BEING DRAWN EXPRESSLY FOR THIS WORK

NEW YORK

The Norman W. Henley Publishing Company

132 NASSAU STREET

1910

THE TROW PRESS, NEW YORK

PREFACE

In general, the writing of works such as that which the author herewith presents, is accompanied by several features the effect of which is to materially lessen the excellent results which such a work should produce.

One of the errors to which we allude, is the tendency of the author on trade subjects to write in too technical a manner, that is, to handle his subject in such a manner that none but the most educated of his readers are able to thoroughly grasp the principles presented.

For instance, since the plumber is seldom to be found who can handle an algebraic equation, it would certainly seem far better to present a necessary principle by means of arithmetic rather than by means of algebra, and if there is no other way than by means of algebra the author should see to it that he fully explains the entire operation at length, in such a manner that the reader who has not had the advantage of instruction in such branches may be able to grasp the subject. In other words, the author should stand in the same position to his readers that the teacher does to his pupils. It is his duty to honestly instruct, and not merely to fill his pages with facts which, though valuable, are presented in such a manner as not to be easily understood by the average reader.

A second serious though unintentional error on the part of many authors is the omission of minor details. While to the author, who is naturally a man of experience and education in his special line of work, the statement of simple, and to him obvious, facts seems a matter of foolishness, ofttimes, to many of his younger and more inexperienced readers, the statement of these simple things is a matter of utmost importance, and a means of establishing the main principle more strongly in their minds.

The author of this work frankly confesses to surprise at the absence of knowledge of rudiments which he knows from long

11

experience to exist, and, knowing that this condition does exist, has no apology to offer for the statement of various facts in his writings which certainly should be known and understood. Indeed, it is his firm belief that one of the chief factors in obtaining whatever success has come to him in his line of work, is the fact that he has never hesitated to give the minor details and to state simple facts. Certainly if these are not thoroughly understood, the main subject under consideration cannot possibly be digested as thoroughly as it should be.

A third defect that often creeps into trade text books is the lack of systematic treatment of the various subjects considered.

A book so written cannot give to the reader as clear an understanding as a work which takes up the various subjects in proper order. By this we do not mean to infer that there is only one order that may be properly followed, but merely to emphasize the fact that the mere statement of facts is not sufficient. There must be a proper order.

Knowing the tendency toward these errors the author has honestly endeavored to avoid them, and to give his readers such information as will be of practical use to them.

THE AUTHOR.

November, 1910.

CONTENTS

CONTENTS

INTRODUCTION

THE intention of the author in presenting this work has been to produce something in the nature of a text book, which should not only appeal to the beginner as a book of instruction, but to his more advanced brother as a book of reference, as comprehensive as our allotted space would allow.

Starting then, with the consideration of the tools of the plumber, the author has in his earlier pages taken up briefly the subject of the manual work of the plumber, following which come several chapters on the various phases of trapping, venting and drainage. This is followed by chapters on certain important classes of plumbing construction. The latter part of the work is devoted to the general subject of hot and cold water supply, and to several special subjects, including a chapter on mechanical drawing, which is especially designed to meet the requirements of the plumber.

As generally applied to-day, the word "plumbing" includes not only the drainage and vent systems, which in reality are parts of the same system, but also the water supply, both hot and cold water piping. Originally by the word "plumber," was meant a lead worker, but the common significance of the term is now entirely different.

Many of the workmen of large firms doing plumbing construction are specialists along certain lines of their trade, but in general, the present-day plumber is required to understand and work at both branches of his trade. It therefore becomes necessary in any comprehensive treatise on the subject of plumbing, to consider both the drainage and water supply systems.

Both these systems have in the past undergone great changes, and are at the present time undergoing change. In general these changes mark great progress, and while it is difficult to see how plumbing construction can be perfected much beyond the point which it has now reached in some sections of the country, it is

15

entirely in the nature of things to look for still further improvement. In conjunction with such improvement, we believe that a less complicated system is to be the result, and the attainment of such a result should be looked upon with favor.

In the interest of improved plumbing, the author takes the liberty of calling special attention to the merits of what is known as " continuous venting." It is his firm conviction that the universal adoption of this system of venting would mark one of the greatest strides forward that has ever been taken in plumbing construction.

These final remarks are made, as the author believes, for the best good of the plumbing fraternity, a body of men with whom he has been closely affiliated for many years, and among whom he is glad to count many friends.

STANDARD PRACTICAL PLUMBING

CHAPTER I

THE PLUMBER'S TOOLS

THE tools which the plumber is now called upon to use in connection with his work are of quite different nature to those used previous to the advent of the present methods of construction.

This change is due, in the first place, to the fact that the plumber is now provided with manufactured lead traps, bends, offsets, etc., and it is no longer necessary for him to make these things himself.

Furthermore, it is a fact that the use of lead for all purposes of plumbing construction, whether on the drainage system or vent system, in the installation of fixtures, or in the lining of tanks and safes, has been, and is being, superseded by the use of other materials.

To be sure, it is principally on large work in the larger cities that lead work has been entirely given up, but the tendency is strongly that way on smaller work in all parts of the country.

It is the purpose of this chapter to explain the uses of some of the more important tools, to give some advice as to the selection of proper tools, and to show the advantages of certain tools of recent construction.

The plumber's " kit " should include the following tools: Gas pliers, pocket pliers, screwdriver, compasses, rasp, file, saw, compass saw, rule, tape, plumb bob, hammer, monkey wrench, bit brace and bits, pointed copper, hatchet copper, rosin and grease box, spirit level, $2\frac{1}{2}$-in. and $3\frac{1}{2}$-in. ladles, pothook, tap borer, bending pin, turn pins Nos. 1, 2, and 3, 1-in., $1\frac{1}{4}$-in., $1\frac{1}{2}$-in., and 2-in. drift plugs, shave hook, dresser, small mirror, wiping cloths, 1-in., $1\frac{1}{4}$-in., $1\frac{1}{2}$-in., and 2-in. sand plugs, cold chisels, calking tools, joint runner, 1-in., $1\frac{1}{4}$-in., $1\frac{1}{2}$-in., and 2-in. bending springs, lead-pipe cutter, and 10-in. and 14-in. pipe wrench. A more complete kit may contain numerous other tools, such as chipping knife,

The plumber is used for lifting pots of hot metal.

The plumber uses a bending pin for throwing up an edge on lead pipe in preparing it for wiping. For instance, in wiping a pipe onto a drain trap, a hole is cut into the side of the trap of less diameter than desired, and by means of the bending pin the metal outside the hole is beaten out to form a collar into which the pipe may fit, the collar then being beaten close down to the pipe. The bending pin would be used in the same way for connecting a branch into a lead pipe. There are three styles in use, as shown in the illustration, the use of the different forms being a matter of taste of the workman. The form having one end bent and the other straight is probably mostly used.

The tap borer is used in boring a hole of any size into the side

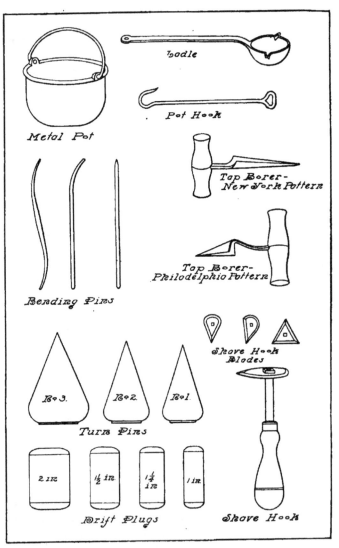

Fig. 1.—A Few of the Plumber's Tools.

of a lead pipe. Such a hole may be made entirely with the tap borer, or it may be started first with a bit. The latter is usually the preferable method, as on heavy lead pipe it is slow work getting the hole started, and so much pressure is necessary that light pipe is in danger of being crushed. The tap borer is made in two styles, the New York pattern being long and sharply tapered, and the Philadelphia pattern short, with a taper less sharp.

Ratchet tap borers are also used to a considerable extent.

Turn pins are necessary in expanding or flaring the ends of lead pipe. The plumber generally requires three sizes, Nos. 1, 2, and 3. Turn pins should be made of boxwood, dogwood, or lignum vitæ.

The shave hook, as its name indicates, is used for shaving off the oxidized surface of lead pipe, in order to obtain a bright surface. This is always a necessary operation, as solder will not adhere to any but a clean, bright surface, free from all oxidation. Shave-hook blades are made in three styles, as shown in illustration—oval, half oval, and triangular.

The selection of the form of shave-hook blade is a matter of taste on the part of the workman, although the oval pattern is probably mostly used.

Drift plugs are used for forcing through lead pipe to take out any dents or uneven places in the pipe, and are made in the diameters of the bores of the several sizes of lead pipe. The material of which drift plugs are made is the same as for turn pins, either boxwood, dogwood, or lignum vitæ.

In Fig. 2 are shown other tools which the plumber commonly uses.

The dresser is a tool used in shaping and smoothing up lead pipe and sheet lead.

Most dressers manufactured and sold are of hard wood, but many plumbers prefer to make their own of soft wood. The softwood dresser does not mar the lead as the hard wood does.

The bending of lead pipe is done in several ways, one of which is by the use of sand.

The pipe is filled with sand and the ends securely plugged, after which the pipe at the bending point is heated slightly, in which condition, if the sand is closely packed, a very perfect bend

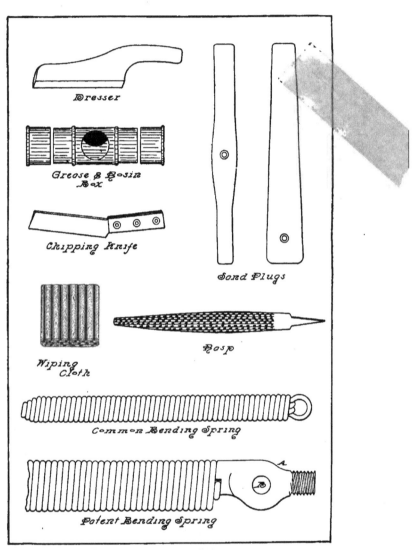

Fig. 2.—A Few of the Plumber's Tools.

may be made. The sand plugs shown in illustration are used for plugging the ends of pipe to be bent in this manner. These plugs are made in two styles, as shown.

The grease and rosin box is a device which is to be found in most plumbers' kits.

When rosin, grease, etc., are not kept in some such receptacle they become scattered among the tools, and are not only hard to find when needed, but adhere to the tools and get them into dirty condition.

The chipping knife is used for chipping off the uneven thin edges of wiped joints.

The upper side of the blade is made thick, so that it may be struck with the hammer.

The wiping cloth is used in making wiped joints. When the molten metal has been poured onto the pipe, and has finally reached the right consistency, the workman works the mass of metal with his wiping cloth into the form of the symmetrical wiped joint.

There are two kinds of wiping cloths, ticking and moleskin. The latter is the more expensive, but not necessarily the preferable style, as ticking wiping cloths are preferred by many plumbers. The best ticking wiping cloths are made of a high grade of herringbone bed ticking. When properly made, a ticking wiping cloth is of 16-ply, that is, 16 thicknesses. Ticking wiping cloths may be folded so that the grain of the cloth will run lengthwise or crosswise of the cloth. Most plumbers prefer their cloths made in the former manner, although many use the cross-grain cloth. In Fig. 3 is shown the proper method of folding wiping cloths, both ticking and moleskin. No. 1 shows the shape and proportions of the cloth from which the wiping cloth shown in Nos. 2, 3, 4, and 5 is to be made. The dotted lines show the creases or folds in the cloth after it has been made up.

No. 2 illustrates the first operation, which consists in folding the two edges of the cloth to the center of the piece of ticking, and No. 3 the second operation of folding from the center to the side. The partly folded cloth is then reversed, as shown in No. 4, and the two narrow ends folded over so that they meet in the center. No. 5 shows the final fold.

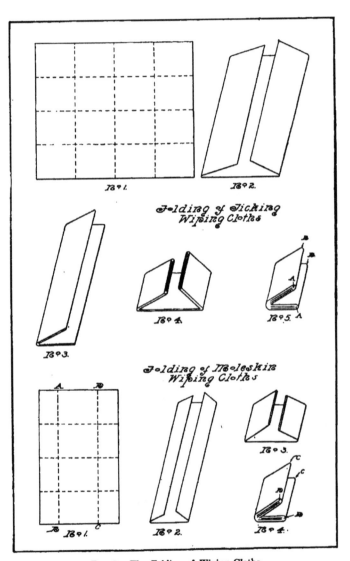

Fig. 3.—The Folding of Wiping Cloths.

After completing the folding, the cloth should be secured at the points A A·and B B. This is done by taking several stitches with needle and thread in such a way that the thread is not exposed on the wiping edge.

In Fig. 3, No. 1 at the foot of the page shows the proportions for a moleskin wiping cloth of the same size as the ticking cloth already described. From a comparison of the wiping cloths of the two materials it will be seen that the area of moleskin required is only half that required of ticking.

The reason for this is that the moleskin is so heavy that if made 16-ply it would be too thick. However, in order to give firmness to the cloth, it is well to paste onto it, in folding, one thickness of stout paper. This paper should be of the size and cover the area shown by A B C D. If paper is used, the two sides should be folded over, as shown in No. 2, and the two edges pasted to the paper, and the moisture allowed to dry out under a slight pressure before proceeding with the folding. No. 3 shows the second operation, and No. 4 the third and last, after which the corners of the cloth should be secured as in the case of the ticking cloth.

After completing the number of wiping cloths required, it is a good plan to grease them with hot grease and then put them under a heavy pressure for about twenty-four hours. When this is done they will hold their shape to much better advantage.

Most plumbers use mutton tallow on their wiping cloths, which aids very materially in the working of the cloth in wiping joints, and, indeed, the workman is usually much averse to parting with an old and long-used wiping cloth, as it has become thoroughly saturated with grease, smooth, and free from any fuzz that a new cloth is bound to show. Special preparations are on the market for greasing wiping cloths, which produce excellent results.

To those who make their own wiping cloths the following table of sizes will be of value. In the first column is given the size of the completed wiping cloth, the first-named dimension being that. of the wiping edge.

The figures in the second column show the dimensions of cloth to be cut for the several sizes.

Sizes of Ticking Wiping Cloths

Size of Wiping Cloth	Necessary Dimensions of Ticking
4 in. × 4 in.	16 in. × 16 in.
3½ " × 3½ "	14 " × 14 "
3¼ " × 3¼ "	13 " × 13 "
3 " × 3½ "	12 " × 14 "
3 " × 3 "	12 " × 12 "
2¾ " × 3 "	11 " × 12 "
2½ " × 3 "	10 " × 12 "
2½ " × 2½ "	10 " × 10 "
2¼ " × 3 "	9 " × 12 "
2 " × 3 "	8 " × 12 "
1½ " × 3 "	6 " × 12 "

Sizes of Moleskin Wiping Cloths

Size of Wiping Cloth	Necessary Dimensions of Moleskin
4 in. × 4 in.	16 in. × 8 in.
3½ " × 3½ "	14 " × 7 "
3¼ " × 3¼ "	13 " × 6½ "
3 " × 3½ "	12 " × 7 "
3 " × 3 "	12 " × 6 "
2¾ " × 3 "	11 " × 6 "
2½ " × 3 "	10 " × 6 "
2½ " × 2½ "	10 " × 5 "
2¼ " × 3 "	9 " × 6 "
2 " × 3 "	8 " × 6 "
1½ " × 3 "	6 " × 6 "

The quarter- and three-quarter-inch sizes are not standard sizes, and therefore not generally carried in stock, although many plumbers claim that they must have cloths of these odd dimensions. It is difficult to name any complete set of wiping cloths, as one plumber will often require different sizes than another workman, and also because of the variation in size of joints made in different sections of the country.

Ordinarily, however, a set of wiping cloths complete enough for the workman would include the following cloths: 4 in. × 4 in., 3¼ in. × 3½ in., 3 in. × 3 in., 2½ in. × 3 in., 2 in. × 3 in., 1½ in. × 3 in., the latter being of the flange pattern, with the rounded wiping edge.

To return to Fig. 2, the rasp shown is a necessary tool in the work of the plumber.

This should be an ordinary coarse wood rasp, and is used for such purposes as beveling or tapering the ends of lead pipes.

In recent years the bending of lead pipes has been largely accomplished by the use of bending springs, instead of by the old-time methods which were not only slow but required a considerable amount of skill.

These springs are made to fit into the bore of the lead pipe, when the latter may be bent without danger of collapsing, after which the spring may be withdrawn.

These springs are often damaged in withdrawing them from pipes, owing to the fact that attempts are sometimes made to pull them out. The spring should be wound up, thus decreasing its diameter sufficiently to allow its easy withdrawal. Turning the spring so that it unwinds is a very bad practice also.

Recently a patented bending spring has appeared on the market, which has several features which make it superior to the common spring. The spring is firmly secured to a malleable iron head A, as shown in Fig. 2, this head being provided with a hole B, and at its end with a half inch pipe thread. Through the hole a piece of pipe may be thrust, and used as a lever to wind up the spring in withdrawing it. A half-inch pipe may be screwed to the end of the spring, and by means of it, withdrawn from the pipe after the bend has been made. This attachment allows a bend to be made at any distance from the end of the pipe, whereas in the use of the common bending spring, any bend made at a distance from the end of the pipe greater than the length of the spring, could be made only with much difficulty and waste of time.

The hammer is a tool concerning which the plumber is usually very particular; especially in his use of it in calking cast-iron pipe. In Fig. 4 are shown several styles of hammer used by the plumber. The hammer shown in No. 4 is generally advertised as a plumber's hammer, but is not used so extensively as the other styles shown, which are known as machinist's hammers. Nos. 1 and 2 are very commonly used. No. 3 has the advantage of having the same face on either end, which is regarded as a desirable feature by many workmen, as the hammer never needs to be turned around to get the striking face in the right position. Hammers are made in the following weights: 1 lb., $1\frac{1}{4}$ lb., $1\frac{1}{2}$ lb., $1\frac{3}{4}$ lb., 2 lb., $2\frac{1}{2}$ lb., and 3 lb., the weight usually being marked on the end of the handle. This weight is exclusive of the handle. The 1-lb.

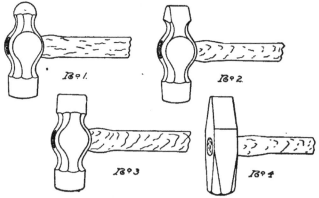

FIG. 4.—Plumbers' Hammers.

hammer is too light for the plumber's use; the $1\frac{1}{4}$-lb. weight is about right for calking, although $1\frac{1}{2}$-lb. hammers are often used; $1\frac{1}{2}$-lb., $1\frac{3}{4}$-lb., and 2-lb. hammers are used for cutting extra heavy pipe. The plumber ordinarily requires two hammers: one for calking and another for cutting. The heavier weights of hammers are used chiefly in the calking and cutting of large extra-heavy cast-iron pipe on water mains, and similar heavy work.

Calking tools, which are indispensable to the plumber, are tools concerning which he is especially particular. Each workman generally has his own particular ideas as to the calking tools that meet his desires. So true is this, that many workmen have their calking tools made to order, instead of obtaining tools ordinarily carried in stock.

These tools are made in great variety, and the workman who does his work to best advantage must be provided with a considerable number of them, most of which are designed for use in special places, or under special conditions.

These tools may be obtained ground for inside or outside calking.

In Fig. 5 are to be seen various styles of calking tools, some of which may not have been previously seen by all of our readers.

The plumber's cold chisels are of numerous variety, ranging from an 18-in. brick chisel to very small styles.

B represents a blunt cold chisel much used in cutting soil pipe, which is not so easily gotten out of order as the thinner and sharper chisels, such as A. C, D, and E represent different styles of regular calking tools, having blades of different lengths and thickness. F is known as a throat iron, and is very useful in calking such fittings as bends, where there is little room for a direct blow. G and H represent right- and left-hand offset calking tools. It often happens that lines of soil pipe are run in corners, and it is clearly seen that tools of this description are very useful in calking the part of the joint that is on the back side of the pipe. K is another tool for the same purpose.

L is a picking-out chisel, used in picking out the lead of a calked joint, its shape being such that the work may be done to advantage.

M is a stub-calking iron with which almost a direct blow can be given, and of greater force than can be gotten with the regular calking irons, as there is no springing of the tool.

N and O represent yarning irons, the former stiff, and the latter having a spring blade. They are used in forcing the oakum into place, one tool being preferred by some workmen, and the other by others. P is known as a ceiling iron, and is used in calking joints in such positions that a downward blow cannot be delivered in the usual manner. A joint very close to the ceiling, for instance, may be made with this tool, the blow of the hammer being delivered on the offset near the handle.

W, in Fig. 6, represents a special form of yarning iron, having but one offset, which many workmen find preferable to other styles.

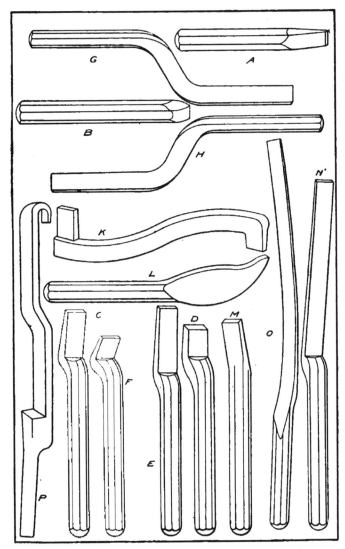

FIG. 5.—Various Styles of Calking Tools

The other tools in this illustration are special forms of chisels, which will be found very useful to the plumber.

R is a hammer head chisel and S a hammer head gouge, both of which are used in such work as cutting through floors, timbers, etc., and should be ground and tempered to withstand as well as possible the striking of nails and similar rough usage.

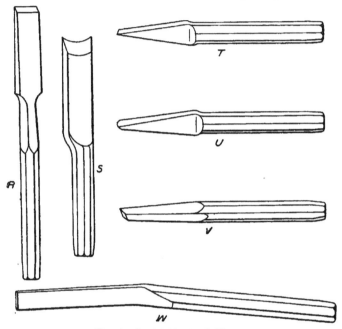

Fig. 6.—Special Plumbers' Chisels.

These tools will be found preferable for hard usage to the common wooden-handled chisels. The three tools shown by T, U, and V, are respectively cape and half-round cape chisel, and diamond point chisel.

A very important feature in the making of calking tools is the forming of them in such a manner that they shall be rigid under a blow, with as little spring as possible. In offset tools, for instance, the offset should be as straight as possible, as a sharp offset will make the tool spring, and often render it unfit for use. This is one of the chief objections to calking tools handled by most jobbers of such goods.

There are many other varieties of special calking tools and chisels which might be mentioned, but those already described constitute the principal types of such tools.

In Fig. 7 are shown several special plumber's tools, some of which are of comparatively recent origin, while others have been in common use for many years.

The 5-wheel lead pipe cutter is a tool well-known and highly valued. The only point against it is that it will not cut larger than $1\frac{1}{2}$-inch pipe. This is a point which the 4-wheel cutter shown in the illustration overcomes, a point of considerable importance nowadays, as the use of two-inch pipe is constantly increasing, as it is a size which is being more extensively used on waste lines for such fixtures as kitchen sinks, laundry tubs, etc.

The lead pipe expanding pliers is a tool which has been devised to do the work of the several sizes of turn pins. By pressing the lever handles together, the conical end opens and spreads the pipe. The end of the cone is knurled, which tends to prevent the expanding cone from slipping out of the end of a heavy pipe in expanding it.

It will be seen that as the cone opens, it forms an·ellipse instead of a true circle, and to make the expanded end of the pipe perfectly round, the expander must be constantly turned as it is being used.

The asbestos joint runner is a most valuable tool to the plumber, although, strange to say, there are many plumbers who do not possess the tool, and still adhere to the old methods of using clay, putty, oakum, etc., in making calked joints.

As the illustration shows, the asbestos rope is wound around the pipe, both ends bent back, and secured by the clamp, allowing a triangular opening into which the metal may be poured. On vertical joints the use of the joint runner is not necessary, but on horizontal joints it is of great service in preventing the escape of the molten lead when it is poured into the hub.

The brass pipe wrench is to-day a necessity with the plumber who desires to put up neat brass and nickel work. As shown in

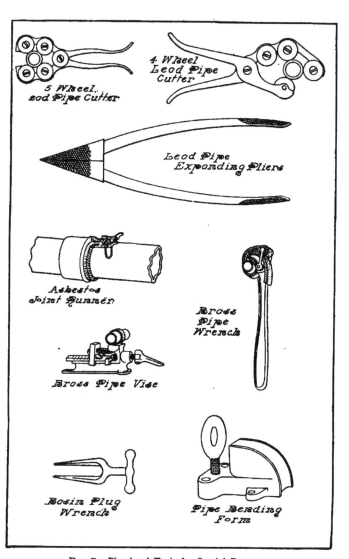

FIG. 7.—Plumbers' Tools for Special Purposes.

illustration, the wrench is arranged for brass tubing, the curve in the head of the wrench preventing the crushing of the tubing. When being used on brass pipe, the strain comes on the nose of the wrench or near the point. The grip is made by means of a stout band or strap made of heavy ducking, by means of which a powerful grip may be secured without marring or scratching the pipe, as would result in the use of a common pipe wrench. To make the strap work properly, it should be rosined.

The brass pipe vise operates in a similar manner by the use of a rosined strap of ducking. When such a vise is not at hand, brass and nickel pipe may be held without scratching by means of

FIG. 8.—Wooden Vise Blocks for Holding Brass Pipe.

wooden blocks, as shown in Fig. 8, a separate block being used for each size of pipe.

These blocks may be made by boring a hole of the right size through a split block, and then planing the surfaces that come together slightly, so that the surfaces will not meet when held in the vise.

The basin plug wrench is a simple but very handy device. It is used for preventing the turning of the bowl plug of a wash basin when the locknut underneath is being set up, and also for holding the plug when it is to be disconnected. The plumber often has trouble in holding the plug from turning, and in many cases has been known to use his dividers to do the work of the wrench, usually springing and otherwise damaging them.

The pipe-bending form is of cast iron, screwed to the work bench or to a plank, and is used in making bends on wrought iron, brass, and lead pipe. By adjusting the eye bolt to the work, the bending may be easily accomplished.

There are many tools which the plumber usually has in his kit, or the employer owns, which are not shown in the accompanying illustrations. Most of the fundamental and most necessary tools have been shown, however, and briefly described, and at various other points certain other tools will be mentioned.

CHAPTER II

WIPING SOLDER—ITS COMPOSITION AND USE

SOLDER, such as used by the plumber, is composed of lead and tin.

The proportions in which these two metals are used vary considerably with the use to which it is to be put.

The plumber requires both bright solder and wiping solder, the proper consistency of the latter being a matter of great importance to him in the making of wiped joints. Bright solder is made of one part lead and one part tin.

The proportions for wiping solder are not so definite as for bright solder, as different workmen are accustomed to different degrees of fineness in their wiping solder. In general, however, the proportions may be laid down as three parts of lead and two parts of tin. Ten parts of lead and six parts of tin is a proportion sometimes used. Many of the best workmen make their own wiping solder, such a course enabling them to obtain solder that is suited to their individual requirements.

Nothing but the purest grades of lead and block tin should be used.

A test used by some plumbers to prove wiping solder, is to pour a small quantity of the melted metal onto a cold surface, when, if it is of about the right quality, it will have when cool a mottled appearance.

If it is too coarse—that is, if it has too much lead, it will have a granular appearance. If it is too fine—that is, if it has too much tin, it will have a very bright appearance.

While lead melts at about 612 degrees and tin at 442, the melting point of wiping solder is about 450 degrees, and of bright solder about 375 degrees.

There are certain substances which act very injuriously to wiping solder.

For instance, the presence in a pot of wiping solder of a very small amount of zinc, will make it entirely unfit for use.

Antimony and iron are also injurious.

The greatest amount of trouble, however, arises from the presence of zinc, for this metal is used extensively in the manufacture of plumber's brass work, such as bibbs, ferrules, nipples, solder unions, etc., and in wiping these fittings onto lead pipes, more or less of the zinc is taken up by the solder. This is especially true in the use of the cheaper grades of ferrules and nipples, which often contain large amounts of zinc. It is a customary practice of the plumber to dip his brass work into the wiping solder, in order to tin it, and this is one of the quickest ways in which the solder may be spoiled.

The experienced plumber can usually tell very quickly whether there is zinc in his wiping solder, as it works up roughly and crystallizes in a different manner than good solder. Solder is also often damaged by carelessly overheating it. This burns out the tin and leaves the solder coarse.

When impurities are known to be present, the solder may be purified in the following manner: Heat the solder red hot in the first place. If the solder is heated so as to appear red hot in the light, it is too hot, and should be heated only so that it shows a faint red in the dark. When this heat has been reached, throw into the solder a lump of sulphur, which will mix with the impurities of the solder when it is stirred, and carry them to the surface. Any oxidized tin or lead formed in overheating will also separate out in the form of a powder and rise to the surface. The impurities should be thoroughly skimmed off with the ladle, and after the solder has somewhat cooled, it is well to throw in some tallow, which will liberate the sulphur, and also a lump of rosin, which will further improve it.

After this refining process has been completed, the metal will usually be too coarse, owing to the burning out of some of the tin. Therefore the solder should be tempered with new metal until it has regained its right consistency.

When wiping solder is being used it should be stirred occasionally, in order to thoroughly mix the lead and tin, for the latter being the lighter, tends to rise to the top.

CHAPTER III

JOINT WIPING

THE art of making wiped solder joints is acquired only by experience, and written instructions concerning the subject amount to but little. To be able to make the various forms of wiped joints in a perfect manner is the ambition of the young plumber, and it may be said that comparatively few actually reach a high standard in this branch of the work.

In modern plumbing construction the use of lead and solder is very limited, for the reason that the employment of lead for nearly all purposes in plumbing construction has been replaced by the use of other materials.

Indeed, the use of lead is now very largely confined to short lengths of lead waste and vent pipe, and in a great deal of work no lead whatever is used. This is a great change from the conditions that obtained years ago, when the older plumbers of to-day were working at their trade. In those days, all traps, bends, etc., and even soil pipe, were made of lead, and made by the workman himself. In addition, lead was used entirely for the lining of tanks; lead safes were extensively used, and a large amount of ornamental lead work was constructed. It is not strange, therefore, that skill in the manipulation of lead and solder has declined greatly in recent years, and indeed, it may be said that the skill in this line of work formerly required is no longer a necessity.

The reason for the use of the wiped joint is that this form of joint is stronger than other forms, and presents a better appearance.

The wiped joint should be symmetrical, both to secure uniform strength and neat appearance. The two illustrations shown in Fig. 9, show poorly constructed joints.

Wiped joints are made in a variety of shapes and sizes. In some sections of the country, it is customary to wipe a short, thick joint, while in others, long, thin joints are made. Joints excessively long or excessively short are unsatisfactory. If solder is to be economized, it is better to make the saving in length, rather than in thickness, for a short, thick joint has greater strength than a long, slender joint. The strength of a wiped joint depends not only upon the amount of solder used, but upon the quality of the solder. A joint may be well wiped and of symmetrical shape, and

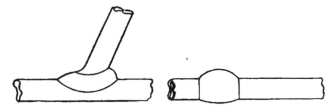

Fig. 9.—Poorly Shaped Wiped Joints.

still be a poor joint, owing to its being porous. When porous, the joint will "sweat" as it is termed, that is, drops of water will ooze through the solder. This is caused by the poor condition of the solder, due usually to a lack of the proper amount of tin. Solder when made of the proper proportions of lead and tin is much stronger than the lead, and it is the tin that gives the solder its strength by cementing the mass of metal together.

In Fig. 10, several kinds of wiped joints are shown, also the method of preparing the lead pipes which are to be joined together by the joint.

The simplest joint is the round joint of Nos. 1 and 2. This joint may be wiped upright or underhand, that is, horizontally.

Nos. 1 and 2 in Fig. 10, show two different methods of preparing the pipe. In No. 1 the female end of the pipe is prepared with the tap borer or the rasp. If the latter is used, care should be exercised to prevent the inside of the pipe from being roughed up by the striking of the end of the rasp against it. The male end is then rasped off to fit the female end.

In the case of No. 2, which is preferable to No. 1, the female end is flared out with the turn pin, the inside surface being shaved to give a clean, bright surface. It is essential that the two surfaces

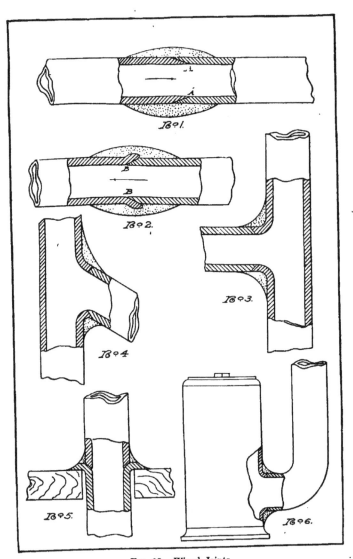

Fig. 10.—Wiped Joints.

that fit together should be bright and free from all tarnishing, in order that the solder may adhere and make a perfect joint between the two pipes.

The next step is to shave off the surface of each pipe lengthwise, as far as the joint is to extend, this being done with the shave hook.

All burrs or rough edges should be made smooth. A very important feature is to join the two pipes together in such a way that anything flowing through the pipe when it is in use, shall have the least possible opportunity to catch on the inside or male end.

Thus, in Nos. 1 and 2, any lint or other material in the waste, would have less opportunity to catch at A A and B B if flowing in the direction of the arrows, than if flowing in an opposite direction. In making a perfect joint, the solder should be able to penetrate into the joint between the two pipes, but it should not be allowed to penetrate into the interior of the pipe, where it would form in sharp points which would catch and hold matter flowing through the pipe.

Before the joint is ready to be wiped, the surface of the pipe beyond the joint and on both sides of it, should be protected, so that the solder may not adhere to it at any point beyond the joint. This may be done in several ways. The universal, old-style method was by means of soil, the soil being allowed to remain on the pipe after the work was completed, it being considered ornamental. The use of soil is practiced to quite an extent even now, but its use is decreasing. Soil is made of lampblack and glue, and when properly made, should stand the following test: Apply the soil to a piece of lead pipe, and allow it to dry. If the lampblack rubs off, it shows too much of this material. If, when the pipe is bent, the soil cracks and breaks off, it shows too large an amount of glue. It may be tempered to stand both these tests.

Fig. 11 shows a round joint and a branch joint set up, ready for wiping, with soil applied.

Another method of preventing the adhesion of solder outside the joint, is by means of paper pasted onto the pipe. The paper covers the same surfaces that are shown covered with soil in Fig. 11. In the case of the round joint it is a simple matter to put on the papers, but in branch joints and other joints of irregular shape, it is often a difficult matter to cut the paper in the proper shape. Another disadvantage in the use of this method is that sometimes the paper is poorly pasted, or poor paste is used, and the solder works under and sticks.

The most up-to-date method, and one which is being rapidly adopted by plumbers, is the use of plumber's paste. This paste when heated, forms a sort of enamel coating over the surface of the pipe. It bakes onto the pipe and does not flake off, protecting the pipe perfectly and being easily washed off when the work is complete. Only specially prepared paste will answer for this work,

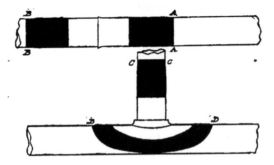

Fig. 11.—Joints Prepared with Soil, Ready to be Wiped.

as common pastes will cook and flake off. The use of paste for this purpose accomplishes good results with less labor than either soil or paper. In the use of soil, it is applied before the pipe is shaved. Referring to Fig. 11, it will be seen that the soil must be applied to make a sharp line at A A, B B, C C, and around the outer curve D D, but inside these lines it may be applied without care, as these surfaces are to be shaved.

The round joint, the preparation of which has been described, is now ready to be set up and wiped. A common method of holding the work in position for wiping is shown in Fig. 12. The plumber will often support his work on bricks, and hold it in position by means of them, and, indeed, many workmen prefer this method to the use of special devices for this purpose. There are many devices on the market, however, designed to hold the work in position, one of these being shown in Fig. 13. In wiping a branch joint, a third pipe holder may be used to hold the branch pipe in position. The use of the pipe holders will be clearly seen. They are driven into the work bench or into a plank, and by means

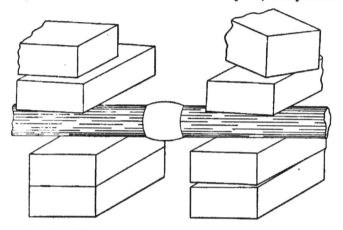

Fig. 12.—A Common Method of Holding Pipes for Wiping Joints.

of the slotted upright piece the work can be held at any height or at any desired angle. There are no bricks or other obstructions to

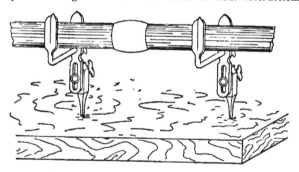

Fig. 13.—Use of Pipe Holders in Wiping Joints.

get in the way of the workman, and there is less liability that the work may become dislodged.

As already stated, it is an impossibility for the novice to learn the art of joint wiping from books. He must practice under the direction of some person who understands such work. There are certain suggestions which can be made, however, which will be of much value to the beginner. After the work has been set up, place a large piece of paper underneath it to catch the solder. The next thing is to be sure that the solder is at the right heat. A very good method of testing it, is to thrust into the molten solder a shaving or a piece of paper rolled up.

If the shaving or paper takes fire, the metal is too hot, but if the material chars quickly, the solder is right to use. Some experienced plumbers can tell the condition of the solder by holding the ladle in the solder until it is of the same temperature, and then quickly holding it to his cheek. This test, however, requires experience. When sure that the solder is at the right heat, take the ladle in the right hand and fill it about three quarters full.

Pour the solder onto the joint very lightly at first, so that it may not burn through.

Move the ladle backward and forward, pouring over the entire surface, and even out beyond the joint at either end, in order to heat the pipe thoroughly, and to a temperature of the same degree as the solder. This is a very important part of the work, cannot be hurried, and is a point not often fully appreciated by the beginner. Continue pouring, and with the catch cloth in the left hand under the joint, catch the solder as it falls off, and throw it back onto the joint.

Gradually the solder becomes soft yet firm, and when it has reached this condition, get the joint roughly into the shape required. Then, quickly laying down the ladle, take the wiping cloth in the right hand and form the joint as desired. It is almost useless to attempt to explain this last operation.

Some workmen use two wiping cloths in wiping a joint, while others use only one.

A very important point is to wipe the thin edges quickly, as the metal cools at these points almost immediately, and if this is allowed to happen, a good joint cannot be wiped. When the joint is nearly formed, attention must be given especially to the bottom of the joint. The heat of the joint will usually cause the solder to run off at this point, and the workman must with his cloth, prevent this, and prevent the joint from getting out of shape at this point. While the solder is being poured onto the joint and the latter is being brought to the right heat, the wiping cloths should be heating, so that when needed they shall not be cold.

If the solder sticks to the cloth, it shows that there is too much tin in the solder.

If there is too much tin the solder will tend to run off from the bottom and make it almost impossible to wipe a perfect joint. It

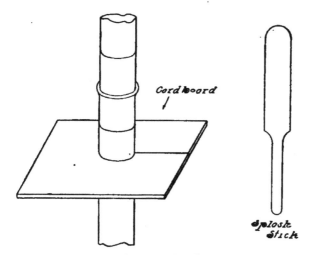

Cord board

Splosh Stick

Fig. 14.—Wiping of Upright Joints.

is well to rub onto the cloth a little whiting or powdered chalk to prevent scratching. It is also necessary to grease the cloth with tallow, which makes it work more smoothly, and acts as a flux for the solder. Grease should also be applied to the lead work as soon as it has been shaved, in order to prevent the surfaces from oxidizing. This action takes place quickly after the lead is shaved, and prevents the proper adhesion of the solder to the lead, as it forms a thin coating between them.

A small trowel will be found very handy for gathering up the solder that collects under the joint.

It is necessary to give a few suggestions concerning the wiping of upright joints, for wiped joints must often be made in this position. In Fig. 14 is shown an upright joint set up and ready for wiping.

Below the joint something should be arranged to catch the solder falling from the joint. The method shown in Fig. 14, consists in the use of a sufficiently large piece of cardboard, fitting closely to the pipe and cut through to the edge, as shown, in order that it may be slipped on. This cardboard may rest on any support that may be conveniently used. Another means sometimes used consists of a funnel-shaped lead collar fitting closely about the pipe and close under the joint, collecting the solder in the manner of a saucer. It is claimed that having this collar close to the joint allows the metal to heat up the joint at this point effectually, and to hold the heat.

In making an upright joint, unless the workman is skillful in pouring the metal from the ladle, it will be necessary to have what is known as a splash stick, which is illustrated in Fig. 14, with which to throw the solder onto the joint.

The plumber may make his own splash stick out of any piece of wood at hand.

It should be about 6 or 7 inches long, ⅛ inch thick, and 1¼ inches wide in the wide part. In getting the solder onto the joint, splash the solder onto the upper part of it and all around it.

With the splash stick keep pulling the solder up onto the upper part of the joint.

When the solder has reached the right consistency and amount on the joint, shape it roughly with the splash stick, then wipe it quickly with the cloth. In all wiping work, the secret of successful work is quickness without any lost motions.

Attention may now be given to the wiping of branch joints, as shown by Nos. 3 and 4 of Fig. 10. With the gimlet or tap borer open the pipe at the point where the joint is to be wiped, being careful not to rough up the inside of the pipe opposite the opening.

The hole should be made smaller than the final requirement, and the lead then beaten out with the bending pin into the form of a collar, the inside of which should be beveled off to receive the end of the branch.

Next bevel the end of the branch pipe to fit into the collar. By the way, in getting the pipes ready for wiping, before anything else is done the pipe should be drifted out with the drift plug and dressed, so that it is in perfect condition. After fitting the pipes, apply soil or plumber's paste, as the case may be. If the latter is used, go over the work with fine sand paper before applying it.

After the paste or soil has been applied, scribe out the shape of the joint with the shave hook, then with the same tool shave off the surfaces that the joint is to cover.

A word of caution is necessary concerning the use of the shave hook. It is necessary only to remove the oxidized surface and thus thoroughly clean it, and entirely unnecessary to cut deeply into the lead. If a deep shave is made, the strength of the lead at this point will be much impaired. As soon as shaved, the joint should be thoroughly covered with tallow. The work is now ready to be set up and wiped. If pipe holders are not used for supporting the work, various methods may be used for holding the branch in position, depending largely on the location of the work and the conveniences at hand. Generally the branch may be supported against a wall or other vertical surface, or if long, it may be bent around to any convenient support and afterwards straightened.

The flange joint, as shown in No. 5 of Fig. 10, is the most easily wiped of the several joints.

It is used where the pipe passes through the floor or through a wall. The pipe coming through the floor should be of sufficient length above the floor to be flanged over. A good method is to cut a hole in a piece of paper of sufficient size, slip the paper over the pipe, and allow it to rest on the floor to collect the solder dropping from the joint. Flange the lead pipe over onto the floor, beating it down smoothly. In flanging the pipe, use the turn pin to turn it over as far as possible.

The edge of the flanged lead may be left as it is, or may be shaved to a sharp edge, as shown in No. 5. If the latter method is followed, it should be shaved before being flanged over. The soil or paste should next be applied, and the surfaces shaved as already described for other joints. After the flange has been wiped, the paper may be cut out around the joint, so that it does not show. It is a good plan, by the way, in using soil or paste, to apply it inside the pipes, so that the solder may not run through into the inside of the pipe any more than possible.

No. 6, Fig. 10, shows a lead pipe wiped onto a trap. There is no different principle employed on this work than in making the branch joint in No. 3. In turning out a collar on the trap, to receive the pipe, care must be taken that the side of the trap is not collapsed, for many traps are now made of such thin material that

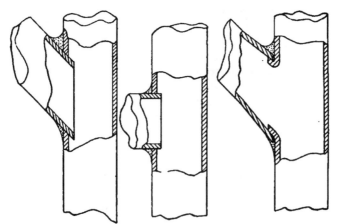

Fig. 15.—Wrong Methods of Making Wiped Joints.

any rough usage is liable to produce this result. The use of the lead pipe expanding pliers will be found satisfactory for such work.

In Fig. 15 are shown three joints prepared in a very poor and unworkmanlike manner. In the first place, no branch should project inside a pipe as it not only cuts down the available area of the pipe, but also presents a serious obstruction in the pipe. In one of the branch joints shown, the branch is fitted around the outside of the collar. This is a very poor practice, as it allows the end of the collar to form an obstruction which, especially in the case of waste pipes, is liable to catch threads and other similar materials in the waste, producing final stoppage. This difficulty could be somewhat lessened by beveling the inner edges of the collar, although such work is wrong under any conditions.

When the branch is fitted as shown in two of the illustrations, solder has a much greater opportunity of working into the pipe than in work properly constructed.

It will be noted, also, that the amount of solder used on the joints in Fig. 15 is insufficient to afford the necessary strength to the joint.

As to the proper length of wiped joints, the practice varies greatly. For the smaller joints, however, a length of from $2\frac{1}{4}$ to $2\frac{1}{2}$ inches makes good looking work, and about $1\frac{1}{2}$ inches for a 4-inch joint.

Thus far, attention has been confined solely to the wiping of

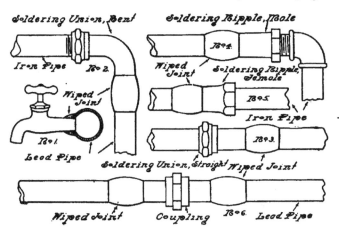

Fig. 16.—Wiping of Brass Work onto Lead Pipes.

two lead pipes together. In addition to this there is a great variety of work such as shown in Fig. 16, that is, work in which lead pipe is wiped to various pieces of brass work. There is comparatively little to be said on this subject, as the principles employed are not different from those already considered.

In wiping bibbs, soldering nipples, unions and couplings onto lead pipe, the pipe is flared at the end with the turn pin, and properly shaved. The brass piece is then set into the cup thus formed, and the lead beaten down to the brass. As far as shaving, soiling or pasting and greasing, the work is the same as that already considered. Before the brass work is ready to be set up and wiped, however, the end to which the joint is to be wiped, must be well tinned. The brass end is first filed off until a thoroughly clean, bright surface is obtained, and it is then tinned with a copper. This is a much better method than the common one of dipping the brass into the pot of solder, which always results in leaving in the solder more or less zinc which is present in the brass. The flux used in tinning brass work may be either rosin or tallow, or some prepared wiping flux. The latter is usually put up in boxes in the form of a paste, an advantage in its use being that it does not get

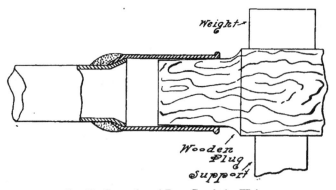

FIG. 17.—Supporting of Brass Ferrule for Wiping.

onto the tools as rosin or grease does, which is kept loosely in the plumber's bag.

The wiping of brass ferrules is a very important feature, though bringing into use no additional principles.

In Fig. 17 is shown the ordinary method of holding the ferrule in position for wiping. A wooden plug of the desired length is driven into the hub end of the ferrule, and this may be supported either by the pipe holder or on any convenient support with a weight to hold it in position.

Several different forms of brass ferrules are shown in Fig. 18, and the various methods of preparing them for wiping.

Ferrule No. 1 is of the tapered pattern, the pipe fitting inside it. No. 2 is of the straight pattern, the pipe being swelled out at the end with the turn pin until it just fits the inside diameter

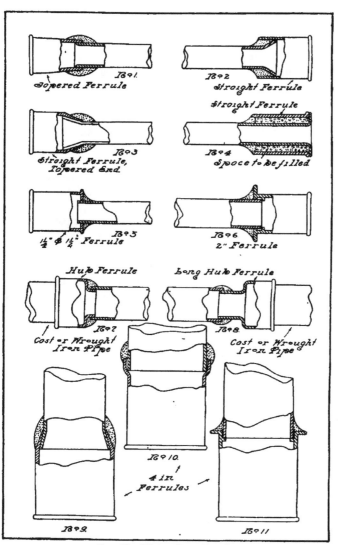

FIG. 18.—Wiping Brass Ferrules.

of the ferrule. If the inside of the ferrule is thoroughly brightened, this makes a strong joint. No. 3 ferrule is a common pattern, with the pipe turned over to fit the taper of the ferrule, the joint being round. In these three connections, if the pipe were fitted outside, the end of the ferrule would present a shoulder which would act as an obstruction. Such a method would be considered very poor practice.

The method shown in No. 4 is an excellent one. The space between the pipe and the ferrule may be calked with paper.

Nos. 5 and 6 show a new form of ferrule in which a flange joint may be used. The flange joint is not only the easiest to prepare and wipe, but less solder is used on it than on the ordinary joint. In order that a flange may be obtained, the ferrule for 2-inch pipe must be cast somewhat different than the ferrule for $1\frac{1}{4}$- and $1\frac{1}{2}$-inch pipe.

Nos. 9, 10, and 11 show 4-inch ferrules of different patterns. No. 11 is of the same general pattern as Nos. 5 and 6, a flange joint being used.

The 4-inch ferrule is usually wiped upright. It is a difficult joint for the beginner, the chief difficulty being in getting the work up to a proper heat. To facilitate this, the ferrule may be heated over a fire, or a bag of hot sand may be laid inside of it.

The glazing of wiped joints should be considered before leaving the subject. As soon as the joint has cooled just sufficiently to be firm, a ladle of semifluid solder is poured onto the joint, and as quickly as possible wiped off. If the metal is too hot it will melt the joint and destroy its appearance. Glazing must be done at exactly the proper time or it will not be successful. A glazed joint looks very bright and is unlikely to be porous.

If it is desired to give the wiped joint a mottled appearance the workman should blow upon it while it is cooling, and some workmen in blowing spit upon the joint with a sort of spray.

In addition to wiped joints, there are two other common joints, the cup joint and the overcast joint.

The cup joint is made very simply, by swelling the end of the pipe by means of the turn pin, setting the end of the other pipe into the cup, and filling the latter with solder by means of the soldering copper.

While this joint is not allowed on the plumbing system as a general thing, it is often used in connecting bowl cocks to lead supplies.

The hatchet copper may be used to advantage in making the cup joint, as it swivels and may be used on the back side of the pipe more handily than the common soldering copper.

The overcast joint is made in the shape of the wiped joint, but with the soldering copper. Most plumbing ordinances prohibit its use, as well as the use of the cup joint, but on work not regulated by ordinance, each is used to quite an extent.

The overcast joint may be rasped and filed into such form that it has an appearance similar to that of the wiped joint.

As previously stated, the making of wiped joints is a matter of considerable skill, gained by experience, and it may also be added that unless the workman keeps in practice, he loses the ability to do the work easily and well, although he soon regains the skill that he has lost.

CHAPTER IV

LEAD WORK

PLUMBERS' lead work has changed greatly within the last twenty-five years.

In the first place, there is not nearly so much of this work done at the present time, different methods are used for constructing the work, and furthermore, whatever lead work is used on the plumbing system is now nearly all manufactured in such form that it is ready for use without the necessity of being worked up into shape by the plumber. Twenty-five years ago, most of the tanks used on the plumbing system were lined with sheet lead, whereas sheet copper has now quite generally taken its place. Occasionally, however, tanks are required to be lined with lead, and the method of lining with lead is a subject which the plumber should understand, even under the conditions that exist to-day. In the following remarks relative to the lining of a tank with sheet lead, the instructions for laying out the sheet metal itself, apply equally to either lead or copper.

The roll of sheet lead, which should generally be either 4-lb. or 6-lb., should be laid upon the floor, and with the assistance of his helper, the plumber unrolls it, until it lies flat upon the floor. With his dresser the plumber should then go over the sheet lead, taking out all dents, creases, etc. After being thus worked upon, it is ready to be laid out to fit the tank.

In Fig. 19 is shown a perspective view of a tank, the dotted lines showing the lining, each corner being lettered. In Fig. 20 is shown the method of laying out the sheet, whether of lead or copper, for the tank shown in Fig. 19. It will be noted that the lettering of the respective surfaces in the two illustrations correspond. C E F D is laid out the same size as the bottom of the tank. A C D B and E G H F of the same size as the sides, and A C E G and D B H F of the same size as the ends. The measurements

F H, F G, A C and B D should be cut about an inch longer than the height of the tank, by the way, in order that this extra length may be turned off and tacked to the upper edges of the tank.

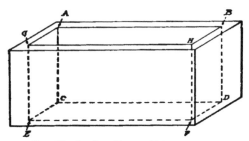

FIG. 19.—Lead or Copper Lining for Tank.

The two sides should be cut about two inches longer than the length of the tank, in order that these strips may be formed around the corners of the tank, to act as a support to the lining, and to

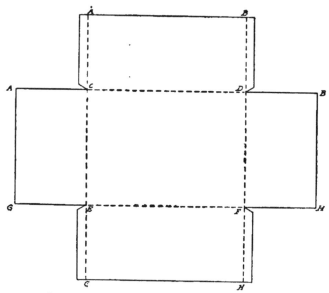

FIG. 20.—Layout of Lead or Copper Lining for Tank.

prevent the solder from flowing in between the lead and the sides of the tank. These strips should be secured to the ends of the tank with copper nails.

The dotted lines in Fig. 20 show where the lining is to be bent to fit into the tank. In placing the lead in the tank, it should be folded so as to be easily handled, but with as few sharp bends as possible. After being placed in the tank, the lead sides are gradually worked up into place. The strips left on the corners should be securely fastened, and the corners of the lining driven back into place with a wooden wedge. After the lead has been driven into place, and the small corners on the top edge of the tank filled with a piece of sheet lead, the work is ready for scraping, in preparation for the wiping of the seams. A line should be drawn to establish the width of the joint. Then with the shave hook, proceed to scrape the surface, being careful to make a clean-cut edge and not go over the line. When the scraping has been completed, go over the brightened surfaces with tallow or plumber's wiping flux. The joints or seams are now ready to be wiped.

From $\frac{1}{2}$ lb. to 1 lb. of solder should be figured on per foot of seam, according to the size of the tank. On this work a tool known as a plumber's iron is generally used, its purpose being to keep the work heated up. A piece of board should be cut out to fit into the corner at the bottom of the tank, to catch the falling solder. Next take a ladleful of solder in the left hand, and with the splash stick in the right hand, commence to throw the solder onto the seam, shoving it back into place with the splash stick, and taking it from the board at the foot of the seam. Continue this until the work is well tinned, and at the proper heat. When the work has reached this condition, drop the ladle and splash stick, taking the iron in the left hand and the wiping cloth in the right. Pass the iron, which has been previously heated, gently over the surface of the solder, to keep it properly heated, and with the wiping cloth wipe down from the top, a quarter or less of the length of the seam. Do not try to do too much at a time. After getting well started a longer strip can be wiped.

In wiping the seam, the heat is quite likely to cause the sheet lead to leave the wood and rise up, but this can easily be pressed back into place with the cloth.

When near the bottom, plunge the point of the iron into the solder to limber it up, and with the cloth remove the surplus solder. Next remove the board, and finish the joint in the lower corner. While the plumber's iron is generally used, there are some expert plumbers who can wipe a seam without its use. It requires much practice, however, to attain this degree of skill, and, as a rule, the iron is used. The old-style storage tanks were so heavy, especially after the lining had been set in place, that it was difficult to turn the tank over on its side. Therefore the seams were generally wiped upright. At the present time most of the tanks whose seams would have to be wiped upright are tanks used for special purposes, such as acid tanks in factories, etc.

Whenever small tanks are to be lined with lead, the present custom is to turn the tank onto its side and solder the seam with an ordinary soldering copper.

Seams on copper tanks may be wiped or soldered, although, as in the case of lead, such seams are now generally soldered.

A very effective method of supporting a lead lining on the

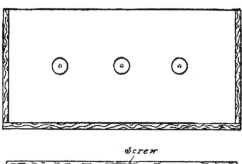

Fig. 21.—Supporting of Lead Lining on Sides of Tank.

sides of a large tank may be seen in Fig. 21. On large tanks special support is necessary, as the lead is soft and very heavy and liable to creep on the vertical sides. This method consists in cutting out a number of shallow bowls in the sides of the tank, the number depending on the size of the tank. These bowls may be made with a carpenter's gouge. After the lead is in place, beat it into the bowls with a round-faced hammer or mallet, and secure the lead to the sides of the tank with a screw, as shown in the detail view in Fig. 21. These bowls should then be scraped bright and covered with tallow. Then, with the splash stick, throw the solder into the bowl in the same manner as for an ordinary joint. When the metal is ready for wiping, wipe the bowl quickly, leaving its surface flush with the lead lining. This covers the head of the screw, and makes a strong and permanent support for the heavy lead sides, which otherwise would be liable to sag in time.

In addition to the subject of lead linings, there is also something to be said regarding the running of lead pipes. The bending of lead pipes was considered to some extent in the chapter on plumbers' tools.

Too much importance cannot be attached to the proper supporting of lead pipe.

Lead is a peculiar metal, and deteriorates much more rapidly if improperly put up, as is well known by the older lead workers. Lead in time seems to lose its life and grow rotten, and has not the sustaining strength that it has when new. Again, lead under heat becomes soft, not that its atoms expand in bulk to the extent that occurs in some other metals, but when heated, the atoms making up the body, under a slight expansion readily slip by each other. It is due to this action that a piece of lead pipe will bend more readily when heated than when cold. For this reason, great care should be exercised in the running of lead pipe, that it be well supported, in order that its own weight may not cause it to sag. The sagging of lead pipe carrying hot water is more common than the sagging of cold-water pipes. Very often lead pipe which is supported only by clips will be found supported at intervals of three and four feet. While such work as this looks good when new, it will be but a very short time before the pipe will have a wavelike appearance throughout its entire length, due to the sagging of the pipe between its supporting points. The sags will often cause the pipe to dip two or three inches from the horizontal. The sagging of lead pipes not only makes a very unworkmanlike piece of work, but such pipes cannot be entirely drained, water always remaining in the sags to freeze and burst the pipe in the event of the vacancy of the premises during cold weather. In addition, such sags, when they occur on hot-water pipes, interfere with, and often entirely interrupt the circulation of hot water.

To be well supported, clips should be placed every eighteen inches on a horizontal line. This will result in good work, work which will retain its proper alignment for many years. One of the best methods of supporting horizontal lines of lead pipe, and a very easy method, is to nail up strips of board and run the pipe on the edge of the board. Suppose, for instance, that the pipe is to be run under a floor. The plumber would naturally arrange the work as far as possible so that the pipes would follow the timbers

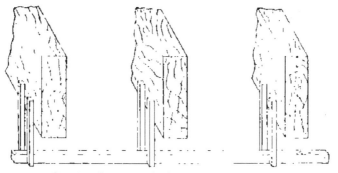

Fig. 22.—Support for Horizontal Line of Lead Pipe.

through the spaces rather than cross the timbers. The latter method often requires much cutting and consequent weakening of timbers, and there is also the possibility of sagging between timbers. When conditions are such that the pipes can follow along the timber, nail narrow strips of board to the side of the timber, giving the strips such pitch as would be required for proper drainage. The pipe should be run on the upper edge of this strip, supporting it with clips as often as is necessary to hold it from slipping off. This, of course, does not need to be often, as the clips do not in any way support the weight of the pipe.

Work run in this manner will look as well, and be in as good condition ten years after being installed as at the time it is put up, provided the proper weight of pipe has been used to withstand the existing pressure.

A modification of this same idea can be applied to pipes run horizontally in the cellar. Suppose a single line of lead pipe is to be run through the cellar. Take strips of board, furring strips, for instance, supporting these strips to the timbers above, as shown in Fig. 22, and shortening the supports in order to give the pipe its proper pitch. A very good idea is to run a line through the cellar, to serve as a guide in securing the proper pitch.

When a number of pipes are to be run side by side, as is often required, let the board selected be of sufficient width to hold the desired number of pipes, and the same means of support described above may be used.

This makes an excellent support, and not only are the pipes always protected from sagging, but in the event of repairs, the workman has simply to mount his steps, when he can look directly down upon all the pipes, select the one on which he wishes to work,

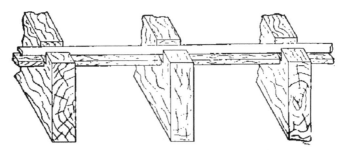

Fig. 23.—Supporting of Lead Pipe between Timbers.

and many times complete the necessary repairs without removing the pipe from its position. Any moving or bending of pipes on repair work should be avoided whenever possible, as the pipe will always stretch more or less, and get somewhat out of shape.

When pipes must be run across timbers, instead of in the direction in which the timbers run, the method shown in Fig. 23 may be used to give support to the pipe between timbers. This method consists simply in nailing strips of board between the timbers, on which the pipe may rest.

An objection to using metal clips in supporting lead pipe is that, owing to the softness of lead, the clip will work into the pipe, sometimes sufficiently to weaken the pipe to a considerable extent.

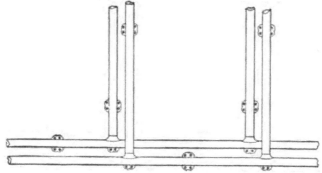

FIG. 24.—Use of Lead Tacks.

This result is due to the weight of the heavy lead pipe coming upon the clips. Lead tacks, soldered to the pipe and screwed to the support, are also much used on lead supply work, both on concealed

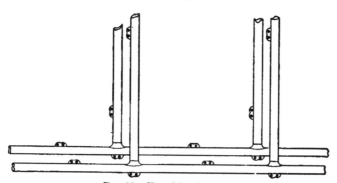

FIG. 25.—Use of Lead Tacks.

and on exposed piping. The use of lead tacks is shown in Figs. 24 and 25.

In Fig. 24 they are shown in pairs, and in Fig. 25 singly and alternately on opposite sides of the pipe.

These tacks are used on both horizontal and vertical lines of lead pipe.

As already stated, lead pipe is not now used to the extent that it formerly was, but has now been replaced by galvanized wrought iron and brass.

In many respects this change is for the best. While the plumber is unable to display the skill in installing pipe of other kinds than lead, wrought iron and brass are free from many of the evils that accompany the use of lead pipe.

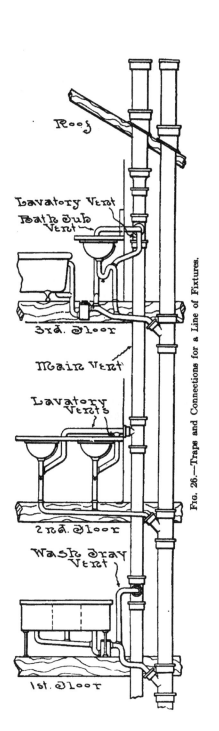

Roof

Lavatory Vent

Bath Tub Vent

3rd. Floor

Main Vent

Lavatory Vents

2nd. Floor

Wash Tray Vent

1st. Floor

Fig. 26.—Traps and Connections for a Line of Fixtures.

CHAPTER V

TRAPS

The subject of traps is a fundamental one, inasmuch as upon the proper operation of the trap depends the operation of the entire plumbing system, from a sanitary standpoint.

Defined, the trap is a vessel holding a quantity of water, whose purpose is the prevention of the passage of gases and odors from the sewer or cesspool, and from the plumbing system itself, into the house.

In order to protect the house from such danger, a trap is required not only under each plumbing fixture, but also on each floor drain, cellar drain, rain leader, etc.

The use of traps under the various fixtures, and their connections, is to be seen in Fig. 26. The subject of venting, which is so closely associated with trap work, will be considered in another chapter.

It may be said that all traps used in plumbing construction are based upon one or the other of two fundamental types. These are shown in Fig. 27, the two types being known as the S trap

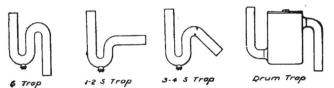

S Trap   1-2 S Trap   3-4 S Trap   Drum Trap

Fig. 27.—Fundamental Types of Traps.

and the drum trap. These two forms of trap are more commonly used than any others, and concerning their comparative excellence there has long been much debate. By many the S trap is considered the best form of trap, inasmuch as it is self-scouring and therefore more easily kept from becoming foul. The chief argument against the S trap is the fact that it may easily lose its seal by siphonage, such action resulting in establishing direct communication between the sewer and the interior of the house. The characteristics of the S and drum traps are exactly opposite; where one is weak the other is strong. The drum trap holds a large body of water, a large part of which is inactive. Therefore it is not to be expected that this form of trap will be so free of filth as the S trap; in fact its opponents claim that the drum trap is in the nature of a small cesspool. On the other hand, the drum trap is far less liable to siphonage than the S trap, a 4-inch drum trap being found by test to be practically nonsiphonable under conditions generally existing in the plumbing system.

In the use of these two forms of traps a neutral position would appear to be more logical than the radical position so generally

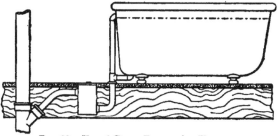

Fig. 28.—Use of Drum Trap under Floors.

maintained by the plumbing fraternity, there being places where either one will certainly do better work than the other. For instance, when vented and used in connection with such fixtures as lavatories, also in the construction of water-closets, main traps, etc., the S trap is the better and·more convenient form to use, for while holding the advantage of being self-cleansing, its size in many of these instances, and the size of its connecting pipes, eliminates almost entirely the danger of siphonage. Many times it is essential that to insure perfect work, the delivery from the trap should be as rapid as possible, and it can readily be seen that delivery from the S trap more nearly satisfies such requirement than the delivery from the drum trap. On the other hand, the drum trap is especially well adapted to use beneath floors, for instance, in bath-tub work, Fig. 28 showing such a connection.

As a rule, the waste pipe from such a fixture as the bath tub has none too much fall, particularly when the trap is at some distance from it. Under such conditions a better pitch can be secured in the use of the drum trap, and in addition, the cleaning facilities are much better in the case of the drum trap. Another point which recommends the drum trap is its great depth of seal, this being an important feature of the trap, particularly if attached to a fixture not often in use, for with a shallow seal evaporation soon breaks it.

Although not considered the best practice, it often happens that two or more fixtures enter the same trap, as for instance, bath and lavatory, or sink and laundry tubs, and when so installed the drum trap is almost a necessity, as its construction allows several waste pipes to enter it at different points at the bottom, while a pipe of larger size from the top forms the outlet.

From these two traps scores of other traps have sprung into existence. In the illustrations shown in Fig. 29 will be found various forms of these traps now in common use. There are traps which have valves of one kind or another. In general these valves are very simple, consisting usually of a ball resting against a seat, the ball being displaced when waste enters the trap, and reseating itself after the waste stops running. In these traps, which also have the ordinary water seal, dependence is made for additional protection upon this valve or mechanical seal as it is called. When new, such a trap may do good work, but the trap soon becomes foul, and the valve likewise, in which condition it not only fails to perform its work, but becomes actually an obstruction around which substances may collect and eventually form a complete stoppage of the trap. Most plumbing ordinances now prohibit the use of this class of traps. There is another class of traps having one or more partitions within the body of the trap. Such traps usually have the advantage of being compact, convenient for use in many places, and make a neat appearance. However, when such internal partitions project above the water line in the trap, danger is always present, from the fact that sand holes or other imperfections may exist, under which condition direct communication with the sewer is established. A particularly bad feature of such partitions is that serious flaws may exist, and remain

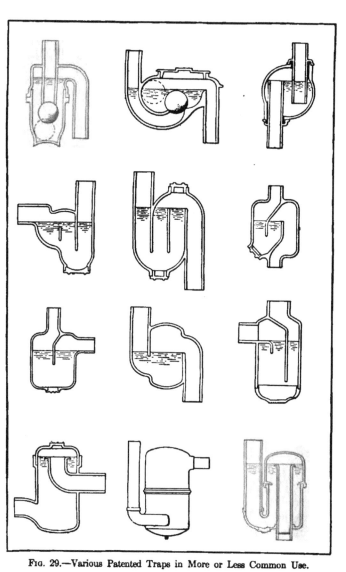

Fig. 29.—Various Patented Traps in More or Less Common Use.

undetected, for whatever leakage may come from them shows only inside the trap, never outside. If it could be detected from the outside the faulty trap might be replaced, thus obviating the continuance of the resulting danger for an indefinite length of time. Many ordinances now discriminate against this form of trap.

There is also a class of traps so constructed as to give the waste in passing through it a centrifugal motion. This result is obtained by connecting the inlet into the trap on a tangent instead of into the center. This causes the waste to take a whirling and lifting motion. This trap is made in the form of the drum or round trap, but while possessing very great scouring and self-cleansing properties, it is liable to lose a portion of its seal, due to the momentum acquired. Thus, many different classes of traps might be named, each presenting some feature that would appear of value. Many of these features have much merit, especially when the trap is new, but when put to the test of time under actual working conditions, many apparently excellent traps have either failed entirely or only partially achieved the results claimed for them.

In Fig. 30 may be seen several additional forms of traps. Each of these traps is of patented form, having advantages and disadvantages which the reader may discern after having followed the foregoing remarks on trap construction.

It will be noted that two of the traps shown in Fig. 30 are specially adapted to use under floors, and have the advantage of a cleanout accessible without the removal of flooring. The trap constantly being sought for, and which may some day be brought out, should be simple in construction, self-cleansing, nonsiphonable, have a good seal, and no internal partitions, depend upon no mechanical device, and have as few corners or places where filth may collect as possible. In addition, facilities must be provided for the cleaning of such a trap. Although there are many excellent traps now on the market, it does not appear that perfection has yet been reached, and therefore until such a trap does appear, the present forms must be used, and judgment exercised in deciding which form is best adapted to the special work in hand. For the past few years there has been much money and energy expended by manufacturers in the attempt to produce a trap that would be non-

siphonable, siphonage, by the way, being the greatest obstacle to
the attainment of a perfect trap. Many times the manufacturer
has flattered himself that the desired result had been reached, and
in many cases has been successful in convincing city health officials

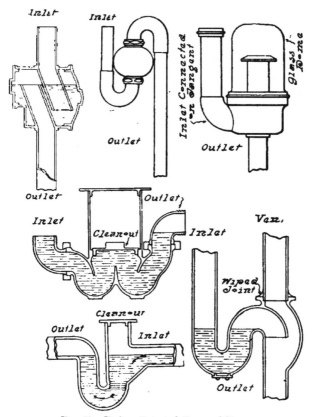

FIG. 30.—Various Patented Forms of Traps.

to that effect, and in procuring from them permission to install his
form of trap without venting, a subject which will soon be considered. It is extremely questionable, however, whether the trap
has yet been produced which can honestly be said to be entirely

free from the danger of siphonage under all practical working conditions, and after the trap has reached a more or less foul condition incident to its use for a considerable length of time. It is not to be questioned that great strides have been made in the right direction, but it would appear that any trap for use in connection with a plumbing fixture should still be provided with special means to protect it against the action of siphonage. The nearest approach to the desired end is to be found in the modified forms of the drum trap, of which there are many excellent makes.

The results which have been obtained in testing several of the modern traps which are claimed to be nonsiphonable are of much

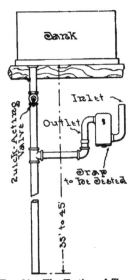

Fig. 31.—The Testing of Traps.

interest, and tend to show how closely some of them are approximating in their operation the result which is desired.

The general method of testing traps is illustrated in Fig. 31. A tank holding about 200 gallons is generally used to provide the flush, and from this tank a 1½-inch pipe is carried down a distance of 35 or 45 feet, the end of the pipe being open, to allow the waste to be emptied upon the ground or to be connected to a drain.

At a point several feet below the tank a branch is taken out, at the end of which the trap to be tested is attached, as shown.

A quick-opening valve having a full water-way should control the flush, by which means the pipe may be quickly and completely filled. The suction created through this length of pipe is great, and puts a most severe test upon the trap, a test much more severe than it is subjected to under ordinary working conditions.

There is no trap, it might be said, which will not lose at least a small part of its seal under an extreme test of this nature.

Traps having a 4- or 5-inch seal have lost in these tests, within the first minute, from 1 to 2 inches of their seal, and often a greater amount. However, in many cases a continuation of the test did not result in further loss of seal.

Many traps under this severe test lose their entire contents, and traps, by the way, which are widely advertised as nonsiphonable.

Those traps having the characteristics of the drum trap, have in general withstood severe tests better than those forms which follow the S type.

It should be noted that traps thus tested are new traps, having no collection of filth in them that is the result of use in actual work, and it is a question whether traps that had been in use for a few years would give such good results under test.

When the nonsiphonable trap becomes an accomplished fact from all practical points of view, there would seem to be no end to the changes that would result in the plumbing system. It will not be a matter of great surprise to see within the next few years, the plumbing system installed without the use of trap vents. When this result comes the decrease in the complex form and in the cost of the plumbing system will be very great. Such a system, however, will not be acceptable until the problems involved shall have been solved beyond a question of doubt.

In considering the perfect trap, especially if of the drum-trap form, an additional danger occurs to us which should be overcome. We refer to the entrance of sewer gas through the trap when the cleanout cover is removed from a trap connected as shown in Fig. 28. This will happen in any trap whose cleanout is not submerged, and it will also happen if the gasket on the cleanout does not make tight. It is seldom that after the trap is opened the old gasket will make a tight joint, even though it is not destroyed in removing the cover, and it is also seldom that the joint made by a new gasket is tested. Therefore, the perfect trap should be so constructed as to overcome this danger.

The term " trap seal " has been used several times, and it is a matter of importance. Fig. 32 is given as a means of defining it. Under normal conditions, the water in the trap stands at the level A. If, however, it drops below the level B, the trap becomes ineffective, as it no longer prevents the entrance of sewer gas. The

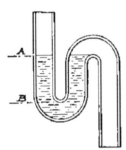

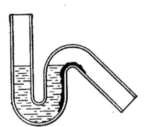

FIG. 32.—The Trap Seal.　　FIG. 33.—Trap Seal Broken by Capillary Action.

water standing between the levels A and B is called the seal of the trap. This seal may be broken or destroyed in a variety of ways. It may be destroyed by siphonage, by capillary attraction, by evaporation, by back pressure, by momentum, and by gusts of wind. Its destruction by siphonage is a matter of such importance that the following chapter will be reserved for its consideration. Defined, capillary attraction is the power possessed by liquids of rising through very fine tubes to a higher level than that of the liquid in which the tubes dip. It is this action which causes a sponge to fill with water. Its application to the breaking of the trap seal may be seen in Fig. 33, which represents string or a collection of lint or other like substances dipping down into the seal of the trap and terminating in the outlet. Capillary action will cause the water in the trap to follow up through this collection of lint and drop over into the outlet. This constitutes a serious danger to the trap seal, and one for which there would seem to be no remedy. It may readily be seen that in the case of a fixture seldom used, whose trap seal therefore is seldom renewed, capillary action by withdrawing the water from the seal a drop at a time, may eventually destroy it entirely, and the length of time in which such a result might be reached is surprisingly short.

As to the breaking of the seal by evaporation, it may be said that the danger is far less in the unvented trap than in the properly vented trap. This is due to the fact that the vent brings in upon the seal a supply of air which naturally increases the rate of evaporation.

Causes which tend to increase the rate of evaporation are increase of temperature, exposure of surface, and air currents passing over the surface of the liquid.

Back pressure exerted upon the trap seal is a pressure generated in the sewer, and acts upon the sewer side of the trap. A poorly vented sewer may produce such a pressure owing to the expansion caused by a sudden rise in temperature, as might be occasioned by the sudden entrance into the sewer of a large amount of steam or hot water. Tide water backing into the sewer might also produce back pressure. The result of this pressure, unless certain precautions are taken in the construction of the plumbing system, is the saturation of the trap seals with sewer gases, which finally are given off into the interior of the house.

The breaking of the trap seal by momentum is occasioned by the rushing out of the waste from the trap with such force that a part or the whole of the seal is carried with it. This is a danger that exists to some extent in traps working under centrifugal motion.

The breaking of the trap seal by gusts of wind is not a common occurrence, although it sometimes happens. The trap of a water-closet, for instance, located on a top floor, and connected to a soil pipe running through the roof, may lose a few drops of its seal from time to time, owing to gusts of wind passing over the opening of the roof pipe.

CHAPTER VI

THE SIPHONAGE OF TRAPS

As already stated, the trap seal is broken more frequently by siphonage than by any other means. In fact, siphonage is the greatest obstacle that confronts the trap, and it is the one thing that prevents the attainment of the perfect trap.

In order to study siphonic action in connection with the trap, it will be necessary first to consider the action of the simple siphon, and for this purpose Fig. 34 may be used. The purpose to which the siphon is applied is the transferring of liquids from higher to lower levels, and in form it consists essentially of a tube so bent that one arm is longer than the other. The short arm dips into the liquid to be moved, and the long arm delivers the liquid at the lower level. In order that the liquid may be carried over by siphonic action, it is necessary that the air be exhausted in the long arm, or in other words, that a vacuum be created at this point. At the instant that a vacuum is by any means formed in the long arm, atmospheric pressure acting upon the surface of the liquid, no longer having any force counterbalancing it, forces the liquid up the short arm, and over the crown of the siphon into the long, or delivery, arm. Unless broken by other means, siphonic action will continue under these conditions, until the water falls to a point below the bottom of the short arm. When it is considered that atmospheric pressure is approximately 15 lbs. per square inch, it will be seen that with a nearly perfect vacuum, siphonic action is strong and rapid. It is necessary that one arm of the siphon be shorter than the other, in order that the heavier column of liquid in the long arm may exert a pulling force or suction upon the liquid in the short arm. If it were not for this relative difference between the two arms of the siphon, the liquid in each would fall back by virtue of its own weight, and the continuance of siphonic action would be impossible. Therefore, the greater the relative difference in length between the two arms, the stronger will be the action of the siphon, unless, indeed, the long arm be carried to such a length that friction overcomes the advantage gained.

The action of the siphon may be destroyed by admitting air at or near the crown, a principle which, as will be seen in the following chapter, is made use of in connection with the plumbing system, to prevent the siphonage of traps. While presenting what may be considered as the greatest obstacle which the plumbing system has to overcome, siphonage is also one of the greatest aids in procuring a high grade of plumbing construction, inasmuch as upon the prin-

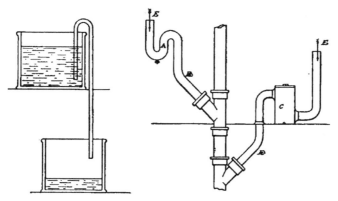

FIG. 34.—The Siphon.   FIG. 35.—The Siphonage of Traps.

ciple of the siphon depends the action of many excellent plumbing fixtures, valves, and other devices. By referring to Fig. 35 it may be seen wherein the connections of both S and drum traps present the same conditions to be noted in the typical siphon shown in Fig. 34. The arm A of the S trap constitutes the short arm of the siphon, and B, the long arm, with the relative difference between the lengths of the two arms often very great. A vertical column of water in the trap of the size of the waste pipe, constitutes in the drum trap the short arm of the siphon, and D the long arm. With atmospheric pressure in each case acting in the direction of the arrow E, all that is necessary to produce the siphonage of the contents of each trap is the formation of a vacuum or partial vacuum in the

long arm. There is usually abundant opportunity in the plumbing
system that is unvented, for the formation of this vacuum. In Fig.
35, for instance, it might be formed by the passage of a heavy volume of waste past the entrance of the branches on the two waste
fittings on the soil-pipe line. The effect and various causes of
siphonage in the plumbing system may best be studied from such
an illustration as Fig. 36, which shows a plumbing system such as
commonly installed years ago, with no line of soil pipe venting
itself through the roof, and without trap ventilation of any description. In such work, the condition most favorable to siphonage is to
be found in the fact that the vertical line of soil pipe terminates at
the top fixture instead of continuing through the roof with an open
end. Suppose now, that a large body of water enters the vertical
line of pipe from several fixtures at the same time. Even though
the volume is not sufficient to entirely fill the bore of the pipe,
owing to its spiral motion in falling, the effect may be nearly equivalent, in which case the air in the pipe is forced ahead of the falling column of water, and a partial vacuum thereby formed in its
rear, the effect of which may be felt to a greater or less degree on
every trap in the building. By this means each of the traps on
the top floor may be siphoned, even the 4-in. water-closet being
susceptible to its action. It may readily be seen that in large
buildings, where there is a large amount of plumbing of this
old-time type, the conditions would often be more severe than
those shown in Fig. 36, and the siphonage of traps therefore
even more certain. Again, let a heavy body of waste pass down
the vertical line of soil pipe from the three floors above the basement. As this column enters the horizontal line, it is naturally
retarded; the waste, as a consequence, backs up and fills the pipe
at this point, and in attempting to pass out produces a partial
vacuum which is certain to be severely felt by the water-closet
trap in the basement. It will be noted in Fig. 36 that the waste
from the upper bath and lavatory, and from all three fixtures
on the second floor has little pitch and is of considerable length.
Such conditions are most favorable to trap siphonage, for the lack
of fall allows the waste to set back and fill the pipe, and as in
the instance noted above, in attempting to pass off, the waste
partially exhausts the air in the pipe, and the siphonage or partial

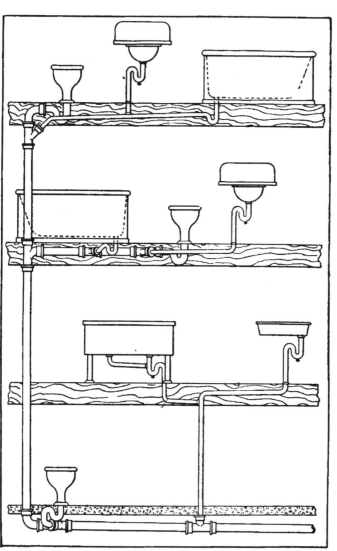

Fig. 36.—Siphonage of Traps in Old-Fashioned Unvented Plumbing System.

siphonage of the traps follows. It should be understood that very often the trap is affected by siphonic action only slightly, possibly only a few drops of the seal being lost at a time. In the event that the fixture is not in constant use, however, it becomes merely a matter of time when enough of the seal will be thus gradually lost to make its destruction complete. Therefore it is plain that even though siphonic influence may not be severe in the case of a certain trap, it still presents great danger.

A stoppage in the waste outlet may have a result similar to that mentioned of fixtures having long wastes without proper pitch. Much old work was put in like that of the kitchen sink and laundry tubs, and here again is abundant opportunity for siphonic troubles. A heavy flow of waste through the horizontal line of soil pipe might siphon either sink or laundry-tub trap; a heavy flow from either fixture might siphon the other; and either fixture might siphon its own trap. Thus it may clearly be seen that the old style plumbing system was susceptible in many different ways to trap siphonage, and the fatal results coming from ignorance of the conditions which actually existed to such a great extent in the plumbing system, and ignorance of the proper remedy for such troubles can hardly be estimated, but must certainly be of great extent.

Fig. 37 shows another unventilated plumbing system, similar in many respects to that of Fig. 36, in which the siphonage of each fixture is a matter of possibility. These illustrations are not exaggerated in any way, but show truthfully the manner in which the unvented plumbing system, with its great and serious defects, was formerly installed.

Fig. 37 shows not only the great possibility of the siphonage of the fixture traps, but shows also other minor defects common to the old-time plumbing system, such as the use of tee fittings on the drainage system, the entrance of waste into the heel of the lead bend, etc.

For the purpose of comparison, Fig. 38 is given, showing a complete modern system of plumbing, with its main line of vents and its branch vents. The great advance which has been made in plumbing installation since the days when such work as that shown in Figs. 36 and 37 was considered sanitary, may easily be seen in comparing the illustrations.

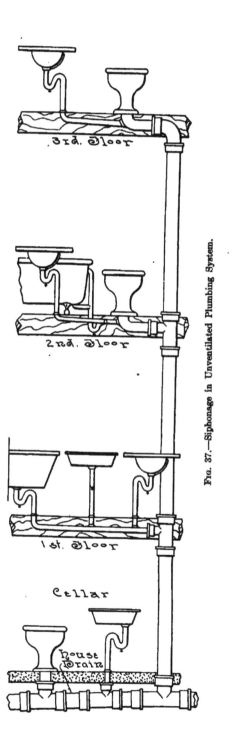

3rd. Floor

2nd. Floor

1st. Floor

Cellar

House
Drain

FIG. 37.—Siphonage in Unventilated Plumbing System.

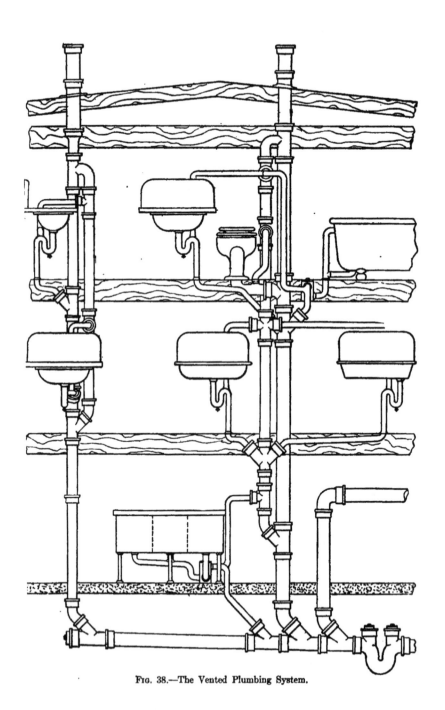

Fig. 38.—The Vented Plumbing System.

The application of the principle of trap venting has, without doubt, been the chief cause of such vastly improved sanitary conditions in the plumbing system. It is the venting of fixture traps which has proved the only practical means of preventing trap siphonage, and this subject in theory and in its practical application will be taken up in a special chapter on the subject of venting.

CHAPTER VII

VENTING

WHILE as a principle it has been known for ages, it is only within a comparatively few years that venting has been applied to the plumbing system as a means of overcoming such troubles as those mentioned in the preceding chapter. As a matter of fact, however, venting to-day stands second only in importance to the trap in a properly installed plumbing system.

Venting may properly be considered under two heads, soil or waste vents and trap vents. There are also two other forms of vent, the local vent and the fresh-air inlet, neither of which apply to our present subject, but which will be considered in later chapters. By the soil or waste vent is meant the continuation of vertical soil or waste-pipe lines above the highest fixtures and through the roof, terminating with an open end. It will readily be seen that the use of this vent prevents all trouble from back pressure in connection with trap seals, the vent relieving all pressure that might be generated in the sewer. The importance of this vent is realized when the plumbing system shown in Fig. 36 is compared with the same system supplied with the soil and waste vent. Not only does this vent relieve the system of back pressure, but it also purifies it, and lengthens its life, and in addition is often an aid in installing the trap vents, as will soon be seen. The soil and waste vent should ordinarily be carried at least two feet above the roof, and always above any opening on the roof, or the windows of neighboring buildings. There is one source of danger to this vent that should always receive attention, particularly in cold climates. Steam from the plumbing system will in cold weather form a mass of frost about the vent opening, and in the case of the smaller sizes of soil pipe often close the opening entirely. All sizes smaller than 4 inches may be closed in this way. Therefore no pipe of less size than 4 inches should pass through the roof, all pipes of smaller size being increased to 4 inches below this point, as in Fig. 59. Some plumbing ordinances require an enlargement of only one size in diameter. This would mean that a 2-inch pipe need be increased only to 3 inches in passing through the roof. The first-named provision, however, we believe to be the better. Vent covers are frequently fitted to the tops of roof pipes, which is certainly wrong in principle. It is better practice to discard even the wire cage which is so commonly used, for even this contracts the opening and allows the frost to accumulate more readily than it would in the open end of the pipe. Trap venting is the subject next to be

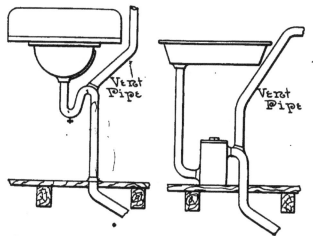

FIG. 39.—The Vented S-Trap.   FIG. 40.—The Vented Drum Trap.

considered, a subject both important and extensive. It has been seen in the preceding chapter that the admission of air to the crown of the siphon will destroy its action. It must necessarily be destroyed, for the admission of air destroys the vacuum upon which siphonic action depends. Briefly stated, then, the trap vent used on the plumbing system is a pipe, as shown in Figs. 39 and 40, whose purpose is to carry a supply of air to the crown of the trap, thereby preventing the formation of a vacuum in the outlet from the trap, and making the siphonage of the contents of the trap an impossibility. In order to perform its work, the trap vent must be connected with the outside atmosphere. This is accomplished by connecting the trap vents of the several fixtures into a main vent, the latter either passing through the roof to the outer air, or connecting into the soil and waste vent above the highest fixture. The trap vent, or back vent, as it is also called, should be connected to the trap at or near the crown, and on the sewer side of the trap. The connection of this vent to the trap and into the main vent may be seen in Fig. 41. The vent should always enter the main line of vent at a point higher than the fixture itself. If connected below

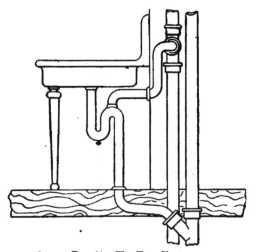

Fig. 41.—The Trap Vent.

the fixture it may easily be seen that in the event of the stoppage of the outlet from the trap, the waste would pass out through the vent into the drainage system and thus continue until the vent in turn was stopped. This condition occurs in the work illustrated in Figs. 42 and 43, the former representing the trap vent connected directly into the main vent, and in the latter the trap vent connected into a vent from another fixture.

When properly connected, waste in the case of a stoppage would be unable to pass over through the vent, and would set back into the fixture, thus giving warning of the existence of trouble.

While in principle the proper point for the connection of the vent is at the crown of the trap, there is an objection to this course from the fact that it brings in the supply of air directly upon the

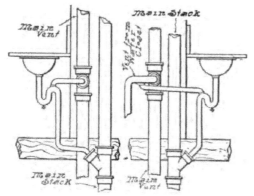

Figs. 42, 43.—Wrong Connection of Vent.

seal of the trap, thereby greatly increasing the rate of evaporation. It is better, therefore, to connect the vent in such a way that this danger may be obviated as far as possible. Fig. 44 shows how this may be done in connection with the several styles of S traps. From

Fig. 44.—Venting of S-Traps.

the nature of its connections, precautions of this kind are not so essential to the drum trap.

In the connection of the vent to the trap, a very important point is the making of the connection in such a way that the possibility of the stoppage of the vent opening by grease, lint, etc., in the waste may be made as slight as possible. In Fig. 44 the danger of such stoppage is present in the case of each of the three traps, but least of all in the half-S trap, and it may be added, also, that in this trap the rate of evaporation will also be less than in the others, owing to the distance of the vent connection from the seal. The stoppage of the vent opening is in reality the greatest obstacle that the vent system has to contend with.

It is a fact that after being in use for a length of time, a large majority of vents connected as in Fig. 41, become almost, if not entirely closed with grease, lint, etc., and in that condition of course become inoperative. Many expedients have been tried in the manufacture of traps to overcome this difficulty, but with little apparent success. Some few plumbing ordinances call for the location of a cleanout on each trap vent, but this is by no means a solution of the difficulty, for the seat of the trouble is always hidden from view, and that a stoppage of the vent exists is almost never known. In addition, the average owner or tenant knows so little concerning these matters that he cannot be depended upon to clear the vent at proper intervals, and in most cases not at all. The knowledge of the great extent of this evil is one of the chief reasons for the great activity in the search for a nonsiphonable trap, such a device naturally not requiring the vent, and therefore being free from this trouble.

Certain cities have even gone so far as to adopt the nonsiphonable traps now on the market, allowing their installation without venting, preferring to take chances with the so-called nonsiphonable trap rather than with the ordinary trap and its attendant closed vent. There is a form of venting known as continuous venting, or venting in the rough, which may be said to be free from the stoppage evil, and the subject is of such importance that the following chapter will be devoted to its consideration. A stoppage of the trap vent is to be considered more dangerous than a stoppage of the waste, as the latter quickly makes itself known by the setting back of the waste into the fixture, while the former is seldom known unless the work is taken apart.

Little has so far been said concerning the vent and waste connections of drum traps, and a consideration of the subject will be of value. A great majority of drum traps installed are probably connected as shown in Fig. 45. The chief argument against this style of work is that if the trap screw gasket does not happen to be tight, there is direct communication with the drainage system or the sewer and the house. Such conditions would also arise while the cover was removed during the cleaning of the trap. This trouble may be avoided by a connection such as in Fig. 46. The chief objection to the connections of Fig. 46, however, is the fact that there is of necessity a greater length of pipe in which waste may stand and possibly cause the fouling of the outlet. On the whole, however, Fig. 46 represents a very satisfactory arrangement. The connections of Fig. 47 also prevent the escape of gases when the trap screw is off or not tight, but the objectionable feature in allowing the outlet pipe to project into the trap is that it presents an obstruction in the body of the trap, and around it filth may collect, making the stoppage of the trap more probable. The vent connection, however, is good, and more free of the danger of stoppage than most of the other connections shown. This fact applies also to Fig. 49.

The method of taking the vent connection off the trap-screw cover, as in Fig. 48, is quite a common one, and not to be recommended, as each time the trap is to be cleaned it is necessary to twist the vent pipe back out of the way. The connections shown in Fig. 49 are in many respects very good. The cleanout cover being submerged, any leakage is at once apparent, but with the cleanout in this position, it is impossible to prevent the escape of gases when the cover is removed. Many other forms of connection showing modifications and combinations of those illustrated might be given.

In providing a supply of air to the trap vent, one of three courses may be followed. If there are no fixtures above, it may be entered into the soil or waste vent at any point below the roof; it may be carried directly through the roof; or it may be carried into a line of main vent, as shown in Figs. 45 to 49. The only objection to entering the trap vent directly into the soil or waste vent when there are no fixtures above, is that unless the fixture is on the top floor, other fixtures may be located above at some future time. The carrying of the trap vent directly through the roof not only makes an extra roof connection necessary, with considerable extra expense, but as such a pipe is somewhat apart from

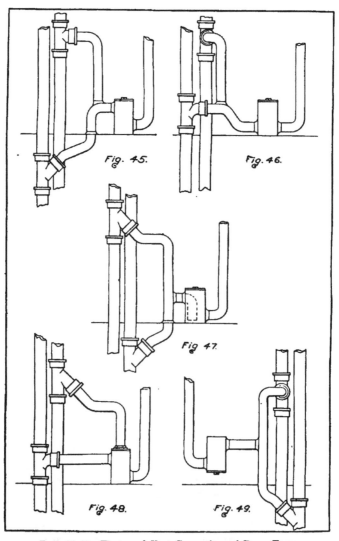

Figs. 45–49.—Waste and Vent Connections of Drum Traps.

the main system, the air in it is colder and the circulation of air therefore less satisfactory. The most approved method, then, is to connect the trap vent into a main line of vent, illustrations of which will be seen later. A very important point in the running of trap vents as well as main vents, is that they shall pitch upward at every point. A considerable amount of condensation and scale forms in the vent pipes, and if there is no pitch on the pipes these accumulations cannot find their way back into the trap, where they may flow out through the waste. The size of the trap vent should generally be the same as that of the trap to which it is connected.

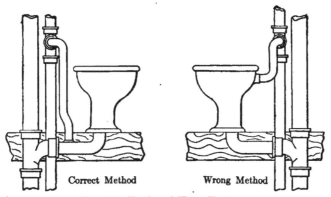

Correct Method   Wrong Method

Fig. 50.—Venting of Water-Closets.

The important exception to this rule is the vent from the water-closet. The waste from the water-closet is 4 inches in diameter, but experience shows that a 2-inch vent is sufficiently large.

Fig. 50 shows the correct and the wrong method of venting the water-closet. When properly installed, a 2-inch vent is taken from the top of the horizontal part of the lead bend, carried above the fixture and entered into the main vent. It is considered poor practice to connect this vent on the vertical arm of the bend, as paper and other substances are liable to collect about the entrance and finally close it. Its location on the horizontal arm of the bend is comparatively free from this difficulty. Another very good method, the principle of which is similar, is the connection of the vent to the vent hub of a vented T-Y fitting, into which the lead bend is calked. This method will be illustrated later. The incorrect method, shown in Fig. 50, consists of the connection of the vent to the vent horn of the water-closet, a method which is now prohibited by nearly all plumbing ordinances. The objection to such a method is that any blow which the fixture may receive, or the settling of floors, will break off the vent horn, for the reason that the vent pipe is usually too rigid to take up any movement of the closet. The water-closet is naturally the fixture most difficult to siphon, inasmuch as it is more difficult to form a vacuum in a 4-inch pipe than in pipes of smaller diameter. Therefore, it is not

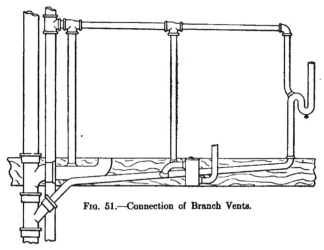

Fig. 51.—Connection of Branch Vents.

necessary to vent this fixture under certain circumstances, for instance, when it is located close to the stack on the top floor. In this location, with no fixtures above it to produce siphonic conditions, there is nothing to be gained in venting. The vents from a number of fixtures may be connected into one line, and this line connected into the main vent, such a method often being more advisable for many reasons than the running of each trap vent separately into the main. When so installed, however, as the several vents enter the branch to the main vent, the size of the branch vent should be increased, as shown in Fig. 51. In the case of a small number of fixtures, however, such as to be found in the bath room, the 2-inch vent to the water-closet need not be increased in size after receiving the vents of the other fixtures, as it is of sufficient size to provide air to the several fixtures.

In order to make sure that no vent shall act as a soil or waste pipe in the event of stoppage of any part of the waste the main branch vent should enter the vertical main line of vent above the top of the highest of the fixtures. Very often a fixture is located at a considerable distance from the main vent to which its trap vent is to be connected. When this distance is 8 feet or more, the trap vent should either be carried independently through the roof or

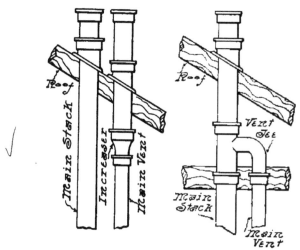

Fig. 52.—Main Vent and Main Stack Separately through Roof.

Fig. 53.—Upper Connection of Main Vent into Main Stack.

enter its main vent at a point above all fixtures. Another necessary provision is the increase in size of pipe used on long lines of vent. After passing 30 feet in length, the size of the vent should be increased one size. This precaution is necessary from the fact that in long lines of pipe, friction will decrease the efficiency of a pipe in delivering an adequate supply of air to the trap. In the running of main vent lines, many of the principles that apply to the trap vent are to be followed. There are, however, several points

which should be considered that do not enter into the subject of
the trap vent. In order to perform their work, the trap vents must
be provided with a supply of air, and therefore the main vent must
open into the outside air. One method of doing this is to run the

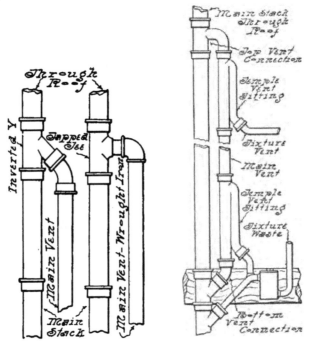

FIG. 54.—Two Methods of Upper Connection of Main Vent into Main Stack.

FIG. 55.—Showing Top and Bottom Vent Connections and Temple Vent Fittings.

main vent directly through the roof, as in Fig. 52. The ordinary
method, however, is to connect the main vent into the main stack
above all fixtures, as shown in Figs. 53, 54 and 55. Below the
lowest waste connection into the stack, the main vent should be
connected back into the stack, as in Fig. 57. This connection is
made in order that all scale and condensation forming in the pipes
may escape into the drainage system, to be washed away. Fig. 58
shows the use of a special fitting for making this connection, which

allows the two vertical lines to be run very close together. In Fig.
59, at B, is shown a wrong method of connecting the main vent
into a trap vent, instead of re-entering the main stack. The same
connection may perhaps be seen more clearly in Fig. 56.

When the lower end of the main vent stack is reduced to receive a trap vent, as in Fig. 56, there is abundant opportunity for
the collection of scale, rust, and condensation in the heel of the
reducing elbow, and no opportunity whatever for it to be washed

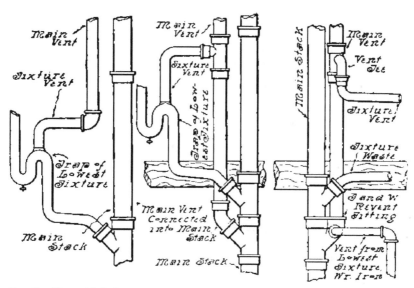

FIG. 56.—Wrong Method of   FIG. 57.—Improved Lower   FIG. 58.—Special Main
   Lower Connection of Main   Connection of Main Vent   Vent Connection.
   Vent.   into Main Stack.

away as in the correct method. The latter connection is the more
rigid of the two also. For these reasons the connection of Fig. 57
is the one now generally called for by the best plumbing ordinances.

Fig. 59 shows the various connections on the vent system, with
various common fittings in use.

In Fig. 55 also are shown main vent connections, and a special

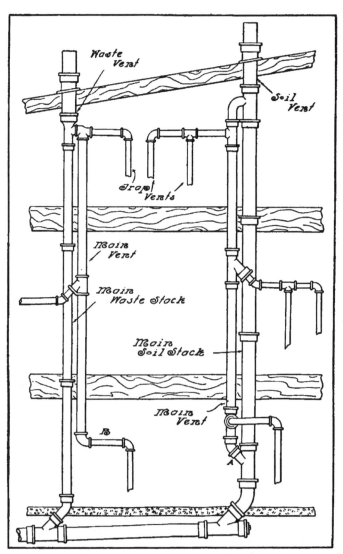

Fig. 59.—Vent System, Showing Main and Trap Vents, Use of Fittings, etc.

form of vent fitting, which is not only excellent in principle, but allows the work to be installed very compactly.

A few words should be said concerning the material used on the vent system. For main vent lines cast iron or galvanized wrought iron pipe is used, and for trap vents either brass, lead, or galvanized wrought iron, the latter being the most extensively used in both cases.

CHAPTER VIII

CONTINUOUS VENTING

As seen in the preceding chapter, the great obstacle to the operation of the trap vent is the collection of grease, etc., about the vent opening into the trap, in such quantity as to completely close the opening. If the vent should be disconnected from the trap it would be found that in a vast number of cases the opening is completely closed, and the vent entirely useless, which condition generally renders the trap easily subject to siphonage. As already stated, numerous mechanical devices have been tried in the attempt

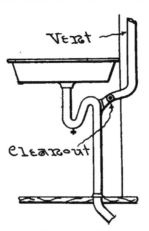

FIG. 60.—Cleanout on Trap Vent.

to regulate this difficulty, but all without avail. Even the use of the cleanout on the trap vent, as seen in Fig. 60, does not constitute a solution of 'the difficulty, although in some cities it is required. The trouble seems to be too deep-seated to be remedied by superficial means. In order to solve the difficulty, a different principle should be applied, and it would seem that in the continuous vent a very satisfactory solution has been found. There may be places where it is difficult to apply this method, but in general it may be successfully done.

In Fig. 61 are shown two examples of the application of the continuous vent to both the S and the drum trap.

This vent system is, by the way, sometimes called "venting in the rough." The principle involved in the continuous vent is readily seen. It consists essentially in the use of a fitting of the

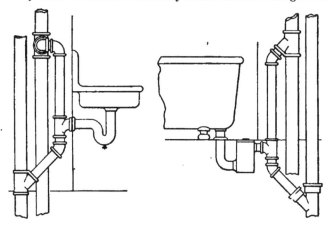

FIG. 61.—The Continuous Vent.

T-Y style, in such a manner that the vent may be taken from the top of it, and the waste from the bottom. This form of installation necessitates the use of the half-S trap, and prohibits the use of other forms of S trap, with the exception of the running S trap. It hardly need be stated that the opportunity of closing the vent opening is far less in this form of venting than in the method of the preceding chapter, which is in common use. This opening is not only further from the trap, and therefore more free from the splashing of the waste as it enters the trap, but the use of the T-Y fitting also tends to make the accumulation of grease about the opening more difficult. Another advantage gained in the use of the continuous vent is that no part of the work need be exposed to view, with the exception of the trap itself. This, as may well be supposed, is often a valuable feature. Generally when this style of vent is used, the material employed on both waste and vent is either brass or galvanized wrought iron, although lead may be used if for any reason it is found to be more desirable.

In a great deal of work on which the continuous vent is used, the cost of stock and labor involved is very much less than when the same work is installed according to the methods shown in the preceding chapter. This is particularly true of certain classes of large work. Fig. 62, for instance, shows the continuous vent prin-

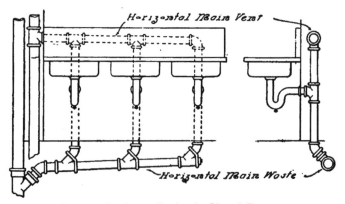

Fig. 62.—Continuous Venting for Line of Fixtures.

ciple applied to a line of fixtures, both front and end views being given. To this type of work the principle is particularly adaptable, and is being constantly employed to a greater extent. The method allows both horizontal main waste and main vent to be run back of partitions, concealed from view. Another material advantage of the continuous vent is the fact that the vent is taken off so far from the trap that the rate of evaporation is far less than under the conditions existing in work as ordinarily constructed. This is a more important feature than is generally acknowledged, for many traps, otherwise properly installed, fail because of the evil due to evaporation. In Fig. 63 is shown a vertical line of fixtures entering a waste stack, the traps being provided with con-

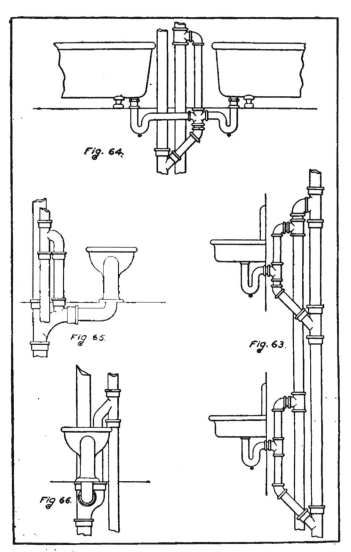

FIGS. 63–66.—Examples of Continuous Venting.

tinuous vents, and in Fig. 64 the same style of work in connection with a double line of fixtures on opposite sides of a partition. Double lines of fixtures are very often to be found on large work, such as apartment and office buildings, hotels, schools, factories, etc., and on such work as this there is no question whatever that the saving in labor and material is very great.

In Fig. 65 is shown a water-closet vented from the vent hub of a vented T-Y, a method which is very acceptable. This particular vent is not generally spoken of as a continuous vent, but it actually is in principle, and is therefore considered in this chapter. Such

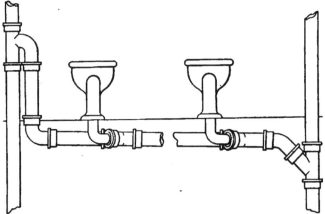

Fig. 67.—Continuous or Circuit Venting of Water-Closets.

work is very substantial, and particularly adapted to locations in which the plumbing is liable to rough usage, as, for instance, in factory work.

Fig. 66 shows the use of special patented fittings designed for vent work, the principle being very similar to that involved in the work of Fig. 65. In this connection it may be said that a great variety of vent fittings are now made, many of which will be noted in later illustrations, which are of very great value in the construction of continuous venting. Another modified form of continuous vent is to be seen in Fig. 67. This style of work, known as circuit venting, is applicable only to batteries of water-closets, but as it often happens that in the plumbing of hotels and other public buildings, extensive toilet rooms are located one above the other, the occasion often arises where the principle referred to may be put to good use. The illustration shows a line of water-closets on one floor only, but similar work on floors above or below would be put in in a like manner. The idea consists in the location at either end of the line of water-closets, of a vertical stack, one for soil and waste, and the other as a main vent. Each vertical line is carried through the roof, thus affording abundant circulation of air for each line of fixtures. Here again a great saving is made in labor and material over the separate vent method, in which a vent is taken from each lead bend. In the case of such work as that of Fig. 67, if fixtures other than water-closets waste into the horizontal soil pipe serving the water-closets, the vents from such fixtures may be run in the ordinary manner and connected into the vent stack.

It may be said that the continuous vent will prove a most valuable feature in the attainment of a perfect plumbing system, and that when its value becomes more thoroughly understood and appreciated, it is bound to be universally adopted. Indeed, it appears strange that it is not already put to more extensive use, as it certainly is a solution of some very serious problems.

CHAPTER IX

HOUSE SEWER AND SEWER CONNECTIONS

HAVING now considered the two fundamental subjects of traps and venting, the entire plumbing system will be considered, beginning at the point where the house sewer connects into the public sewer. Before proceeding with the subject, it will be well to define several terms, which are not always clearly understood.

By house drain is meant that portion of the horizontal drainage system into which all soil, waste, and drainage pipes discharge within the walls of the building which the drainage system serves. The house drain conveys the drainage to a point outside the foundation walls into the house sewer.

By house sewer, lateral or main drain, is meant that portion of the horizontal drainage system which extends from the house drain outside the foundation walls into the public sewer.

By house connection is meant that part of the house sewer which lies between the public sewer and the curb line.

By crock drain or sewer is meant any drain or sewer constructed of vitrified earthenware, hub and spigot pipe.

. By tile drain is meant any drain constructed of hard-baked earthenware pipe, which is laid with open joints, and having no hub and spigot ends. Tile drain is a name often wrongly applied to the crock drain.

The house drain usually ends at a point 10 feet outside the foundation walls, and at this point enters the house sewer, which is generally constructed of vitrified earthenware pipe, although occasionally the cast-iron pipe of the house drain is continued to the public sewer.

No earthenware pipe should be allowed inside the foundation walls of any building, on any part of the drainage system. All plumbing ordinances now make this prohibition. The reason for this is that owing to their nature, the cement joints used on this

101

style of pipe are liable to break or crack, or the pipe itself to suffer like injury, in which event the sewage will leak out and produce conditions unsanitary in the extreme. Breaking of pipe and joints may often occur from various causes, such as settling of the ground, etc.

The house connection is a term not so definitely defined as might appear from the definition above.

In some cities the house connection continues only to the curb line, in others to the fence line, and occasionally to the house sewer at the foundation wall. In each case this part of the drainage system is usually under the care of the municipal authorities, and the plumber allowed to work on it only under certain conditions and restrictions. In many cities a regularly appointed sewer inspector inspects all work done on the house connection, and only those plumbers may perform this class of work who have the proper license and permit from the proper officials.

This chapter will have to do principally with the house sewer.

This part of the drainage system, as before stated, is generally of vitrified earthen pipe. Much care should be exercised in making the connection between the house sewer and the public sewer, as a serious fault at this point renders an otherwise perfect drainage system useless.

Fig. 68 will serve to show some of the points of importance that should be observed. In the first place the branch for the house sewer should enter the street sewer above the center at a point high enough to guard against the setting back of the contents of the street sewer into the house sewer at such time as the former is carrying its maximum amount of sewage. It can readily be seen that in the backing up of sewage into the house sewer there is danger of the latter being closed up with heavy matter from the street sewer.

In addition, a Y branch, pointing in the direction of flow in the street sewer, is preferable to a tee, inasmuch as there is less liability of the collecting of such materials as rags, paper, etc., about the entrance.

An eighth bend into the Y will bring the course of the house sewer at right angles to the street sewer. Sharp, abrupt bends should never be used on this part or in fact on any part of the

drainage system. If necessary to make a turn of 90 degrees, it
should be done by means of eighth or sixteenth bends rather than
by the use of a quarter bend. Precautions should be taken that the
Y branch, or any cement used in making the joint, may not
project inside the street sewer and thus present projections
upon which matter floating in the sewage may catch. The

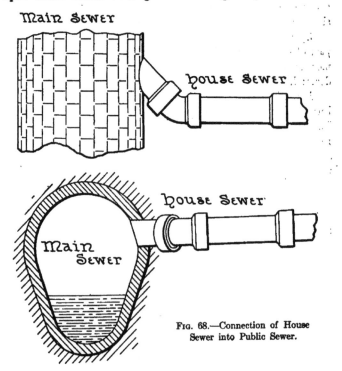

Fig. 68.—Connection of House
Sewer into Public Sewer.

house sewer should be laid on a grade of not less than
1 foot in 100 feet, and more pitch is desirable when possible
to secure it. The trench in which the house sewer or any other
underground drain is laid, should have a uniform slope and on the
bottom depressions should be made to receive the hubs of the pipe.
Each length of pipe should be given a solid bearing throughout its
length. The best foundation for the laying of the house sewer is

a natural bed of earth, gravel, rock, or sand. If such a foundation is not attainable, concrete may be laid beneath the pipe as a support. Chestnut planking also makes a good foundation on which to lay the pipe. Whenever the ground is made, or filled in, or where there is possibility of the settling of the pipe, or danger from the roots of trees, from frost, etc., it is preferable to construct the house sewer of extra heavy cast-iron pipe. The earth about the pipe should always be well rammed.

Special care should be taken in the making of joints on this part of the work. In general this work is done by unskilled workmen, and the attention is not given to it that its importance should demand.

If the joints are unglazed they should first be wet, and the space between hub and spigot completely filled with Portland cement. This cement should be made of one part Portland cement and three parts of clean sand. In the use of pipe having glazed hub and spigot ends the hub should first be calked half full with oakum, and the remaining space filled with Portland cement. This method should also be followed in making the joint between the cast-iron house drain and the earthenware house sewer.

In the case of the last-named joint, if the house sewer is more than one size larger in diameter than the drain, an increaser or reducer should be used in making the connection.

After each cement joint is made and before starting on the next one, all mortar projecting from the inside of the joints should be cleaned off by the use of a swab.

The danger of leaving superfluous cement projecting into the drain may be seen from Fig. 69. Such projections present sharp,

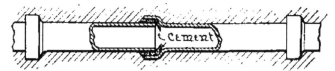

Fig. 69.—Danger of Cement Projecting inside Drain Pipe.

rough surfaces, against which various substances contained in the sewage passing through the pipe may collect.

It often happens that pipe of too large size is used for the house sewer. It is true that it is almost as serious a matter to use too large pipe for horizontal drains and sewers as to use too small pipe. If the pipe is of proper size the sewage flowing through it passes out more rapidly, and with greater scouring action than if running sluggishly at the bottom of a pipe of large diameter. Thus, in Fig. 70 it may readily be seen that as the waste in the smaller pipe

FIG. 70.—Flow of Drainage through Large and Small Pipes.

more nearly fills it than the same amount of waste in the larger pipe, such scouring action must certainly be greater in the small pipe. The solid matter carried by the sewage in the larger pipe has greater opportunity of lodging on the surface of the pipe also. Therefore, if a 5-inch pipe will perform the work in an entirely satisfactory manner it is obviously unwise to use a larger size.

The great danger in the use of earthenware pipes is that they may crack or be broken or that the joints may not be tight, under which conditions the surrounding soil becomes polluted and earth

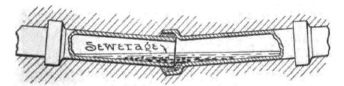

FIG. 71.—Settling and Breaking of Earthenware Pipes.

works into the drain, as in Fig. 71, eventually causing stoppage and the backing up of the house sewage. For this reason an earthenware drain or sewer should not be laid less than 3 feet beneath the surface, or within 25 feet of any well or other source of water supply.

A restriction now laid down by nearly all plumbing ordinances is that no house sewer or drain shall receive sewage from any other house. In many cities two systems of sewers are now maintained, one for the disposal of house drainage, the other for surface water. Under these conditions the rain leaders should not be connected either into the house drain or sewer. Where there is no double sewage system, however, it is allowable to connect the rain leaders into the house sewer and often allowable to connect them into the house drain. When connected into the house sewer, each rain leader should be trapped, in order to prevent direct communication with the house and public sewers.

The main trap is sometimes placed on the house sewer, but it is better to locate it inside the foundation wall on the house drain, where it is more accessible, and often less susceptible to the action of frost.

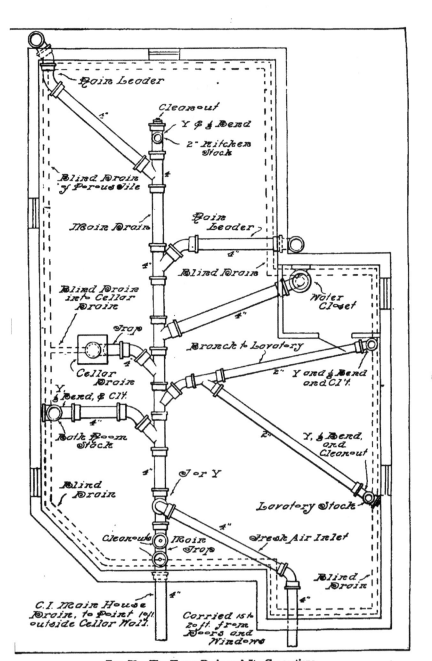

FIG. 72.—The House Drain and Its Connections.

CHAPTER X

THE HOUSE DRAIN

THE house drain is that part of the horizontal soil piping of the drainage system which receives all soil, waste, and drainage pipes of the house. In Fig. 72 is shown a plan view of a house drain, with its various connections, which may be referred to in relation to some of the following considerations.

As previously stated, it connects with the house sewer at a point 5 to 10 feet outside the foundation walls. This provision is made in order that in the event of the breaking of the house sewer, which is generally of earthenware pipe, sewage may not be able to leech back through the foundation walls into the basement

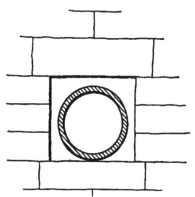

FIG. 73.—House Drain through Cellar Wall.

or cellar. The house drain should never be of earthenware pipe, the proper material for this work being either cast or wrought iron pipe. Wherever the house drain is run underground nothing but extra heavy cast-iron pipe should be used, wrought iron being especially susceptible to chemical action and decomposition when

used underground. Special provision should be made in constructing the foundation wall, to allow a passage through for the house
drain. This is a point, the importance of which seems to be but
little appreciated. The settling of the foundation walls is liable
to crush or crack the pipe at this point unless the danger is guarded
against. Figs. 73 and 74 show the proper method of construction.
The opening should be constructed with a capstone across the top,
and with space on all sides of the pipe.

If the drainage system is to be provided with a main house
trap it is best to place it as close to the point where the house drain
passes through the foundation wall as possible. There is much to
be said for and against the use of the main trap, the subject being
of such importance that a special chapter will be devoted to its
consideration. The house drain should have a grade of one half

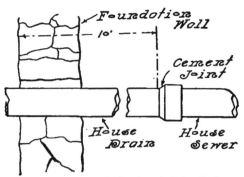

FIG. 74.—House Drain through Cellar Wall.

inch to the foot wherever possible, but in no case should it be less
than one quarter inch. This provision applies to all soil and waste
pipes also.

In running the house drain and, in fact, all other cellar or basement piping, it is always better practice to hang the piping from
the timbers, exposed to view, than to run it underground. The
running and supporting of soil piping thus installed may be seen
in Fig. 75, the supporting of such lines being made by means of
straps and hangers firmly secured to timbers, and by means of
brick or stone piers resting securely on the cellar bottom.

This, of course, cannot always be done, especially if fixtures
are located in the basement or cellar. Some cities require all underground drainage pipes to be inclosed in a boxing of chestnut
planking. This requirement is a good one, but it may be said that
it is followed in comparatively few cases. Into the house drain
are connected not only the soil and waste stacks but also cellar
drainage pipes, rain leaders, yard drains, etc., unless separate
sewers are provided for surface and subsoil water, in which case

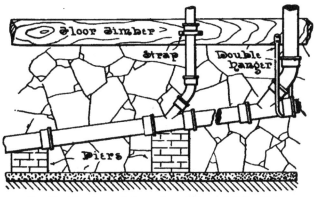

FIG. 75.—Running and Supporting of Exposed Cellar Piping.

the three last-named pipes would enter the surface-water house
drain.

In Fig. 76 is shown an illustration of the house drain, with the
several lines of soil and drainage pipes entering it. All branches
leading into the house drain should be made by means of
Ys. Tees should never be used for this purpose, and T-Ys are
objectionable on horizontal piping. The Y is preferable, for the
reason that waste is carried into the house drain by means of it in
a less abrupt manner, obviating to a large extent the splashing of
the waste against the sides of the pipe opposite the entrance. The
splashing naturally causes substances in the waste to collect about
the entrance of the branch, which will result in impeding the flow
not only in the branch but in the house drain as well. Wherever
right-angle turns are made in the piping, whether it be on hori-

zontal or vertical lines, the change in direction is made by means of a Y branch and one-eighth bend.

In Fig. 77 are shown several examples of the proper methods of making changes in direction in running soil pipe, and in Fig.

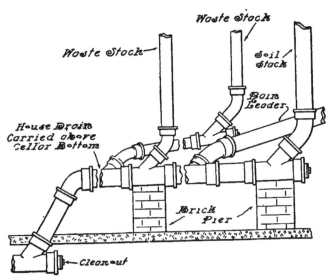

FIG. 76.—The House Drain and Pipes Discharging Into It.

78 are to be seen examples of similar work, in which changes in direction are improperly made. The reasons for considering the connections in Fig. 77 preferable to those in Fig. 78, are those which have been given above.

In Fig. 76 the connections of the waste and soil stacks into the house drain are examples of the methods of connection of Fig. 77. A cleanout should be used at the end of each horizontal run, as seen in Fig. 76.

The supporting of soil piping is a very important matter, one of those points, by the way, which is very liable to be overlooked, both by the plumber and by the architect. It is not an uncommon thing to see the house drain supported from the cellar timbers by rope and wire, or run on the face of the foundation walls with no other support than wooden pins driven into the crevices. Such methods are entirely wrong. Under each vertical line of soil or

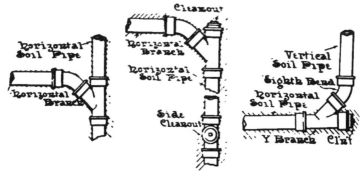

Fig. 77.—Correct Methods of Making Changes in Direction in Soil Piping.

waste pipe, at the point where it enters the house drain, a firm foundation of brick or stone should be provided to sustain the

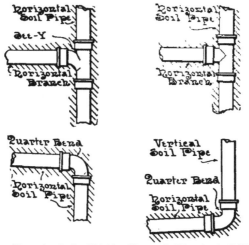

Fig. 78.—Wrong Methods of Making Changes in Direction in Soil Piping.

weight, which in the case of high buildings is often very great. Vertical lines should be supported at each floor by means of

wrought-iron bands placed under the pipe hubs, and securely
screwed to the timbers. Another method of supporting vertical
lines is shown in Fig. 79, from which it will be seen that the pipe
is so cut that at each floor it rests upon a hub. Entire dependence
for support should not be made upon this method, however.

Each line of horizontal pipe that is hung from the basement
ceiling or cellar timbers should be supported at each length. Support is provided by means of pipe hangers of wrought iron. These
hangers should be made in the form of the letter U, so that each
end may be fastened to the timber by screws. Pipe hooks should
never be used for this purpose, as they can be fastened only at one
end, and lack sufficient rigidity. Great damage is often done to

Fig. 79.—Vertical Line of Soil Pipe Supported by Hub at Each Floor.

lines of cast-iron pipe by settling, due to their own weight, a danger
which may be almost entirely obviated by the proper supporting of
the pipe. Another large factor in the weakening of lines of cast-
iron pipe, in imperfect joints, etc., is the settling of floors and
foundations.

The cellar drainage and subsoil-drainage systems are so closely
allied to the main drain that it will be well to consider them in
connection with the present subject.

The cellar drain is usually of 4-inch pipe and receives not only
the surface drainage of the cellar, but the subsoil drainage also.
The drain is formed by a deep well made in the cement cellar
bottom, the hub of a half-S cast-iron trap being cemented into the

bottom of the well. The surface of the concrete cellar bottom is formed so that from all directions it pitches down toward the cellar drain. Just inside the foundation walls and extending completely around the building a gutter is formed in the cement bottom and carried into the drainage well at its top. By means of the graded bottom and the gutter, all water on the cellar bottom, due to leakage through the walls, leakage of pipes and cocks, etc., may be conducted into the cellar drain.

Beneath the cellar bottom the subsoil drain is laid. This is constructed of porous tile without hub and spigot, and laid with

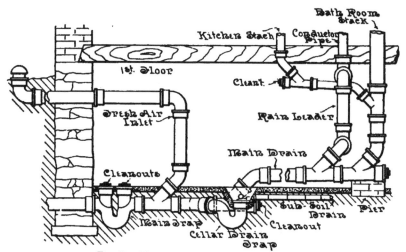

Fig. 80.—The House Drain and Its Connections.

loose, open joints, entirely around the cellar, and from the sides of the cellar into the center of it, wherever necessary. This drain is carried into the drainage well at as low a point as possible, and above the trap. Such a drain is usually employed only where the cellar bottom is damp or wet, and is not usually necessary where the soil is light or sandy.

The drainage well is usually located close to the house drain, the trap connecting into the main through a Y branch. There is danger in the use of the cellar drain, that its trap seal may be broken by evaporation, in which case, if there is no main trap on the house drain, gases and odors from the sewer may enter the cellar or basement through the cellar drain. It is therefore well to provide the trap with a trap screw which may be used to close the opening into the drainage well during periods of drought, when sufficient subsoil water does not enter the trap to maintain a seal. The trap screw may be found of value in some cases, to prevent flooding of the cellar in the event of stoppage of the house drain, or backing up of the sewer. To overcome the danger of loss of seal, in part, at least, it is well to make a deep seal trap by the use of three quarter bends. This provides a very deep seal, which

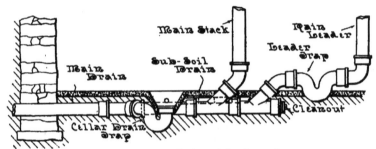

Fig. 81.—The House Drain and Its Connections.

is not easily broken. Such a trap should not be used, however, on any drain carrying other than clear water.

Fig. 80 shows the house drain of a system provided with main trap, and Fig. 81 the house drain of a system which is not thus provided. In each illustration are shown the connections of the cellar drain and subsoil drain, rain leaders, and soil and waste branches.

Fig. 82 shows some features of the testing of the house drain and its connections. In making the water or the smoke test, all openings must be closed before the test can be made, as shown in this illustration. Water is generally admitted, in the water test, through a specially constructed testing plug, which is often placed in the fresh-air inlet opening, owing to its convenience to the water connection. Besides the regular testing plugs and the plug with the water connection, a double testing plug, such as shown in Fig.

82, is generally needed, and a trap-testing plug also. The latter
is shown in Fig. 83. A sectional view of the common testing plug

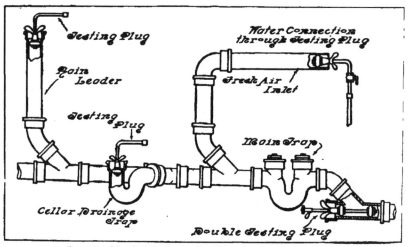

FIG. 82.—The Soil Piping in Readiness for the Water Test.

is shown in Fig. 84, and a sectional view of the double testing plug in Fig. 85. Another very desirable form of testing

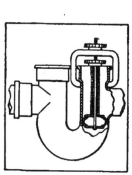

FIG. 83.—Testing Plug for
Running Trap.

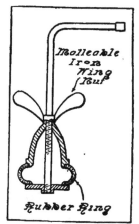

FIG. 84.—Testing Plug.

plug, capable of holding very heavy pressures is illustrated in Fig. 86.

The single testing plug of Fig. 84 operates by the expansion, against the sides of the pipe, of a heavy rubber ring, which is ex-

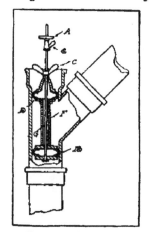

FIG. 85.—The Double
Testing Plug.

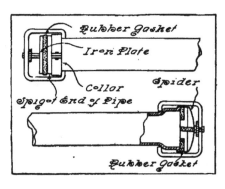

FIG. 86.—Special Testing Plugs.

panded by being compressed between an iron plate and a wing nut working on a screw. The operation of the double testing plug is as follows: The hollow piece F connects the plug D and the plug B

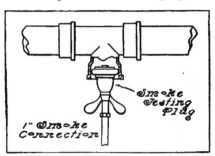

FIG. 87.—Smoke Testing Plug.

rigidly, and inside of it the rod G works. When the wheel A is turned against the nut E, it expands the plug B, and the plug D is expanded without disturbing the other plug, by turning up the nut C.

Figs. 87 and 88 show methods used in giving the smoke test. For the stopping of openings, ordinary testing plugs may be used. In admitting smoke to the system, however, the method shown

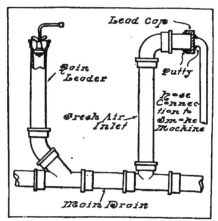

Fig. 88.—Plumbing under Smoke Test.

in Fig. 88 is generally used. Smoke-testing plugs which admit smoke through them, such as in Fig. 87, are also very handy for this purpose.

In " Modern Plumbing Illustrated," * by the author of this work, the subjects of water, air, peppermint and smoke tests are taken up very comprehensively, in all their details, in connection with both large and small work.

---

* "Modern Plumbing Illustrated" by R. M. Starbuck is published by The Norman W. Henley Publishing Co., 132 Nassau Street, New York. Price $4.00.

CHAPTER XI

SOIL PIPING—ROUGHING-IN

THE term soil pipe is used in a popular manner to designate all iron drainage piping, and it is also applied to the cast-iron piping used on the vent system. As a matter of fact, soil pipe is that part of the iron pipe of the drainage system through which the waste from water-closets flows. Other pipe, even though of the same size as the soil pipe, but carrying waste from other fixtures, is called waste pipe. However, the term soil pipe has come to be used so universally to designate all cast-iron pipe, whether used as soil, waste, or vent, that it will be more convenient to refer to it occasionally in this general way.

In Fig. 89 is shown a system of soil piping to which reference will be made later. In this system the main back-air or vent pipes are of cast iron. Wrought iron is being used very largely for this purpose at the present time, and it appears to be replacing the cast iron on this part of the system, in many sections.

In fact the use of wrought-iron pipe for vent work has become almost universal. Long, straight lines of wrought-iron pipe are more quickly run than cast iron, and closer connections can be made.

Several matters which might properly be considered here have already been taken up, such as the supporting of horizontal soil piping, etc. Vertical lines of soil and waste pipe should be supported at each floor by a clamp placed under the hub of a pipe or fitting, and firmly screwed to the timber. This support not only prevents the settling of the stack, but also prevents any side motion of the pipe.

All first-class plumbing ordinances now require the use of extra heavy cast-iron pipe on the drainage system in preference to standard pipe. The reason for this is that the standard pipe being much lighter has more sand holes and defects than the extra heavy.

Unless the standard pipe is cast perfectly, one part of the circumference will be very thin, while the section directly opposite will be correspondingly thick. When in this condition it takes only a slight blow to break the pipe. In the cutting of standard pipe and in the calking of joints, split lengths of pipe and split fittings are much more liable to result than in the use of extra heavy pipe. Many times such defective pipe and fittings are not cast aside as they should be, but made use of, the defects being patched up with tar so that they may not be detected. Principally to make such practices impossible, some ordinances demand the use of soil pipe which has no asphaltum coating.

The weights of different materials used on the plumbing system are, viz.:

Weights of Cast-Iron Pipe

2-inch	Standard	C.-I.	Pipe	Weighs	$3\frac{1}{2}$	lbs.	per	foot
3-inch	"	"	"	"	$4\frac{1}{2}$	"	"	"
4-inch	"	"	"	"	$6\frac{1}{2}$	"	"	"
5-inch	"	"	"	"	8	"	"	"
6-inch	"	"	"	"	10	"	"	"
2-inch	Extra Heavy	"	"	"	$5\frac{1}{2}$	"	"	"
3-inch	"	"	"	"	"	$9\frac{1}{2}$	"	"	"
4-inch	"	"	"	"	"	13	"	"	"
5-inch	"	"	"	"	"	17	"	"	"
6-inch	"	"	"	"	"	20	"	"	"
7-inch	"	"	"	"	"	27	"	"	"
8-inch	"	"	"	"	"	$33\frac{1}{2}$	"	"	"
10-inch	"	"	"	"	"	45	"	"	"

Weights of Wrought-Iron Pipe

Diameter.	Thickness.	Weight per ft.
$1\frac{1}{2}$ inches	.14 inch	2.68 lbs.
2 "	.15 "	3.61 "
$2\frac{1}{2}$ "	.20 "	5.74 "
3 "	.21 "	7.54 "
$3\frac{1}{2}$ "	.22 "	9 "
4 "	.23 "	10.66 "
$4\frac{1}{2}$ "	.24 "	12.34 "

Diameter.	Thickness.	Weight per ft.
5 inches	.25 inch	14.50 lbs.
6 "	.28 "	18.76 "
7 "	.30 "	23.27 "
8 "	.32 "	28.18 "
9 "	.34 "	33.7 "
10 "	.36 "	40.06 "

Weights of Brass Pipe

Diameter.	Thickness.	Weight per ft.
1½ inches	.14 inch	2.84 lbs.
2 "	.15 "	3.82 "
2½ "	.20 "	6.08 "
3 "	.21 "	7.92 "
3½ "	.22 "	9.54 "
4 "	.23 "	11.29 "
4½ "	.24 "	13.08 "
5 "	.25 "	15.37 "
6 "	.28 "	19.88 "

Weights of Lead Pipe

Diameter.	Weight per ft.
1 inch	2 lbs.
1¼ "	2½ "
1½ "	3 "
2 "	3½ "
3 "	4½ "
4 "	6 "

As will be seen later, in the description of the Durham plumbing system, whenever wrought-iron pipe is used for drainage purposes, the fittings used in connection with it should be of cast iron. They should be of the style known as extra heavy cast iron, recessed, and threaded drainage fittings. These fittings should also be used on main vent lines of wrought iron, although it is true that in many cases they are not used on such work.

For fixture and branch vents of wrought iron it is permissible to use galvanized cast or malleable steam and water fittings. In the use of short nipples on either drainage or vent work, special care should be taken in order that they may not be split or crushed in any way. When the nipple is of such length that the distance between the two threaded ends, that is, the part unthreaded, is less than 1½ inches, the nipple should be of " extra strong " pipe.

The term " roughing-in " is applied to the plumbing system when it has reached the point where the first test is to be applied. The " roughing-in " includes the entire soil-pipe system, house drain, soil and waste stacks, main vent lines, all branch wastes and vents. In fact, the " roughing-in " includes the entire plumbing system with the exception of exposed work above the floor, that is, the fixture itself, its trap and waste to the floor, and the vent connection to the wall. Figs. 89 and 110 will give an idea of what is meant by " roughing-in."

In roughing-in, wherever waste pipes are to be run of more than six feet in length, lead pipe should not be used. The use of lead for drainage and vent work is fast going out of date, cast and wrought iron and brass taking its place. The labor involved in lead work, properly constructed, is greater than in the use of other materials; it is less rigid; long lines of lead pipe are liable to sag and form traps; and lead pipe is sometimes subject to the attack of rats, the generally accepted idea being that in their attack they are attempting to reach the water which they hear flowing through the pipes.

To such an extent has lead work been replaced in many parts of the country that the trade of the plumber of to-day has changed almost entirely from that which the old-time lead worker followed. There was a time not many years back when the plumber made his own traps, bends, etc., and a time when lead soil pipe was used. All that is now changed, and although the older plumbers may not agree to it, it would seem that this great change is for the better.

In the running of horizontal soil, waste, and vent pipes, they should have a grade of at least one-quarter inch to the foot, and more than this amount is preferable. Wherever possible, each fixture should have a separate entrance into its stack. This is a practice which is by no means generally followed, and it certainly does

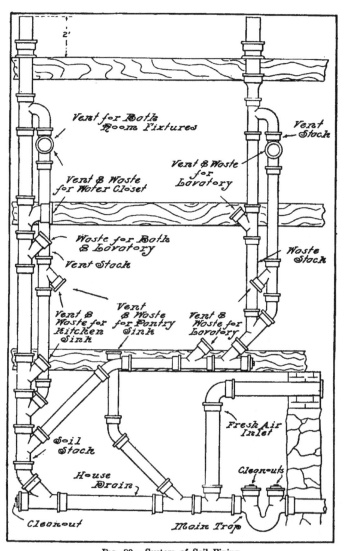

Fig. 89.—System of Soil Piping.

not receive the attention which it deserves. Referring to Fig. 90, it will be noted that the bath tub and lavatory are served by the same line of lead waste pipe. This is not to be considered an unsanitary practice, and many times it would be almost impossible to construct the work otherwise. If the waste pipe should become stopped at any point between the lavatory connection and the stack, it may readily be seen that both lavatory and bath would be affected. If each had a separate connection the stoppage of one

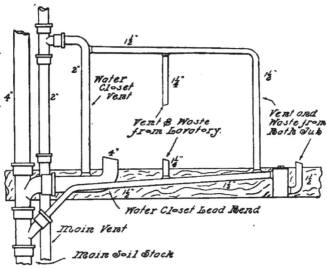

Fig. 90.—"Roughing-in."

waste would not affect the other. It may be stated further that very often the plumber might obtain separate entrance for each fixture, but in a vast majority of cases the work is taken under contract, and the betterment of the work by making separate entrance would result in additional expense to him. In other instances the architect might easily lay out the work and make locations of pipes and fixtures such that separate entrances might easily be made. For instance, in the floor plan of Fig. 91, the relative locations of fixtures and stack are such that each fixture may waste independently into the stack, as will be seen in Fig.

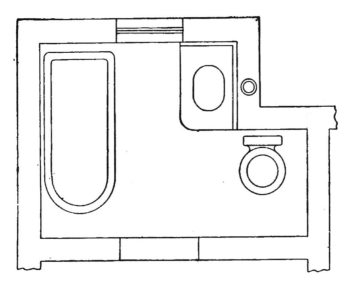

FIG. 91.—Floor Plan of Bath Room.

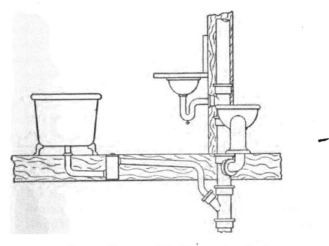

FIG. 92.—Separate Entrance of Each Fixture into Stack.

92, which shows an elevation of the work of Fig. 91. Mention should be made of the practice which is almost universal in certain sections, of connecting the waste pipes from lavatories and bath tubs into the water-closet lead bend. This is a practice followed by a surprisingly large number of plumbers who pride themselves on the excellence of their work; and it is generally allowed both by the architect and the plumbing inspector.

Nevertheless, it is a poor practice, and never to be followed if it is possible to construct the work otherwise. While the practice is bad under any conditions, certain methods of performing this work are far better than others. In Fig. 93 two different methods of

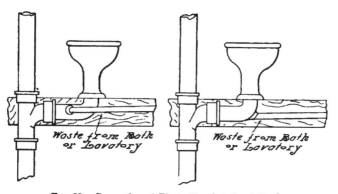

Fig. 93.—Connection of Waste Pipe into Lead Bend.

making the connection are to be seen, into the heel of the bend, and into the upper part of the horizontal arm. The latter is far preferable to the former. When connected into the heel, the opening is in such a position that paper and other matter may fall into the entrance and result eventually in its stoppage. When so connected the connection is often made so low that soil and other waste has an opportunity to set back into the waste pipe whenever the water-closet is flushed. When connected as high up as possible on the horizontal arm, however, neither of these faults is encountered.

The connection of a fixture waste into the vertical part of the lead bend is preferable to the heel connection, but not so good as into the horizontal arm.

In any of these connections, however, another serious fault is to be found. In the wiping of the connection onto the lead bend, small spines of solder are extremely liable to project through into the interior of the bend and cause much trouble by the catching of paper, etc., upon them. When other fixture wastes connect into the lead bend, another serious feature presents itself in the fact that the stoppage of the lead bend results in the disabling of all fixtures connected to it.

No fixture waste should ever pass through more than one trap before reaching the house drain, the effect of double trapping being to cause air-lock between the two traps, which acts to impede the flow of waste through the pipe. Where an abrupt change is made in the direction of a pipe, on the drainage system, a cleanout should be used at that point. End cleanouts should be used as seen in Fig. 89, at the ends of horizontal lines. In running such horizontal lines no dead end should ever be left. By dead end is meant an extension of drainage pipe beyond the last entrance of waste into it. Thus, in Fig. 89, if the house drain were extended beyond the point where the cleanout is, and no waste entered this extension, it would become a dead end. The dead end not only serves no useful purpose, but soon fills with filth, and aids materially in fouling the drainage system.

In the running of drainage pipes, whether on main or branch lines, all offsets should be made at 45° if possible, this giving a much easier passage for the waste than an abrupt offset, such as 90°. Formerly it was customary in making an opening into a pipe for a new fixture waste or branch line of waste to use a saddle fitting, such fitting usually being held in position over the opening cut in the pipe, by wrought-iron clamps, the joint between the fitting and the pipe being made with putty. For obvious reasons this practice is now prohibited, it being a most unsanitary method.

The proper method of performing such work is to break out the pipe at the desired point, and insert the necessary fitting. On such work as this the use of insertable fittings has in recent years become universal. There are several such fittings on the market, and in Fig. 94 two of them are shown. It being desired to insert the fitting A to receive a new line of waste, the pipe at this point is broken out and the spigot end of the insertable fitting calked in.

The fitting A is then set in position, and the part F unscrewed until its hub and the spigot of A are together. The several joints are then calked. The part B of the insertable fitting is provided with a coarse cast thread in which the thread on G works. Such a fitting saves much time and makes more satisfactory work, for in many instances in the insertion of fittings into old pipe, several

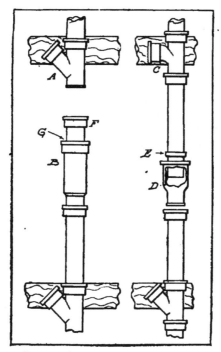

FIG. 94.—The Use of Insertable Fittings.

joints on each side of the fitting have to be sprung in order to get the new fitting into position, and it is then necessary to recalk these joints. The other insertable fitting of Fig. 94 is made on a different principle. It consists of a long hub of large diameter, D, into which a ring of soft lead, E, may be calked when the fitting C has been placed in position.

From what has been stated in previous chapters, it will be seen that in any plumbing system it is necessary that at least one 4-inch pipe shall pass through the roof. Whenever a vent passes through the roof it should extend at least two feet above it.

If a flat roof is used for other purposes than the mere covering of the building, such pipes should extend at least five feet above it.

Whenever a branch line of soil or waste pipe is extended 15 feet or more from the main soil or waste stack into which it is connected, the branch should be carried through the roof.

Soil, waste, or vent pipe should ordinarily not be carried on the outside of any building. Such a prohibition is imperative in a cold climate, but there is not so much to be said against it when practiced in a warm climate, where there is no trouble from frost to be feared. When a building adjoins another of greater height having doors or windows overlooking the lower building, the openings of all roof pipes coming through the roof of the lower building should be at least 12 feet from windows and doors in the higher building, and no roof pipe should be closer than 6 feet to any chimney opening. It is quite customary to use a wire basket or other protector to cover the open end of a roof pipe, but there is something to be said against the practice. The meshes of the basket being somewhat close together furnish opportunity for the collection of frost over the basket in cold weather, resulting in the entire or partial stoppage of the vent opening. The practice, however, would not be open to objection in warm climates and would act as a protection against the entrance through the roof pipe of leaves, etc.

The roof connection is made in a variety of ways, either with sheet lead or with patented roof flanges. In Figs. 95 to 100 are shown several of these connections. Fig. 95 shows a device that is, perhaps, used more extensively than others. It consists of a cast-iron hub riveted to a copper flange, the latter being nailed to the roof as shown.

The roof flange of Fig. 96 is also a patented device, consisting of a lead body attached to a copper flange, having at its upper end an iron ring into which a lead ring is calked. The use of the soft lead ring obviates the necessity of carrying a pot of molten metal to the roof with which to make the lead joint. Fig. 97 shows a flange which may be used on roofs of any pitch, the joint being made by a

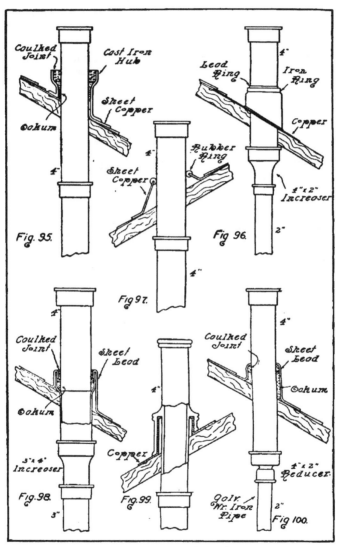

FIGS. 95–100.—Roof Connections.

rubber ring which encircles the pipe. Unless the surface of the pipe is smooth, the rubber is not liable to make perfect contact around the entire circumference, in which case leakage of water down the outside of the pipe will follow. Moreover, the life of rubber is not of long duration, when exposed to the air and weather, and soon loses its elasticity. Fig. 98 shows a method often followed by the workman in making his own roof flange, as does Fig. 100 also. In Fig. 98 the sheet lead is flanged over and down into the

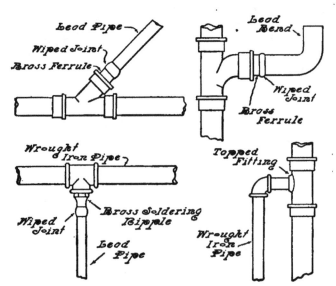

Fig. 101.—Connections between Lead-, Wrought- and Cast-Iron Pipes.

hub. When the lead joint is poured and calked, a very satisfactory piece of work results. In Fig. 100 the sheet lead forms an upright collar around the pipe, and after the joint is poured and calked the end of the collar is rounded over as shown. Fig. 99 shows a very satisfactory roof flange, in the use of which leakage of roof water down the pipe is an impossibility. A very popular feature of this device is the fact that no lead joint has to be poured and calked on the roof. This is a point much appreciated by the workman, as it is often difficult, particularly on steep roofs, to melt and pour the metal for a calked joint. The copper collar fitting up into this device is loose, being held rigidly only at the roof. Consequently, the settling of the roof does not tear away any part of the connection and result in leakage. In several of the illustrations various reducing fittings are to be seen.

Plumbing ordinances lay down special rules for the making of connections between different kinds of pipe. In Fig. 101 are to be seen the common connections, and other connections will be shown later on, in the consideration of special subjects, such as the Durham system. Lead pipe is connected to cast-iron pipe by means of a brass ferrule, to which the lead pipe is connected by a wiped joint, the ferrule being calked into the pipe. One of the figures shown illustrates the lead bend connected in the same way. Lead pipe is connected to wrought-iron pipe by means of a brass soldering nipple. One end of the nipple is threaded and screws into the fitting on the wrought-iron pipe, the lead pipe connecting with the other end by means of a wiped joint. Sometimes in place of the wiped joint a cup joint or an overcast joint is used. The cup joint is made by swelling out the end of the lead pipe, dropping the pipe, ferrule, or nipple into the bell end thus formed, and with a soldering copper the two are soldered together. The overcast joint is made by the use of a soldering copper, the solder being formed around the joint in the form of a wiped joint, and then smoothed over with a rasp or file to give it the smoothness and symmetry of a wiped joint.

Neither of these joints is allowed by plumbing ordinances, although they are used to a large extent in sections that are not under plumbing restrictions. The wiped joint is much stronger and more perfect than either the cup or overcast joint.

Wrought-iron pipe is connected to cast-iron pipe by means of tapped fittings, into which the wrought-iron pipe may be screwed. Wrought iron is also sometimes calked into the hubs of cast-iron pipe if the sizes happen to come right. If not, a coupling screwed onto the end of the wrought-iron pipe will often allow it to be calked.

Before leaving the subject of "roughing-in," the matter of fixture wastes should be considered, as the concealed work on the fixture wastes is constructed during the "roughing in." It will

therefore be appropriate to insert at this point the following table
of sizes of fixture wastes:

	Size of Waste.
Fixture.	*Inches.*
Water-closet	4
Slop sink	3
Pedestal urinal	3
Floor and yard drains..................	3
Horse stall	2
Urinal trough	2
Laundry tubs (3 to 6 parts).............	2
Laundry tubs (1 to 3 parts).............	$1\frac{1}{2}$
Kitchen sink	$1\frac{1}{2}$ or 2
Pantry sink	$1\frac{1}{2}$
Bath tub	$1\frac{1}{2}$
Sitz bath	$1\frac{1}{2}$
Foot bath	$1\frac{1}{2}$
Shower bath	$1\frac{1}{2}$
Safe wastes	$1\frac{1}{4}$
Lavatory	$1\frac{1}{4}$
Group of lavatories (2 or 3)............	$1\frac{1}{2}$
Drinking fountain	$1\frac{1}{4}$
Refrigerator	$1\frac{1}{4}$

The cellar piping is a most important matter of " roughing-in."
There are two common methods of running this piping, the most
common being that of Fig. 102, in which the pipe is concealed underground. The other method is to run it exposed, in which case
it is generally carried on the cellar timbers. The latter method
(Fig. 103) is the preferable one, and when so run support should
be given it according to the method of Fig. 104, but never according to Fig. 105. An important feature in installing cellar piping
is to insure making all cleanouts readily accessible. Such provision
is to be noted in both Fig. 102 and Fig. 103. Many times the
piping cannot be run so that it is practicable to support it from
the cellar timbers because of its distance from them. In that case
the piping should be supported on brick or stone piers, as in Figs.
106 and 107, especially under vertical stacks. When the piping

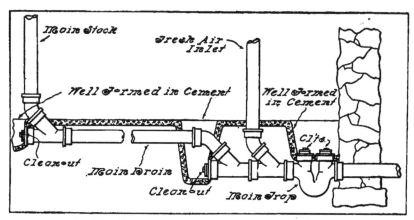

Fig. 102.—Good Method of Running House Drain Underground.

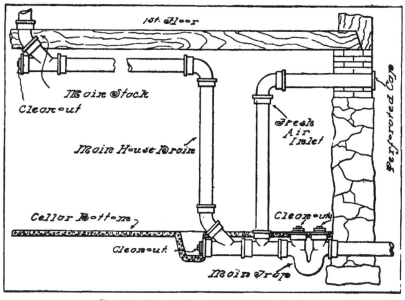

Fig. 103.—Line of House Drain Run Overhead.

is run horizontally through finished rooms and exposed to view the neatest method of supporting it is by means of special pipe-supporting fittings, as in Fig. 108.

The supporting of vertical lines of pipe is shown in Fig. 109. The best method consists of the use of wrought-iron bands or clamps at each floor.

Having completed the consideration of the general subject of

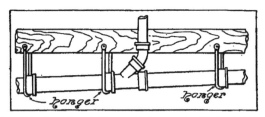

FIG. 104.—The Use of Hangers in Supporting Horizontal Pipe.

soil piping, it will be of advantage to many of the readers of this work to devote some space to certain features pertaining to the practical construction of soil-pipe work, taking up first the operation of calking a lead joint.

In general, this joint is made by first tamping oakum into the hub of the soil pipe, then in pouring molten lead into the hub, after

FIG. 105.—Poor Practice—Use of Pipe Hooks in Supporting Horizontal Pipe.

which it is calked. To many a plumber the simple act of putting in the oakum, tamping it down a little, and then pouring on top of this a little molten lead seems to constitute the whole subject of making a calked joint. There is much more than this to be considered, however, if a successful piece of work is to be done. It is a fact that in many tests applied to the "roughing-in" almost as

much time is consumed in repairing defects in the soil piping
which the test brings to light as was consumed in the construction
of the work. Much of such trouble comes from imperfectly calked

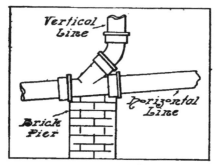

Fig. 106.—Horizontal Line of Pipe Supported by Pier

soil-pipe joints. In making a calked joint the oakum should never
be dropped in loosely, as is often done. It should first be formed
into a tight roll a little larger than the width of the joint to be

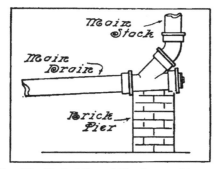

Fig. 107.—Vertical Line of Pipe Supported by Pier.

made. The plumber usually gets his oakum into the right condition by rolling it on his knee. The oakum is then forced into the
hub with a yarning iron and firmly calked with a regular calking
tool, so that a good foundation is made for the lead. In fact, if the
oakum is properly calked, it should be nearly water tight before the

lead is poured. The oakum should fill the hub to within about an inch of the top. It is a mistake to use a great depth of lead, for the reason that while the effect of the calking might be felt at any depth, the really beneficial expansion of the lead is felt only through a comparatively small depth. If the lead is over an inch in depth, it does not feel the effect of the blow on the calking tool sufficiently to cause it to expand properly. As a consequence, the additional metal is of no real value, merely filling space which the oakum might fill at less expense. The lead should not be poured until the metal is hot. The same care does not have to be given to the melting of lead that is needed in melting solder, for the reason

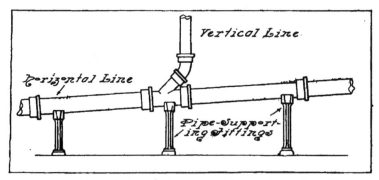

FIG. 108.—Horizontal Line of Pipe Supported by Pipe-Supporting Fittings.

that it contains no tin that may be burned up. It is well to heat the lead close to a cherry red. This heat insures the successful running of the metal, without the necessity of repouring. The lead should fill the hub. The lead is now ready to be calked, and before finishing this operation it is a good plan to thoroughly calk the outer and inner circumferences of the lead, this course insuring an expansion against the sides of the pipe, which are the points where defects are most likely to appear. Calking tools may be ground specially for calking each of these circumferences. When a joint calked as described is finished the hub will be full, whereas if the oakum had been dropped in or loosely calked, the lead, when calked, would have settled down below the top of the hub, necessitating a second pouring many times. When the lead is poured it should be seen that no small fiber of oakum is left reaching up to the top of the hub, as this often is the cause of a leaky joint, the water finding its way along the fiber through the lead.

Another feature on which successful calking depends lies in the quality of the lead used. Calking lead should be as soft as possible,

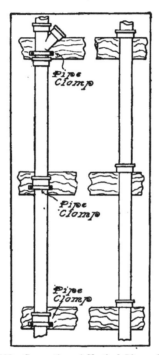

Fig. 109.—Supporting of Vertical Lines of Pipe.

and therefore free from zinc, solder, etc. For this purpose old lead pipe is often melted up, and may be easily made too hard by allowing the solder from old joints on the pipe to be melted with it. The calking of joints on vertical lines of pipe is straightforward work, but in the case of horizontal joints special means must be adopted to prevent the metal flowing out of the hub before it has an opportunity to cool.

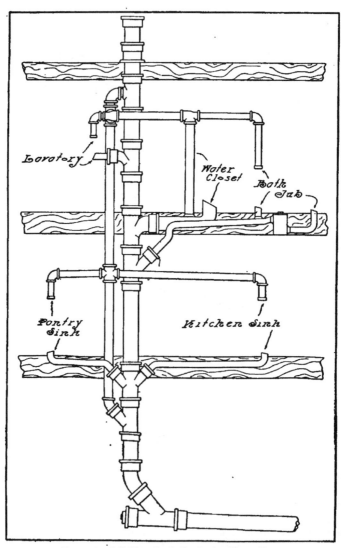

Fig. 110.—Soil Pipe Stack Ready for Water Test.

The old-style method consisted in winding a rope of putty, clay, or flax and putty around the pipe in such a way as to close up the opening between the hub and the pipe. A small opening was then made at the top to allow the metal to flow through. Now, however, special joint runners are generally used for this purpose. They are made of asbestos rope and provided with a special clamp for holding the rope in position and for forming a gate for the metal.

In connection with the calking of lead joints a great variety of tools are used. The plumber is generally very particular concerning his calking tools, and in order that they may be exactly suited to his individual requirements he very often has them made special instead of using the tools ordinarily carried in stock.

The illustration and use of special calking tools is taken up in Chapter I.

In Fig. 110 is shown a system of soil piping which constitutes the " roughing-in " of the plumbing system, and which has been made ready for testing. This system, with its cast-iron stack and galvanized wrought-iron vent work, is typical of the method of construction generally employed on such work, the use of wrought iron for vent work being now more universal than such work as shown in Fig. 89.

CHAPTER XII

MAIN TRAP AND FRESH-AIR INLET

THE use of this trap is open for discussion, and its advantages and disadvantages have been debated more extensively probably than any other subject relating to the drainage system.

Its advocates have strong arguments in its favor and its opponents advance sound arguments against it.

When the main trap is made use of on the plumbing system it

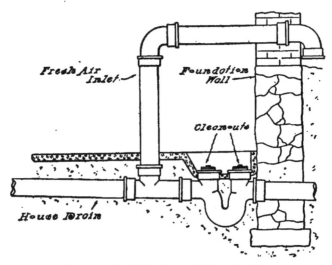

FIG. 111.—The Main Trap and Fresh-Air Inlet.

is located on the house drain and as close to the point where it leaves the building as possible. Fig. 111 shows the connections of the main trap and fresh-air inlet, the latter being a necessity wherever the main trap is used, as will be seen later. The purpose of this trap is to safeguard the building against the entrance into it

141

from the sewer of sewer air and gases. The chief argument against the use of the main trap is that each soil and waste stack passing through the roof should have an unobstructed path throughout its course to the public sewer, in order that it may act as a vent for the sewer. In other words, the non-use of the main trap is advocated in order that every roof connection in the town or city may become a part of a great ventilating system for the public sewer system. It is not to be denied that every system of sewers needs ventilation, and that better provision is needed than is generally provided. The closed, unventilated system without ventilation of any kind is undoubtedly an exceedingly foul and filthy affair and a source of great danger to the community.

It is a question, however, whether the use of the house plumbing system as a sewer vent is desirable, and it is a question whether other adequate means cannot be provided for performing this work with as great efficiency.

At present, in most cities, the chief means of sewer ventilation is through perforated manhole covers in the streets. Needless to say, the amount of ventilation provided in this way is entirely insufficient for the amount of work to be done, and in addition it may be said that in many cases the perforations of the manhole covers become filled with dirt and in the winter time with ice and snow. Moreover, the venting of sewers into public thoroughfares is an unsanitary practice, but one which the public has become accustomed to, and therefore gives small attention to. Other means than this should be provided. One plan has been advanced which would seem to have many valuable features. It has been proposed to erect at available high points on the sewer system large ventilating stacks through which to exhaust the sewers of foul air and to draw into them a supply of fresh air. This method would entail considerable public expense, but would seem to be an object worthy of the outlay, inasmuch as it affects the public health to a large degree. Such a method seems to be far preferable to venting the sewer at all points in the community, where in heavy weather gases are bound to settle down and become a source of danger to the entire people.

It may be a point not generally appreciated, but a fact, nevertheless, that there are very few plumbing systems that have been in use for a period of years which are not defective in various ways. The settling of foundations and floors is bound to produce defective soil-pipe joints, and even result in the cracking of pipe and fittings in some instances. The action of the acids and gases from the house sewage often results injuriously to lead and iron work, and especially to wrought iron. Many other causes of defects in the plumbing system might be named, and it is safe to say that in a large majority of instances the plumbing system would fail under the tests applied to it when first installed.

The point of all this is that through the various defects in the drainage and vent system abundant opportunity is offered for the entrance of sewer air and gases from the sewer into the living rooms of the house.

The purpose of the main trap is to overcome this trouble and to prevent the occurrence of the same conditions from various other causes. For instance, the main trap prevents the entrance of sewer air through the cellar drain, floor drain, and other traps in the event of loss of seal. In the case of fixtures seldom in use the fixture trap often loses its seal through evaporation; fixture traps often lose their seals through siphonage and other causes. Danger is avoided under such conditions by the use of the house trap.

When water-closets are removed from their position, to be renewed or for the making of repairs, direct communication between the house and sewer results unless the main trap is used, as also in the case of repairs or renewals on the cast-iron drainage system, such as the inserting of fittings to receive the waste from new fixtures, etc.

These are a few of the many ways in which the house may become open to the entrance of sewer air, and the facts as presented certainly make a strong argument in favor of the use of the main trap. Some of the minor arguments against its use are the facts that it is liable to freeze when located in cold places, that it will close up with heavy substances in the sewage, and that it presents an obstruction to the free passage of sewage from the house. The two first-named arguments appear to have little weight, as practical experience shows that the trap seal seldom freezes, and that it is very seldom that a main trap becomes stopped up. The waste from the house is generally warm, and, with the exercise of good judgment, the trap can be so located or otherwise protected that it need not be in danger of freezing.

To be sure, the trap prevents the outflow of sewage as rapidly as a free passage would allow, but this fact seldom is found to be the cause of special trouble, and the fresh-air inlet aids materially in the easy passage of the sewage.

The trap used under each fixture is liable to stoppage and presents an obstruction to the rapid outflow of waste, but the facts are never used as an argument in favor of discontinuing the use of the fixture trap. No more should the same arguments avail in discontinuing the use of the main trap.

The first point named in opposition to the use of the main trap is without doubt, then, the strongest argument against it, and really the only one, and it would seem that the weight of argument is in favor of the use of the main trap.

In connection with the main trap the fresh-air inlet is always necessary. For the ordinary house having a 4- or 5-inch house drain the fresh-air inlet should be 4 inches.

Its purpose is twofold. Its chief end is to convey into the drainage system a supply of fresh air and to create a circulation of air through the drainage system and through the roof pipes. It also makes the passage of waste through the house drain easier, as it prevents air lock between the outflowing waste and the seal of the main trap by venting the house drain at a point near the trap.

An objection to the fresh-air inlet is that, in the case of a down draught, foul odors may be driven out through the inlet. These odors, however, do not come from the sewer, and are therefore not so much to be feared. Valves of various kinds have been used to admit fresh air and to prevent the escape of foul air, but in general they are not to be depended upon and are usually looked upon as a failure. Because of the occasional escape of odors the fresh-air inlet opening should never be located within 20 feet of any door or window. This often necessitates the running of the fresh-air inlet out into the lawn, yard, or to the curb, in which case, at the point where it comes to the surface a ventilating cap should cover its end in order that nothing may enter or be thrown into it. The fresh-air inlet is strictly for purposes of ventilation, and under no circumstances should drainage of any description be allowed to enter it. When carried only to the outside face of the foundation wall the fresh-air inlet should be provided at its end with a perforated cover, or, as shown in Fig. 111, with a bend pointing down.

The main trap is sometimes located on the house drain or house sewer underground. When so located the chief precaution necessary is to make it easily accessible, and this may best be done by placing it in a well at such depth as to be protected from the frost, as shown in Fig. 112. When placed underground the fresh-air inlet for the main trap is generally carried straight to the surface,

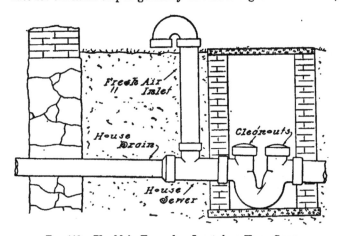

FIG. 112.—The Main Trap when Located on House Sewer.

as in Fig. 112, in which case its open end should be protected by a bend.

The best practice calls for the connection of the fresh-air inlet to a tee or Y placed next to the main trap. Until within a few years the custom was to connect it into the cleanout hub on the house side of the trap. This method not only deprived the trap of one of its cleanouts, but brought cold air so directly upon the seal of the trap that the water often became chilled.

Even though the trap seal should not become cold enough freeze, the mere chilling of it should be avoided, for when sewage becomes chilled the grease contained in it separates out and collects on the cold surfaces exposed to it.

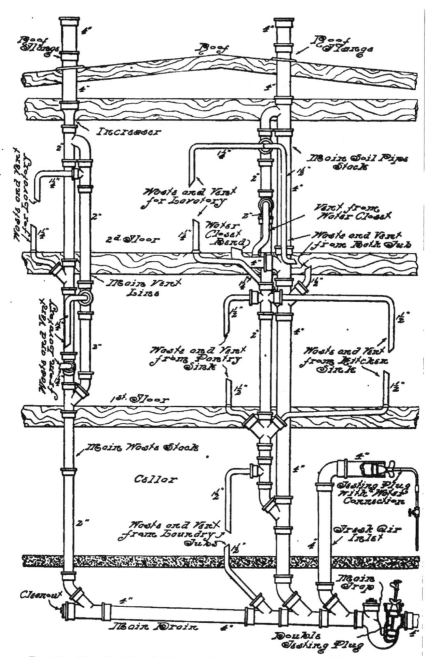

FIG. 113.—"Roughing" for the Plumbing System, with Main Trap and Fresh-Air Inlet.

In order to avoid this trouble the fresh-air inlet is now generally connected as mentioned above, thus making the entrance of cold air less direct. The fresh-air inlet should always be connected on the house side of the main trap. If connected on the sewer side it would act as a direct vent for the sewer and be unable to perform the duties for which it is designed. The fixture trap vent, however, should always be connected on the sewer side of the trap. There is sometimes confusion on the part of people respecting the connection of these two forms of vents, but there should not be, if due consideration is given to the different purposes of the two.

In Fig. 113 is shown an elevation of a plumbing system which is provided with a main trap and fresh-air inlet.

In this illustration is shown only the roughing, with the ends of vents and wastes sealed, preparatory to the water test. In the main trap is shown a double testing plug and in the fresh-air inlet a single testing plug, with water connection, the fresh-air inlet usually being a handy place for connecting the water to the system in testing.

CHAPTER XIII

FLOOR DRAINS, YARD DRAINS, CELLAR DRAINERS, RAIN LEADERS, ETC.

THE subject of floor drains pertains more especially to large work of a public nature, such as public toilet rooms of hotels, schools, factories, etc., apparatus rooms and hose towers of engine houses, washrooms of stables, etc., and in general seldom appears in residence or other similar work. In general, the remarks on the cellar drain, made in a previous chapter, apply also to floor and yard drains.

Whenever a double system of sewers is provided, one for house drainage and the other for surface water, these drains should be connected to the surface house drain, but in the absence of the double system they may be connected to the house drainage system. Floor drains should be at least 3 inches in diameter and be provided with deep seal traps, with cleanouts of the same size.

An example of floor-drain connections may be seen in Fig. 114. The floor should be graded so that all water falling on it may run into the drain. It is very customary to use the drain having a bell trap as shown in detail in Fig. 114. This trap is a very shallow one, whose seal is easily lost from evaporation. It is preferable to use a plain drain without the bell attachment and use a deep seal cast-iron trap, as shown. All yards, areas, or other similar surface should be provided with a drain similar to that of Fig. 114. Whenever connected to the house drain direct, each should be separately trapped. Two or more drains of this character may often be connected into one main, in which case each separate drain does not require a separate trap, but a trap placed on the main may be used instead to protect the several drains. It is often convenient also to connect floor and yard drains into rain leader pipes, under which conditions the trap on the rain leader offers sufficient protection without the trapping of each drain. In fact, connections of this kind have an advantage over separate trap connections in the fact that when dependence is made on the one trap the several drains may be depended upon to renew and maintain its seal with much more certainty than a single drain could be depended upon to maintain the seal of its own trap. Stable wash racks or other wash racks from which waste, carrying sediment or solid matter, issues, should not be connected to any part of the drainage system

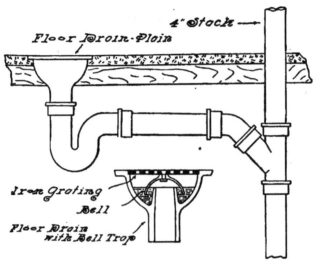

FIG. 114.—Floor Drain.

unless a catch basin with trap is provided to prevent such matter from passing into the drainage system.

All rain leaders should be trapped on plumbing systems which are not provided with a main trap, but on the trapped system the trapping of rain leaders is not necessary, as the main trap affords protection to the roof leaders. In general, the least number of traps possible to afford ample protection is preferable to the use of a greater number, as double trapping is attended with greater danger of stoppage and with a much slower outflow of sewage, owing to air lock between the traps. Whenever rain leaders are run to the roof inside the building they should be constructed of soil pipe,

but when run outside they may be of galvanized sheet iron to a
point not less than five feet from the ground, at which point they
should enter a soil-pipe branch. In Fig. 115 are shown the customary rain-leader connections. When the rain leader is run inside
the building, of cast iron, the connection with the roof gutter

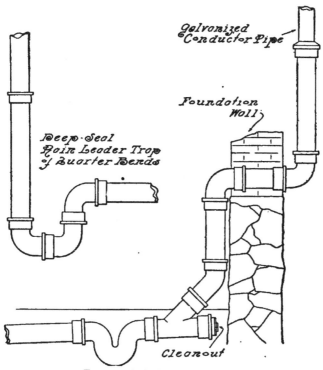

FIG. 115.—Rain Leader Connections.

should be made by means of a brass ferrule, calked into the soil
pipe, to which is wiped the lead or copper pipe connecting with the
gutter. The opening of the gutter connection should be funnel-
shaped and provided with a wire basket as a protection against the
entrance of leaves, twigs, etc., into the conductor pipe and drainage
system.

When two or more rain leaders enter the same branch, and no soil or waste pipe enters between or back of them into the same branch, a single trap on the branch may take the place of a separate trap on each leader, this trap, of course, being placed on the sewer side of the leader entering nearest to the house drain. The size of rain leaders should depend on the amount of roof drainage each one is required to take care of, but should never be less than 3 inches in diameter. As already stated concerning cellar drainage, traps of floor and yard drains, rain leaders, etc., should have as deep a seal as practicable. The depth of seal is limited in the ordinary cast-iron trap, but a trap can be made, such as shown in Fig. 115, which will provide any depth of seal desired. The trap is constructed of quarter bends, and may be made of any additional depth by using a straight piece of pipe on the outlet leg of the trap between the two bends. A seal of great depth would be an unsanitary device if applied to the house-drainage system, as it would provide a lodging place for a large quantity of waste, which would soon putrefy and render the system more impure than there is any necessity for. The water passing through floor and yard drains and roof leaders is clear, however, and depth of seal need, therefore, not be limited. Drainage from fixtures should never be allowed to enter any of these drains.

In connection with the cellar work of the plumbing system, the use of the cellar drainer is a very important feature under certain conditions. It often happens that the street sewer is at such a high level that the house drain, in order to gain sufficient pitch, must be carried above the cellar bottom. In this event, it is clear that the cellar drainage into a catch basin supplied with a trap, such as described in a previous chapter, will not answer the purpose, as it is located so low that it cannot deliver into the house drain by gravity, in the ordinary manner.

The cellar drainer, of which there are several makes, is made use of extensively under these conditions. This device is generally operated by the pressure of water in the house supply system. In Fig. 116 is shown the connections for the cellar drainer and the manner in which its work is performed. Cellar drainers are made to act automatically. When the water accumulates in the catch basin in which the drainer is located it gradually raises a float,

When it has risen to a certain point it opens a valve, which admits the water supply, which discharges the water collected in the catch basin. This water is discharged into a sink installed for the purpose, or, if it so happens, into any similar cellar fixture which may be convenient. This sink should be trapped and vented just as any

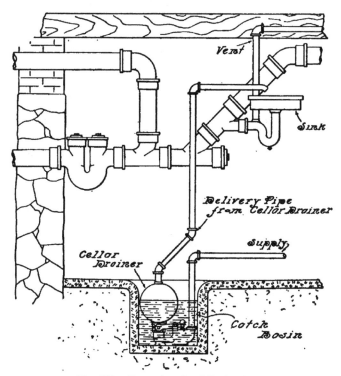

FIG. 116.—Connections for Cellar Drainer.

other house fixture. The action of the cellar drainer depends upon the creation of a partial vacuum by passing water or steam under pressure through a jet, thereby producing a suction which draws the water out of the catch basin or other receptacle into the discharge pipe, the pressure forcing it up to the point of delivery. It will be observed that both surface water and the water used in operating the drainer are discharged.   When the float falls it closes the valve and the device is ready for its next operation.

Some manufacturers claim that the cellar drainer will lift water through 12 feet, but it would appear that 8 to 10 feet is about the limit.   Even so, however, the drainer covers a wide range of work.   It is made in various sizes, capable of caring for 50 gallons to 1,200 or more gallons per hour.   The minimum pressure required is generally about 15 lbs.   The greater the distance through which the water is to be lifted the greater will be the amount of water necessary to operate the drainer.   In addition to its use in connection with the drainage of cellars, it is often used in draining cesspools, wheel pits, catch basins, into which refrigerator lines discharge, and for many other purposes.

The subject of the disposal of sewage and surface water collecting at points below the sewer level has become a very important matter, and as it relates to large work, will be taken up at a later point, in a chapter devoted to that subject.   It will readily be seen that in handling large volumes of drainage from public toilet rooms located underground, the use of any such device as the cellar drainer would be out of the question entirely, such work needing powerful apparatus working on a different principle, and often required to discharge many thousands of gallons per hour.

CHAPTER XIV

FIXTURE WASTES

ANYONE who is acquainted with the work of the plumber well knows that it is not fine fixtures and nickel trimmings that make up the sum total of a sanitary plumbing system. Indeed, the sanitary character of the plumbing system depends much more upon the manner in which the concealed piping is installed than upon that part of the work which is exposed to view. A bath room, for

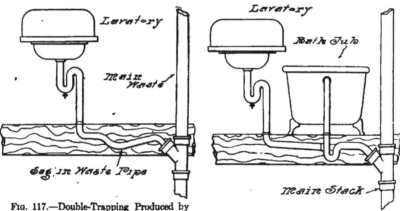

FIG. 117.—Double-Trapping Produced by Sagging of Waste Pipe.

FIG. 118.—Lavatory Double-Trapped.

instance, may be provided with every luxury in the form of high-grade fixtures and brass work and trimmings, and apparently be all that could possibly be asked for, and at the same time the piping under the floor and in the partitions may be of the most unsanitary character and of the poorest workmanship.

In Fig. 117, for instance, the sagging of the lead waste results in double-trapping the fixture, which is always a serious matter. In the running of long lines of lead waste, the proper supporting

154

of the pipe is a matter of much importance, and a matter which is often sadly neglected. Another instance of the double-trapping of a fixture is to be noted in Fig. 118. The latter does not come

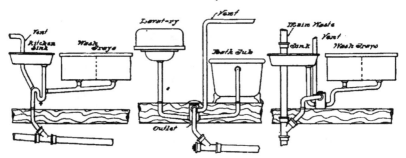

FIG. 119.—Kitchen Sink and Wash Trays Served by One Trap.—Poor Practice.

FIG. 120.—Lavatory and Bath Tub Connected into Drum Trap.—Poor Practice.

FIG. 121.—Sink and Wash Trays Connected into Drum Trap.—Poor Practice.

so much from carelessness as it does from ignorance on the part of the workman, or from an attempt to complete the work with the least possible expense to the plumber. These glaring errors, however, are very much less in evidence in sections that come under

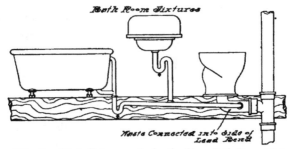

FIG. 122.—One Waste Entrance only for the Three Bath Room Fixtures.

the plumbing inspector's control than in the smaller towns that are not thus favored.

Many of the most objectionable features connected with the installation of fixture wastes, however, come from the neglect to provide proper facilities for carrying the waste away, rather than from work that is installed with such errors as those shown above. It is a very common practice, for instance, to serve two fixtures by one trap, as in Figs. 119, 120, and 121. This practice arises

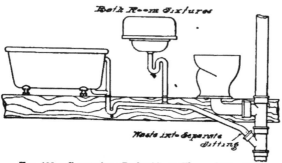

FIG. 123.—Connections Preferable to Those of Fig. 122.

most often in the case of the kitchen sink and wash trays, and in the case of lavatory and bath tub, and is a practice that is followed in a great many cities having plumbing ordinances which require a separate trap under each fixture. Briefly stated, the principle

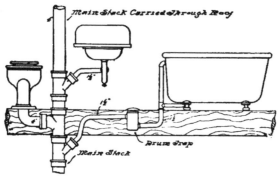

FIG. 124.—Separate Waste Entrance for Each Fixture.

involved is, that as far as possible, each fixture should be separately trapped, and have a separate entrance into the drainage system, and the consideration of the latter is the chief feature of this chapter. It may, perhaps, be considered to best advantage in the case of bath room connections. The work shown in Fig. 122, in which the wastes from all three fixtures of the bath room are provided with but one entrance into the drainage system, is very often

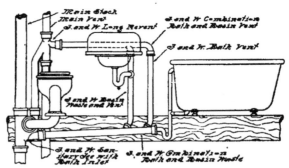

FIG. 125.—Separate Waste Entrances by Means of Special Fittings.

to be seen even in cities which pride themselves on their high standard of plumbing. It cannot be denied, however, that this is very poor work. Fig. 123 shows an improvement in providing a second entrance for the bath and lavatory. This would in general,

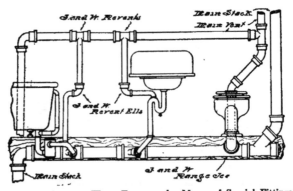

FIG. 126.—Separate Waste Entrances by Means of Special Fittings.

no doubt pass muster as a fairly good piece of work, but it cannot be compared with the work of Fig. 124, in which each fixture is provided with its own separate entrance into the drainage system.

Fig. 124 certainly represents the most sanitary and workman-like arrangement of waste connections. In such work a stoppage on either waste affects that fixture alone, and has no influence on the working of any other fixture, while in the other work mentioned a single stoppage at certain points is able to prevent the use of two, or even all three, fixtures.

The special fittings which have recently appeared on the market in such numbers and in such variety of form are of the greatest aid in obtaining separate waste entrance for fixtures, but in addition provide means of obtaining continuous vents. Two examples of the use of special fittings are to be seen in Figs. 125 and 126, and at various other points in this work other similar instances may be noted.

CHAPTER XV

WATER-CLOSETS

THE water-closet, without doubt, has received more earnest attention in its development than any other plumbing fixture or device. Its use has also had more influence in the working out of the details of the present sanitary system than any other feature that is connected with plumbing construction. It is not the pur-

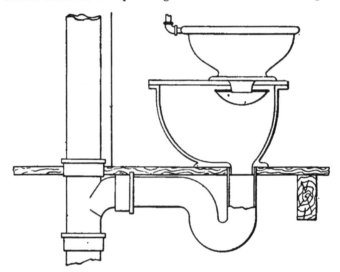

FIG. 127.—The Pan Water-Closet and Its Connections.

pose of this work to enter into the historical features of the development of plumbing, and therefore simply passing mention will be made of the old-time styles of water-closets, in order that comparison may be made between the present fixtures of sanitary construction and the old-time fixtures with their numerous sanitary defects.

The pan closet, shown in Fig. 127, was for a long time universally used on good work and was considered as a most efficient fixture. This fixture was developed in the natural course of the evolution of the water-closet, but in our knowledge of to-day it is difficult to conceive of a more filthy arrangement. Its use is now everywhere prohibited, although even now found to some extent in some sections on old work.

As shown in Fig. 127, the pan closet consists chiefly of the bowl, the receiver for the waste, the pan and a system of levers for operating the pan.

The waste entering the fixture, fell into this pan, which was

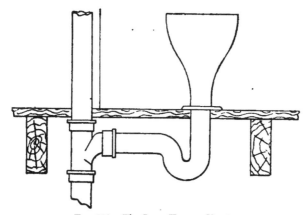

Fig. 128.—The Long Hopper Closet.

of copper, and contained enough water to make a seal over the lower end of the bowl. The system of levers was used to upset the pan and throw its contents into the receiver. The latter soon became covered with filth and the pan also became corroded and filthy. Beneath the pan closet the S trap added to the general filthiness of the fixture. The unsanitary features of the pan closet, as may well be seen, were of such an extent that they cannot easily be exaggerated.

Following the pan closet came the valve and plunger closets, showing an improvement in several points over the first-named fixture. These closets, in their day, were looked upon as perfect fixtures, although from our present standpoint they appear filthy and unsatisfactory in the extreme.

The long hopper closet, shown in Fig. 128, was another type of water-closet formerly in extensive use. This form of water-closet depended for its trap upon the S trap located below it, as shown in the illustration referred to. These traps were either of lead or cast-iron. Very often in old-time bath-room work this trap was the only one in the room, all other fixture wastes being connected into it and depending upon it for their trap seals. It will readily be

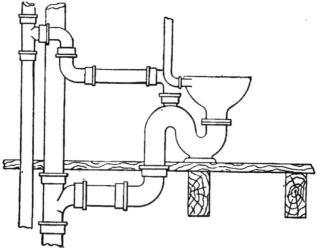

FIG. 129.—The Short Hopper Closet.

seen that such work, without venting of any description, was very far from being comparable to the sanitary work of to-day. The short hopper closet of Fig. 129 is still another form of water-closet of the earlier type, somewhat better than its predecessors, and even now somewhat in use on poor work, but still full of defects, as the water-closet is now understood.

The old-style water-closets, then, were full of defects of all kinds. Some of the features which were objectionable in these fixtures are the following: They had large surfaces, both on the earthenware itself and on the mechanical parts, which were either entirely dry or insufficiently flushed, and therefore presenting opportunity for the collection of filth. Mechanical devices, such as many of them had, are in themselves objectionable. Many of the earlier forms of water-closets were without flushing rims and the devices used for spreading the flush over the surface were entirely inadequate to their purpose.

The old-style fixtures presented dead ends that were unsupplied with water and ventilation; the flush provided was insufficient and not properly applied; the trap, not being a part of the fixture itself, necessitated the use of a special trap, which added greatly to the fouling surface, etc. Many other objectionable features might be named, to show that the old-style forms of water-closet were very filthy affairs, giving out dangerous odors and gases, and at all times constituting a serious menace to the health of the inmates. However, as in everything else, these fixtures continually grew in excellence as the process of evolution went on, and the present sanitary and perfect operating water-closet would not be possible if it had not been for the earlier attempts and the constant effort to reduce their imperfections.

Some of the features which the water-closet should possess, and which the better types of to-day do possess to a large degree, are the following. The fixture should have a trap, with a liberal seal, the trap forming a part of the fixture, in order to reduce the exposed surface, and to increase its efficiency in other ways; all surfaces exposed to soil should be thoroughly scoured by the flush; the flush should be abundant for its purpose, without undue waste of water; the flush should be strong, but noiseless as possible; the trap seal should be open to view; no mechanical devices should be used in the water-closet bowl; and all waste entering the fixture should be quickly and completely removed. The water-closet should be made as compact and of as simple shape as possible, and so formed as to prevent spattering and to allow soil entering it to fall into the trap rather than upon an exposed surface. It is necessary to construct the fixture of strong material, as it is often subject to rough usage; its surfaces should be smooth, both inside and outside; and the glazing should be such that it will not craze. The glazing of water-closets, until within recent years, was liable to crack or craze, thus allowing moisture and filth to be absorbed by the fixture, making of it a most unsanitary device. As known to the reader, the water-closet of to-day, as well as other fixtures, are open, free from the boxing or sheathing that surrounded each fixture of the old-time plumbing system. The open fixture is far more sanitary than the sheathed fixture. The latter not only presents corners and joints which become filled with filth, even under the best of care, but the sheathing incloses an unventilated space, these two features acting to maintain in the room in which the fixtures are located, a less pure atmosphere than is to be found when the fixtures are open.

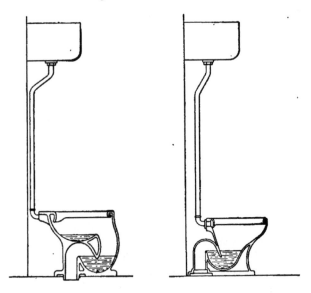

FIG. 130.—The Washout   FIG. 131.—The Washdown
Water-Closet.   Water-Closet.

Following the types of water-closets mentioned above came the washout water-closet, which is in extensive use to-day, in some sections of the country. This fixture is shown in Fig. 130 and was a very great improvement over previous forms of water-closets. As compared with more recent types, however, the washout water-closet is seen to have certain serious defects. As seen in the illustration, this fixture has a flushing rim, a trap within itself, and a pool of water directly below the seal. The soil falling into this pool is removed by the force of the flush, the greater part of which is directed to this point. While there is no difficulty in removing the soil from the pool, in so doing the force of the flush, owing to the work of removing the soil, and to the construction of the fixture, is used up by the time it reaches the trap. Therefore the flush has not sufficient strength to remove the contents of the trap with force, the result being that the waste from this part of the fixture is carried off more by overflow than by any other stronger force. In the washout water-closet the depth of water in the pool is not sufficient to submerge the soil, a point in which certain other water-closets are not lacking. Other defects in this form of fixture are that it has a large amount of fouling surface, and that it is noisy, the latter objection being due to the falling of the water from the pool into the trap.

The washdown water-closet, shown in Fig. 131, though appearing earlier than the washout, is superior to the latter in several ways. In the washdown closet the soil falls directly into the trap. Therefore the flush acts more directly and more strongly in removing waste from the fixture than in the washout, in which, as just observed, the soil must first be forced from the pool into the trap before being carried out of the trap. The washdown water-closet is provided with flushing rim and presents a smaller amount of fouling surface than the washout.

Although the washout and washdown fixtures were great improvements over other water-closets that had been brought out, it remained for the principle of siphonage to be applied to the action of the water-closet to make possible the high-class fixtures of the present day. The application of this principle has, indeed, resulted in a fixture of such perfect action and of such sanitary excellence that it is difficult to see how the fixture can be further improved.

In Fig. 132 is shown a sectional view of the siphon-washdown water-closet, the action of which is the following: The construction of the fixture provides a horizontal leg on the outlet of the fixture, which is somewhat contracted in area as compared with the vertical part of the outlet. When the waste of the fixture, in flushing, reaches the contracted horizontal leg, its passage is retarded to a considerable extent, which allows the entire outlet passage between the trap and the horizontal leg to completely fill with water. This solid plug of water, in passing off, creates a vacuum, and results in establishing the action of siphonage. This

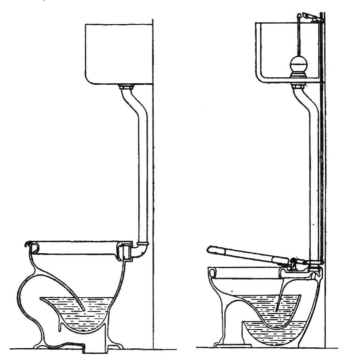

Fig. 132.—The Siphon Washdown
Water-Closet

Fig. 133.—The Siphon Water-
Closet.

action is very strong, and quickly and forcibly pulls the entire contents of the trap out and into the drainage system. After the siphon breaks enough water enters the fixture to form the trap seal. Two or three flushes of the siphon water-closet may usually be obtained if desired, by allowing the supply to fill the flush tank to a higher level. After the first siphonic action breaks, the incoming flush quickly fills the outlet of the fixture a second time, and when the right conditions are reached, the fixture again siphons. The scouring action of this fixture, both within itself and on the connections into the drainage system, is far superior, it is clear to see, to that of any of the fixtures previously considered.

Another form of siphon water-closet is to be seen in Fig. 133. This type has two traps, one above the other. The second trap is not provided as a means of protection against the entrance of sewer air, but to aid in the formation of the siphon. As the flush enters the fixture from the flush tank, it divides, one half going through the flushing rim, scouring the bowl, and aiding in discharging the contents of the fixture. The other half of the flush passes through the passage shown in the illustration, directly into the lower trap. This jet forces the air between the two traps through the water of the lower trap, thus producing a partial vacuum, and forming a siphon, which rapidly draws out the contents of the fixture. This division of the flush not only siphons the fixture, but obviates the spattering which occurs in water-closets when the entire flush is thrown directly into the bowl, and at the same time, a more energetic passage of water through the lower trap is secured, which entirely prevents the possibility of anything remaining in the trap after the siphon has operated. Another good feature of this type of water-closet is that it is comparatively noiseless.

In addition to showing the features of this special type of fixture, Fig. 133 also shows apparatus for automatically starting the flush tank. The ordinary method is by means of the chain and pull, but in public toilet rooms, where it is often desirable not to depend on the individual using the fixture to flush it, the flush tank may be operated by the releasing of the water-closet seat. As will be seen from the illustration, this is accomplished by levers which operate a rod which in turn acts on the flush valve.

In Fig. 134 is shown another form of water-closet, known as the siphon-jet type, which represents the most perfect water-closet which has yet been devised.

The action of this fixture is the result not only of a contracted horizontal outlet leg, but also of a special jet or passage, which throws a strong stream or jet of water directly up into the rising arm of the trap. The jet is formed by a passage cast on the outside of the bowl, communicating with the point at which the flush enters the fixture, and delivering the jet through the opening at the bottom of the trap. This jet aids the flush that enters the bowl through the flushing rim, in quickly filling the outlet leg, and in producing the necessary vacuum, upon which the action of the siphon water-closet depends. This type of water-closet is exceed-

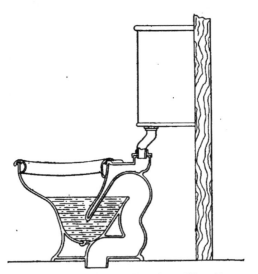

Fig. 134.—The Siphon-Jet, Low-Down Water-Closet.

ingly strong in its action, and as already stated, represents the most advanced type now in use.

The siphon water-closets, then, show the following desirable features: Their action results in the rapid withdrawal of the entire contents of the fixture, which is comparatively noiseless; the scouring action is very strong; there are no unflushed surfaces; there is no waste of energy as seen in the wash-out type; all soil entering the bowl is submerged, and the fixture is very compact and graceful in design.

In Fig. 134 the flush tank shown is of the low-down pattern.

This style of tank has now come into very extensive use, until at the present time it has almost entirely superseded the high tank in many sections of the country.

The low-down tank is no more efficient than the high tank, but to many its appearance is more tasteful than the high tank. The low-down tank combination is more compact, and may be used in many places where it is difficult or impossible to obtain the necessary elevation for the high tank. The low-down tank is also more accessible in case of repairs than the high tank, which

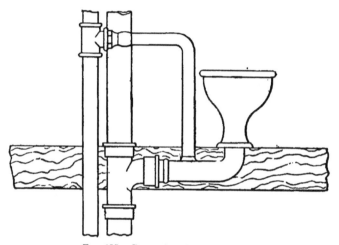

Fig. 135.—Connections for Water-Closet.

must often be taken down in order that the working parts may be gotten at.

The high tank generally delivers its flush through a 1¼-inch pipe, its ability to throw a large volume of water into the fixture quickly, depending upon the elevation of the tank. The absence of elevation of the low-down tank is surmounted by providing a connection of larger size between the tank and water-closet. This connection is usually 2 inches in diameter, which is of sufficient size to throw enough water into the bowl to make its action entirely satisfactory.

Whenever the low-down tank is used, it is necessary to use in connection with it, a water-closet of the siphon type, as satisfactory results cannot be obtained from the use of water-closets of less positive action.

Owing to the nature of its construction, the water-closet must be connected to the drainage system in a different manner than other fixtures.

Fig. 135 will show the manner in which these connections are generally made, when the drainage pipes are of cast iron. As shown, the connection is made by means of a lead bend con-

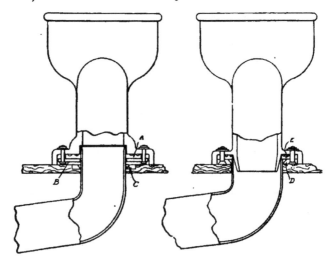

FIG. 136.—Water-Closet Floor Connections.

necting to the outlet of the water-closet. The lead bend is wiped to a 4-inch brass ferrule, and the latter calked into the cast-iron fitting. The vent is generally taken from the lead bend, the proper point of connection being on the upper part of the horizontal section of the bend.

The lead bend and water-closet may be connected in several ways. The simplest and least satisfactory method is by means of the putty joint, the top of the lead bend being flanged over onto the floor, after which a ring of putty is laid on top, and the base of the water-closet screwed down onto the putty. The putty spreads and forms a joint between the lead bend and the water-closet. The objections to this method are, that if the fixture receives a blow, or the floor settles, the joint cracks, allowing a leakage of water around the base of the fixture. The oil of the putty works into the flooring and discolors it.

In Fig. 136 are shown types of floor connections, which it will readily be seen, are far superior to the putty connection. In the method shown at the right, the lead bend is brought up above the floor a short distance, and to it the brass floor flange D is soldered. On the flange, the rubber gasket E is placed, the bolts inserted, and the fixture set in position, after which the nuts are screwed onto the bolts, and the latter made tight. This draws the rubber gasket up against the base of the water-closet, making a gas-tight and water-tight joint.

In making the floor connection seen at the left in Fig. 136, the floor is cut to receive the flange C, which is soldered to the lead bend, the exposed upper edge of which should be smoothed, in order that there may be no rough places on which substances in the waste may catch. The upper part of the lead bend may be painted with white lead to which the edges of the rubber gasket will strongly adhere. The flange B is then dropped into place, the rubber gasket forced on, the bolts put in, the closet set in position, and the bolts drawn up. The flange C takes the weight of the lead bend, thus taking all strain off the base of the closet. The flange B being loose, accommodates itself to any unevenness in the setting of the bowl. In these last two respects, the connection last named is superior to the first named.

The floor connections described are for use only when the cast-iron drainage system is employed. Other methods must be employed when the Durham system is in use. The connections of the water-closet in use on the Durham system are shown in Fig. 137, from which it will be seen that no lead is used in the work. The floor connection is made by means of a brass floor flange, screwing into the iron bend. This floor flange is shown in separate detail in Fig. 137.

In roughing-in the connections for the water-closet, the vertical part of the bend should pass through the floor so that the center will be right to receive the outlet of the fixture. To accomplish this, it is necessary to know the water-closet that is to be used, in order to know how far out the outlet will come. To find the center of the outlet of a water-closet that is in position, be governed by the screw holes on the side of the base. When there is one screw hole on each side of the base, the center of the outlet will usually be opposite these holes. When two holes appear on each side, the center will generally be found midway between them.

After the bend is in position on roughing work, a circular disk of sheet lead should be cut out and soldered into the end of the bend, in order that it may be sealed against the entrance into it

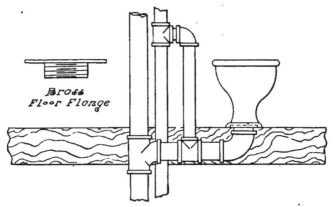

Fig. 137.—Connections of Water-Closet on the Durham System.

of refuse of any kind. If the bend projects through the floor far enough, the end may be mashed in and soldered across the top edge.

In a large majority of cases, the water-closet connection is made into a T-Y fitting, as shown in Fig. 135. It is better to make the connection into a Y fitting and bend, but in most work this is impossible, as such a connection takes up more space than can be allowed, and brings the fixture too far out into the room, as will appear from Fig. 149.

The use of the Y and bend provides the smoothest possible path for the waste, but on vertical stacks, the use of the T-Y is not considered poor practice. It should never be used on horizontal work, however. It often happens in the installation of lines of water-closets in factories, schools, and similar buildings, that the Y and bend can be used to advantage, as shown in Fig. 138.

In this work, the vent for each fixture is taken off the short piece of lead pipe, which is used instead of the lead bend. The work shown in Fig. 138 is especially practicable when the building construction and the purposes of the building are such that it is not undesirable to run the horizontal line of soil pipe on the ceiling of the floor below the line of fixtures.

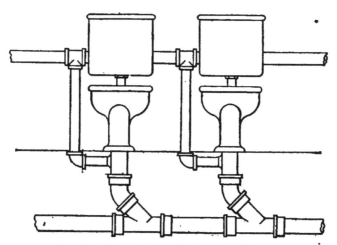

Fig. 138.—Connections for Line of Water-Closets.

If the work cannot be installed as in Fig. 138, the Ys may be used so that their branches point horizontally, in which case a lead bend must be used in connecting each fixture.

In other instances it is desirable to run the horizontal line above the floor. This method necessitates the use of a special form of fixture with its outlet above the floor. If the line of soil pipe is to be exposed to view, it may be supported on special pipe-supporting fittings. These fittings are made to adjust to any pitch at which it is desired to run the pipe. Work of this description may be seen in Fig. 139.

The principles of the venting of water-closets are taken up under the chapter on venting, from which it will be seen that the

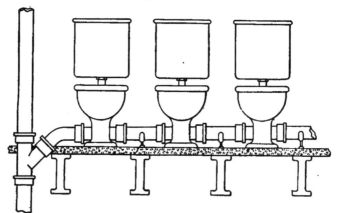

Fig. 139.—Soil Pipe for Line of Water-Closets Supported by Supporting Fittings.

common method consists in taking it off the lead bend, as in Fig. 141. The venting of water-closets from the bowl itself, as in Fig.

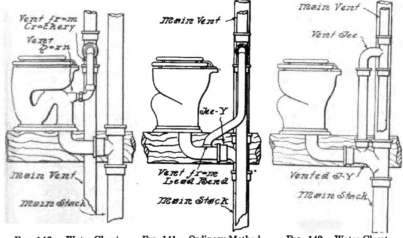

Fig. 140.—Water-Closet Vented from the Bowl.

Fig. 141.—Ordinary Method of Venting Water-Closets.

Fig. 142.—Water-Closet Vented from T-Y.

140, is no longer considered good practice. In addition to the regular method of venting, special waste fittings provided with vent openings are now much used, one of the simplest of these appearing in Fig. 142.

Several of these fittings are to be seen in Figs. 143 to 146. The fitting of Fig. 143 is a common stock fitting, known as the vented T-Y. This fitting is an excellent one, and where practicable to use it, the work may be made very rigid and substantial, and the labor called for is considerably less than in venting from the lead bend in the usual manner. The chief objection to its use is that it brings the water-closet farther out into the room than is desirable, in many cases. Fig. 144 shows a fitting constructed on the same general principles as the vented T-Y, but with the hub, to which the lead bend is connected, much closer to the wall. This advantage is secured by constructing the waste entrance in such a way that it enters the main body of the fitting spirally, on the side. These fittings may be secured with the hub on either the right or left hand. The vent is taken off the fitting in a manner similar to that of Fig. 143.

Fig. 144 also shows the use of a special revent fitting, which has an offset, allowing a connection between the vent hub of the waste fitting and the main vent line. It will readily be seen that the use of these two fittings effects a great saving in labor in the construction.

In Fig. 145 is shown a fitting of different character, for use on horizontal lines of soil pipe, whereas those shown in Figs. 143 and 144 are for vertical lines.

If this fitting is used for the lowest water-closet on the system, the main vent line may often be connected into its vent opening, answering at the same time as the vent for the water-closet itself.

Fig. 146 shows the same fitting as in Fig. 145, used on a horizontal line of soil pipe serving several water-closets. The waste openings of these fittings, it will be observed, point out in such a direction that lead bends must be used in making the connections. The vents from these fittings may be constructed of ordinary pipe and fittings, as in Fig. 145, or with special revent fittings, as shown in Fig. 146.

Figs. 147, 148, and 149 show excellent methods of wasting and

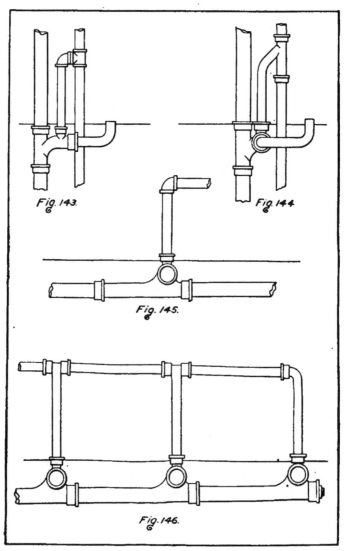

Fig. 143.

Fig. 144.

Fig. 145.

Fig. 146.

Figs. 143-146.—The Use of Special Water-Closet Waste and Vent Fittings.

venting water-closets by means of special fittings. The method of Fig. 147, in which the temple vent fitting is used, is probably the least common of the three, but is nevertheless to be considered a specially good one, and there would appear to be little reason for · its limited use.

It often happens, especially in tenement and apartment houses, that water-closets on the several floors, back up to each other on opposite sides of a partition. Under such conditions, a good method of wasting and venting is seen in Fig. 150, by the use of a vented double T-Y. An improvement on this method, however, is that of Fig. 151, in which a special fitting known as a sanitary cross with double vent is made use of, in connection with the double revent fitting shown.

It will be noticed that while the use of these special fittings must necessarily save a considerable amount of labor as compared with ordinary methods, other advantages are also gained. They often make the drainage and vent piping and their connections much more compact, and reduce the number of joints greatly. The latter is a feature of importance, as the smaller the number of joints there are on any plumbing system, the less liability there will be of defects and of stoppages.

Other special water-closet waste and vent fittings of much value are to be seen in Figs. 152 to 155.

The fitting A in Fig. 152 is a double T-Y with double vents. When this fitting is made use of, the double vent fitting shown will be found of more advantage than vents of pipe and ordinary fittings. From the top of the double-vent fitting, a short revent fitting similar to that of Fig. 144 may be used, or the connection made with pipe and fittings. If the latter method is adopted, the reader will easily see that it cannot be accomplished, either with cast- or wrought-iron pipe, without the use of several more joints than appear in the work of Fig. 152. Another fitting, similar to A, is shown at B, it being provided with a single vent instead of a double vent.

It would appear that as efficient work may be accomplished with B as with A, as far as the venting of the two water-closets is concerned, and the number of fittings used with A and the labor necessary will certainly be greater than in the case of B. C shows

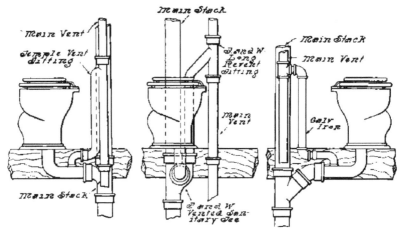

FIG. 147.—Water-Closet Vented into Temple Vent Fitting.

FIG. 148.—Use of Special Waste and Vent Fittings.

FIG. 149.—Venting of Water-Closet with Wrought Iron Pipe.

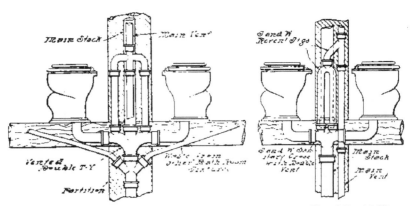

FIG. 150.—Waste and Vent for Water-Closets on Opposite Sides of Partition.

FIG. 151.—Use of Special Waste and Vent Fittings.

still another vented waste fitting, similar to that of Fig. 144, but with an extra inlet for the waste of another fixture. The revent fitting connected to the vent opening of the waste fitting, is also provided with an additional opening to receive the vent from the fixture entering the special waste inlet of the waste fitting. The revent fitting may be secured with the additional opening located as shown, or on either side of the fitting. If the bath waste enters the additional opening of the waste fitting, and its half-S trap is located within a short distance of the stack, the vent for the water-closet may act also as the vent for the bath trap. Fig. 153 shows a special offset fitting, D, for use in connection with the vented T-Y, when the latter is used to serve a water-closet on the lowest floor, or when no other fixtures enter the stack below the water-closet. This offset connects the vent stack into the soil stack as now generally required, and also serves as the vent for the water-closet.

Fig. 154 illustrates the use of another vented fitting, E, for use in connection with a water-closet entering the end of a horizontal line of soil pipe. This fitting allows the entrance of the lead bend into the end and into its vent opening the water-closet vent may be connected to serve also as the main vent in many cases.

In Fig. 155 are illustrated a multiple waste and vent fitting, G, and a double revent fitting, F. The waste fitting is provided with two vent hubs, a waste opening for the water-closet and another for any other adjacent fixture. One of the vent hubs is to receive the vent for the water-closet, and the other the vent from the bath trap or other trap that is located below the floor.

The double revent fitting may be obtained in several modified patterns. For instance, another vent opening may be obtained at the top of the fitting, as shown in connection with the fitting H of Fig. 152.

The fitting may also be obtained with a waste opening at K. Such a waste could not be used, however, if the fitting were provided with the branch L, as this would mean that the same pipe served as both waste and vent, which is not right under any circumstances. A waste opening at K would provide a continuous vent with waste for a lavatory or sink.

All the special fittings shown in Figs. 143 to 146, and 152 to

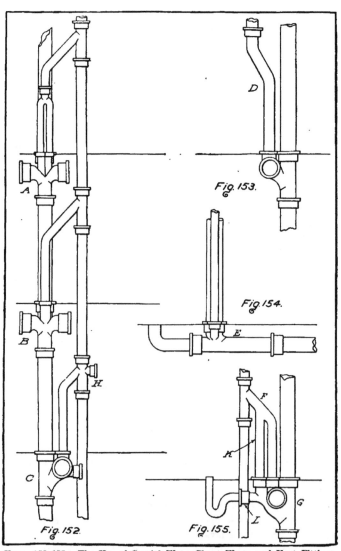

FIGS. 152–155.—The Use of Special Water-Closet Waste and Vent Fittings.

155, with the exception of the vented T-Y of Fig. 143, are known as F and W combination vent, revent, and drainage fittings. They are of great practical value, and are coming into use to a considerable extent. As already indicated, they save a large amount of labor, reduce the number of joints, and make the work compact.

Their use also allows continuous vents to be obtained under almost all conditions. It may be stated that these fittings constitute only a small part of the full line of such special fittings. Others, for use in connection with other fixtures than water-closets, will be seen elsewhere.

Owing to the nature of the waste which the water-closet receives, it should be surrounded with the best possible sanitary conditions. This is especially true, also, of the urinal. With our present knowledge and appliances, however, it is not now so difficult to install these fixtures under difficult conditions and still obtain good results, as it once was.

The water-closet should never be installed in a dark or unventilated place, for light and ventilation are absolutely necessary if this fixture is to be kept from becoming a foul nuisance. When properly provided for in these two respects, however, this fixture need prove scarcely more obnoxious than any other fixture. That this is true, is evidenced by the fact that the atmosphere of the modern well-lighted, well-ventilated bath room, provided with first-class fixtures and a properly constructed sanitary system, is scarcely more tainted than the atmosphere of the remaining rooms of the house.

The location of water-closets in cellars is always poor practice, though quite common in some sections. Whenever thus located, the water-closet compartment should be built with one of the cellar windows opening into it, in order that ventilation and light may be obtained as far as is possible under the conditions.

Whenever possible, the lighting of any room or compartment containing a water-closet or any other plumbing fixture, should be direct, rather than by means of light shafts. Exterior lighting, by means of which the benefit of sunlight may be obtained, is very desirable, as the action of sunlight is especially destructive to filth or germ life.

The natural ventilation of rooms through windows and doors is greater than commonly supposed, but when the water-closet is installed in any room, artificial ventilation is generally needed to keep the atmosphere of the room sufficiently pure. This matter is taken up in the chapter on local venting.

Considerable space has been devoted in this chapter to the venting of water-closets. A few additional remarks on the subject may be of value.

The water-closet is a more difficult fixture to siphon than any other to be found on the plumbing system. It is nevertheless true, however, that it may be siphoned. In a majority of cases, the water-closet trap is siphoned gradually, a few drops at a time, rather than completely at one such operation.

It is undoubtedly true that the venting of water-closets is sometimes demanded under conditions which actually make such provision unnecessary. For instance, when the water-closet is located close to its soil stack, on the top floor, it would be impossible in a plumbing system provided as the modern system is, with roof ventilation, to bring to bear upon its trap seal sufficient siphonic influence to produce even the smallest amount of siphonic action. Many other instances might be noted of water-closets located close to soil stacks in small plumbing systems, where it is really unnecessary to vent them. A water-closet located close to the foot of a stack serving a number of fixtures, or when located on a horizontal line, or when set at a distance from its stack, should always be vented, as siphonic influence on its trap seal under each of these conditions is sufficiently great to make its use necessary.

There are certain practices in connection with water-closet work which should not be followed, and which are of sufficient importance to demand special remark. It is a very common practice to connect the waste from other fixtures into the lead bend of the water-closet, rather than to provide a separate entrance into the stack for these fixtures. There is often a temptation to perform the work in this manner, as it certainly can be done at much less cost, and as it is sometimes difficult to do the work in the proper manner. Nevertheless, the practice is a poor one, for several reasons. In the first place, if the waste is thus connected, a stoppage in the lead bend will not only prevent the use of the water-closet itself, but also of any other fixture whose waste is connected into the bend.

The wiping of a waste into the lead bend cannot usually be accomplished without the forming of spines of solder reaching inside the bend, which will inevitably catch lint and paper and other materials entering the water-closet.

If, however, the waste of another fixture must be connected into the lead bend, it should never be connected into the heel of the bend, as shown in Fig. 156, or into the upright section. It should be connected into the horizontal part of the bend, and as high up on its circumference as possible.

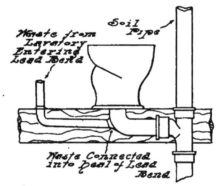

Fig. 156.—Waste Connected into Heel of Lead Bend.

The connection of the vent to the water-closet bowl has been mentioned elsewhere as a poor practice.

The use of offset water-closets is a practice more or less common, but now generally prohibited by plumbing ordinances. This form of water-closet bowl has no trap, but its shape is such that the uninformed person would not generally detect the fact. It is generally used to replace one of the old-time styles of water-closets which depended upon a lead or iron trap below the floor.

Instead of tearing out both closet and trap, the latter is often allowed to remain, and the fixture replaced by an offset bowl, as in Fig. 157. The objections to this course are so apparent as to need no explanation.

The only proper course under the circumstances, is to replace the old fixture and its separate trap with a modern water-closet having the trap within the bowl.

Thus far nothing but tank water-closets have been considered in this chapter. Within the last decade, however, another method for the flushing of water-closets has come into extensive use, which does away entirely with the use of flush tanks.

The device in question is known as the flushing valve, and is made in various forms by the different manufacturers, one of them being shown in Fig. 158.

Flushing valves are also much used in connection with urinals

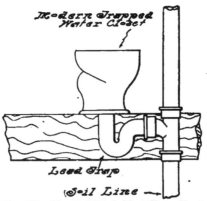

Fig. 157.—The Prohibited Offset Water-Closet.

and slop sinks. Their use thus far has been confined largely to public buildings and large work of a high grade, although in nice residence work they are also being used extensively. The flushing valve is an automatic, slow-closing valve, operated generally by means of a lever or a push button. Although the action of the different valves varies greatly, in general it may be said that its action is as follows:

When the handle or push button is released after the fixture has been flushed, the flushing valve closes automatically by means of the action of a jet or stream of water, issuing from the pressure side of the valve, which passes through a by-pass into the chamber beyond the piston-head, which is thereby forced onto its seat.

The flushing valve may be worked under direct pressure, or under tank pressure. The latter is preferable to direct pressure for this work, as tank pressure is always more uniform than direct pressure, and more positive.

The various makes of flush valves are advertised to work under various pressures, certain types being guaranteed to operate satis-

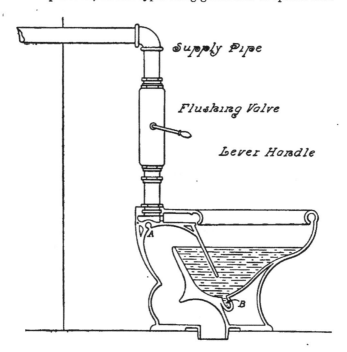

Fig. 158.—The Flushing Valve,—Double-Jet Siphon Water-Closet.

factorily through a wide range of pressure, while other makes are constructed in several patterns, each being adapted to pressure of certain limited range. Generally speaking, however, it may be said that the flushing valve must be provided with a pressure of 10 or 12 pounds to work satisfactorily.

The size of supply pipe for the various makes of flushing valves and for the various pressures varies from 1 inch to 1½ inch. The action and construction of these valves is so different that it is impossible to give exact data without knowing the make of the valve that is in question. Therefore in installing them, it is desirable to secure from the manufacturer the working data and instructions for connecting them under the conditions respecting pressure, number of valves on the system, etc.

In connection with the illustration of the flushing valve shown in Fig. 158, a sectional view of a double-jet siphon water-closet is given. This type of siphon-jet closet is not common and should be of interest to the reader.

It will be observed that one of the jets enters the bowl at A and the other at B, the former throwing a stream of water down the outlet leg, and the latter throwing a stream in an upward direction through the rising leg of the trap. By adding the jet A, the air is driven out of the discharge leg, thus removing the resistance to the jet B.

It would seem that the combination of the two jets must result in a very strong siphonic action, stronger than that obtained in the regular siphon-jet closet.

It is claimed by the manufacturers that this water-closet is designed especially for low-down use, that because of the lack of pressure, due to placing the tank so close to the bowl, much objection to an inefficient siphonic action has been found, which the use of an additional jet has overcome. The jet A is securely trapped. Otherwise, gases from the drainage system might pass up through the discharge leg, into the jet, and thence into the room through the flushing rim.

The frost-proof water-closet is a fixture thus far unmentioned, for which there is a considerable demand under certain conditions. It can readily be seen that it is not possible to use the ordinary water-closet bowl and flush tank in any place that is exposed to freezing temperatures, for the reason that the water in the closet trap would freeze and burst the fixture, and the same thing would happen to the flush tank.

Accordingly, whenever it is necessary to install the water-closet in cold places, the frost-proof type of closet must be used. One form of this fixture is shown in Fig. 159.

As a bowl with the trap included in it cannot be used, a hopper closet is generally employed, protection against the entrance of gases being afforded by a trap placed below the fixture, sufficiently to be below the freezing point. The supply valve is also of necessity placed below the freezing point.

When the seat is occupied, the flush tank fills, due to the open-

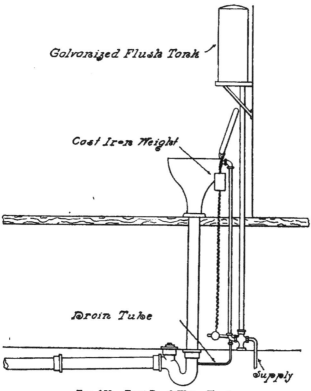

Golvonized Flush Tonk

Cost Iron Weight

Droin Tube

Supply

FIG. 159.—Frost-Proof Water-Closet.

ing of the supply valve by the attached mechanism. When the seat is released, the supply valve closes, and the contents of the flush tank discharge into the closet. After the flushing has taken place, the water remaining in the pipe above the valve, drains off into the water-closet trap, through a small drain tube.

It will thus be seen that when the fixture is not in use, there is no water standing in the flush tank, or at any point in the piping above the supply valve. It is needless to say that this form of water-closet work would not be considered sanitary under ordinary conditions, but under freezing conditions, as found in outhouses, sheds, etc., which are not attached to dwelling houses, such work is the best that can be made of a difficult situation. There are other forms of frost-proof water-closets, in connection with some of them the tank being placed below the water-closet. When so placed, the head due to the elevated tank is lost.

In order to provide sufficient pressure to force the water into the closet bowl, otherwise than under direct pressure, the flush tank is made to act as a pressure tank. When the seat is occupied, the water passes into this tank, compressing the air held in it, until the compression is sufficiently high to prevent its further entrance. When the seat is released, a weight attached tips it up, closes the inlet valve, and opens the discharge. The compressed air of the tank forces the water up and through the water-closet bowl, under about the same pressure as the direct supply.

In many instances, in plumbing systems for such buildings as schools, factories, etc., the range water-closet has in the past been used to some extent.

While the range water-closet is not to be compared to the individual water-closet, as to sanitary excellence, it is a fixture that is in quite extensive use, and therefore deserves attention. The old-style range was a filthy affair, but the present, high-grade makes are far superior in every respect. They are now made of porcelain or enamel-lined, there being no exposed metal surfaces, and otherwise constructed and provided with features which go far toward making this fixture of as high a standard of excellence as it is possible to secure under the conditions that must naturally surround it.

In Fig. 160 is shown one of the modern types of range water-closets, most of which are now operated by means of an automatic flush tank, combined with a strong-acting siphoning apparatus. The tank is connected to the siphon by means of an air pipe. When the tank operates, the flush exerting its influence through the air pipe, exhausts the air in the upper trap to a certain extent,

thereby forming a partial vacuum. The result of this action is
that the atmospheric pressure exerted on the surface of the water
standing in the opening from the range into the trap, sends the
water forcibly over into the trap, filling it, and producing siphonage, which quickly discharges the contents of the range. After
this operation ceases, the range fills to its regular height and is

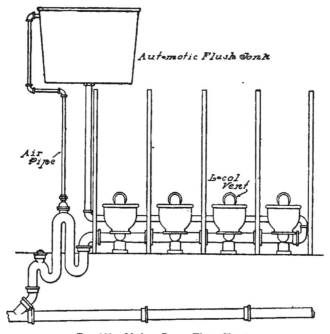

FIG. 160.—Modern Range Water-Closet.

again in readiness. The automatic flush tank may be regulated
to flush at any desired interval. Each bowl is thoroughly flushed
and cleansed at each flush, and the flush from the tank being also
connected to the end of the range waste, adds much to rapid discharging of the contents of the range.

One of the chief objections to the old-style range water-closet,
is that it was poorly flushed. This objection, then, has been very
largely removed in the best makes of the present day, the flushing

and scouring features of such fixtures as that shown in Fig. 160, being very satisfactory.

Another feature that has always been very objectionable in this fixture, is the fact that the waste matter entering the range has given out into the room through the seat openings, a constant stream of foul odors, between successive operations of the flush. This has been very largely overcome by the employment of efficient local ventilation. The subject of local ventilation, by the way, is considered at length in the following chapter.

In the range shown in Fig. 160, it will be observed that each bowl is provided with a local vent connection of large size. These are carried into a ventilating duct which should connect into a well and constantly heated flue.

When a strong ventilation is thus provided, it results in reducing to a minimum, the objection above mentioned, due to the standing in the bowls of the waste matter. Whenever it is possible, a special flue should be provided for ventilating purposes, which should be heated especially for this work, if need be.

In connection with some forms of range water-closets, in which separate bowls are not used, the ventilation for the fixture is provided by a single large pipe attached to the end of the range.

It would appear, however, that the individual local vents are the most direct in their action, and therefore the most efficient. It will thus be seen that the modern range water-closet, constructed of high grade, noncorrosive material with separate bowls, thoroughly flushed, as described above, and provided with strong ventilation, is a far superior fixture to the old type—much more sanitary and satisfactory in every respect.

CHAPTER XVI

LOCAL VENTILATION

LOCAL ventilation has been greatly improved in recent years, until now it seems difficult to understand how in its most perfect form it could be further improved upon. As it has generally been known in the past, the local or seat vent is a pipe connected to the water-closet principally, but also to the urinal and the slop sink, at such a point and in such a manner as to carry off into the outer atmosphere the odors incident to the use of the fixture to which it is attached. It may be stated that the local vent has no connection in any way with the back vent system, the purpose of the two forms of vents being entirely distinct. In Figs. 161 and 162 are shown the common methods of applying local ventilation to water-closets—the method first introduced.

It has been used mostly in connection with the water-closet, and is made of galvanized sheet iron or copper pipe, generally of 2 in. diameter. In its original form, the local vent was attached to the water-closet by a horn cast onto the side of the bowl and at a point above the water line.

The action of the local vent depends upon the fact that heated air rises. Whenever possible it should be connected into a heated flue, as in Figs. 161 and 162. The heat rising in such a flue creates a strong suction on the lines of local vent, usually powerful enough to draw into it all odors arising from the use of the fixtures connected to it.

These odors are carried up through the flue, and are discharged into the atmosphere at a point where they cannot become a nuisance. When it is impossible to connect the local vent into a heated flue, it may be carried through the roof, and a draught created by burning a small gas jet in it. A very important point is that the local vent pipe should always enter a flue above all openings into it. If otherwise connected, foul odors from the vent might escape through flue openings into rooms of the house.

In Figs. 161 and 162 are shown the two methods of constructing local vents, one consisting of a separate vent from each fixture to the flue, the other making use of one main pipe into which

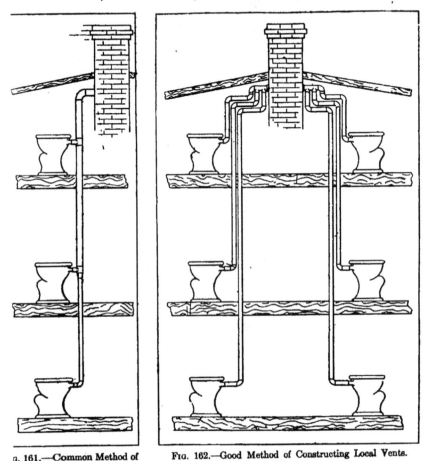

G. 161.—Common Method of Constructing Local Vents.

FIG. 162.—Good Method of Constructing Local Vents.

the separate vents are branched. The separate-vent system of Fig. 162 is by far the preferable.

Whenever local vents from several fixtures are connected into a main line of vent, the latter should be of an area equal to the combined areas of the individual vents. The venting of lines of water-closets, such as found in public toilet rooms, is illustrated in Fig. 163.

In this work, the individual vents are connected into a main

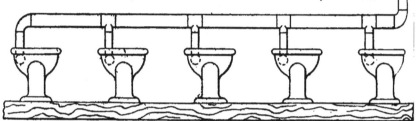

FIG. 163.—Local Venting for Line of Water-Closets.

horizontal line which is carried into a heated flue. There is not the objection to the use of a main local vent on public work that there is in residence- and dwelling-house work.

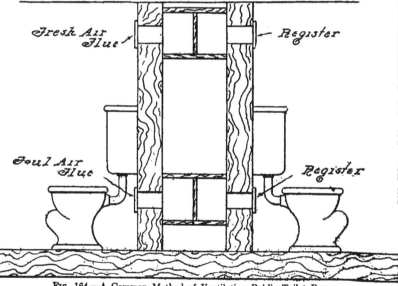

FIG. 164.—A Common Method of Ventilating Public Toilet Rooms.

The use of the local vent system described above, is still common in dwellings, residences, etc., but for large toilet rooms or public toilet rooms, this system after a time, gave place largely to another system, which is illustrated in Fig. 164. It will be clearly seen that this method does not follow closely the definition of local vents, but the subject is not complete without a consideration of it.

The illustration shows a double line or battery of water-closets, each water-closet compartment being provided with a register communicating with the foul-air duct or flue at the rear of the

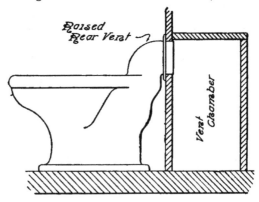

Fig. 165.—Water-Closet with Raised Rear Vent.

battery. Also at intervals along the line of water-closets, registers are placed at the ceiling for the purpose of bringing into the room a supply of fresh air. Thus it would seem that with provision for exhausting the foul air, and for admission of fresh air, this system would give perfect results.

Its weak point, however, is the fact that in order to enter the foul-air duct through the register at the side of the fixture, the foul odors and gases must first be drawn out of the closet bowl, and this gives them an opportunity to become more or less diffused in the atmosphere of the room, which is a serious objection. It may be stated at this point that much appears in the author's work "Modern Plumbing Illustrated," concerning these two methods of toilet-room ventilation, which is not given here.

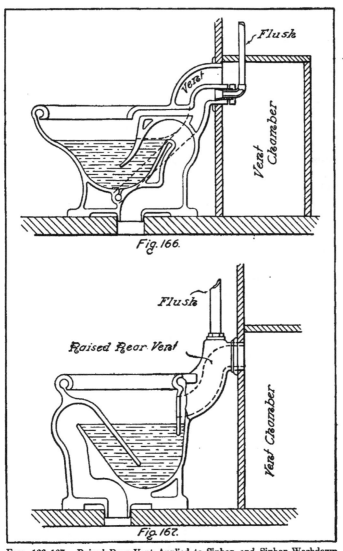

Figs. 166-167.—Raised Rear Vent Applied to Siphon and Siphon-Washdown Water-Closets.

There is a form or method of local ventilation which has neither the objectionable feature of diffusing the odors generated, nor the objectionable feature of the method first described, which is its inadequate size of vent. The method here alluded to is the method which calls for the use of water-closets having raised rear vents, a method which gives most excellent results.

In Fig. 165 is shown one of the modern types of water-closet with the raised rear vent attached. It will be seen that instead of being of only 2 in. diameter as was the form of local vent first described, this vent is 3 to 4 in. in diameter. Furthermore, the raised rear vent is in no way unsightly, but on the other hand really adds to the appearance of the fixture. In Figs. 166–169 are shown sectional views of the most common types of water-closets with the raised rear vent applied. This is to show that the principle is one that can be easily applied to any of the modern types of water-closets. The additional expense of such a fixture over the common type is very slight.

From these four illustrations the principle of the raised rear vent is easily understood. The opening of the vent into the fixture is above the water line, and the course of the vent from the opening into the vent chamber is upward throughout. As gases and odors are generated in the use of the fixture their easiest path of escape is through this raised rear vent into the vent chamber, and thence to the outer air. Into this vent chamber each water-closet of a battery is vented. Experience shows conclusively that not only does the raised rear vent ventilate the fixture to which it is attached but it acts most satisfactorily as a ventilation for the entire room. So fully is this fact acknowledged that the State of Massachusetts now requires all public toilet rooms to be ventilated in this manner.

There has been a widespread attempt in all parts of the country to overcome the foul odors of large toilet rooms by the use of disinfecting and deodorizing devices, but this is by no means a proper solution of the difficulty, and furthermore, those rooms in which such devices are used have an atmosphere almost as repulsive as that of a room in which no attempt at caring for the odors has been made. The expense of constructing ventilating flues and ducts is small in comparison with the results obtained. If pro-

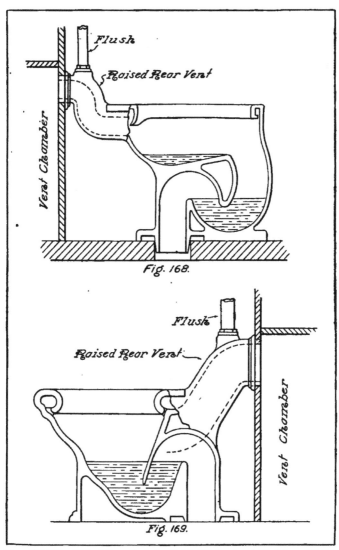

Flush

Raised Rear Vent

Vent Chamber

Fig. 168.

Flush

Raised Rear Vent

Vent Chamber

Fig. 169.

FIGS. 168–169.—Raised Rear Vent Applied to Washout and Washdown Water-Closets.

vision is made for such flues and ducts when the building is first
planned, the additional expense will be very slight indeed, and not
to be considered when the advantages to be gained are taken into
account. There is a great variety of methods in which the ventilation system may be installed. Fig. 170, for instance, shows a

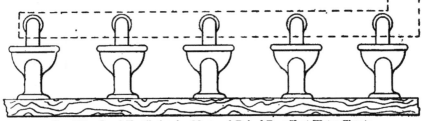

FIG. 170.—Local Ventilation by Means of Raised Rear Vent Water-Closets.

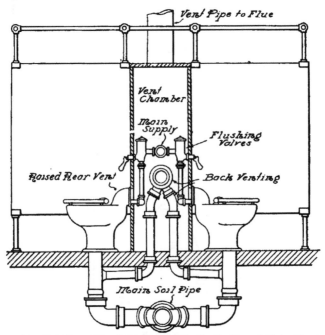

FIG. 171.—End View of Local Vent System for Double Line of Water-Closets.

common method of running a galvanized iron duct back of the partition against which the water-closets stand, thus concealing the work entirely. In Fig. 171 is shown another common and excellent method applicable to a single or double line of water-closets.

The vent chamber runs the entire length of the line of fixtures, and into it the raised rear vent of each fixture is connected. From the top of the vent chamber a pipe is carried to the flue which is to be used for ventilation. An excellent feature of Fig. 171 is that the vent chamber may be used also as a utility chamber. Its convenience in this respect may be seen from the fact that the supply pipes, flushing valves, and the back venting for the double

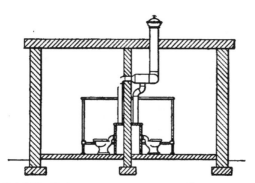

FIG. 172.—Local Ventilation for Comfort Station or Similar Toilet Building.

line of fixtures may be located in this chamber, entirely concealed from view. When so used, a door should be cut into the chamber, to allow entrance for repairs. In Fig. 172, which represents such a toilet room as might be found in a comfort station, a method slightly different is shown. In this instance, there being no flue built into the walls, a galvanized iron flue is carried through the roof, and into it the vent pipes from the two vent chambers are connected.

A ventilator at the top of the flue will add greatly to the effectiveness of the system. It used to be considered that unless local vent pipes could be connected to a heated flue they could not be effective.

This is no longer considered true, although if they can be so connected the results will be so much the better. Many toilet rooms are now provided with local ventilation in which it is impossible to use a heated flue, but this does not prevent excellent results being obtained from a flue or duct carried through the roof as in Fig. 172. In this case, however, as much assistance as possible should be given by the use of a ventilator, an electric fan placed in the flue, or a gas jet so placed. Local ventilation

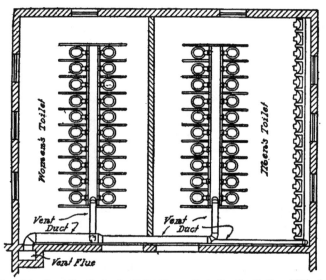

FIG. 173.—Local Ventilation for Toilet Rooms, Including Ventilation of Urinals.

may be provided in old buildings as well as in new ones, the only difference being that in old buildings the piping must often be exposed to view. However, when properly installed, such ducts are by no means unsightly. The writer recalls an old-time building in which local ventilation has recently been installed with results entirely satisfactory. The toilet rooms in this building are without natural light and without communication with the outer air, conditions under which results are generally most difficult to obtain. In this instance the pipes had to be installed exposed to

view.   There was no heated flue at hand, and the ducts were consequently run through the roof with a ventilator at the outer end.
Such excellent results as are obtained under these poor conditions
speak well for local ventilation and for water-closets with raised
rear vents.

As previously stated, local ventilation may be applied with
splendid results to urinals as well as to water-closets. A system
of local ventilation in which urinal ventilation is provided is shown
in Fig. 173.   This method of ventilation has been in use for some
little time and is worthy of far greater use than it has yet obtained.
Both architects and plumbers would do well to talk it and recom-
mend its use more generally.

CHAPTER XVII

MODERN IMPROVED PLUMBING CONNECTIONS

WITHIN a comparatively short time, a large number of especially efficient waste and vent fittings have appeared, which have great merit and have done much toward simplifying and improving waste and vent connections. In these days when the tendency is toward complication, anything which will simplify the plumbing system is to be encouraged.

The author, personally, is inclined to date these improvements

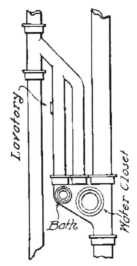

FIG. 174.—A Modern Vented Waste Fitting.

from the introduction of continuous venting, believing this system to be the indirect cause of many of these improvements. The fittings referred to present three most excellent features—they make it possible to gain a separate entrance into the drainage

201

system for each fixture; they allow the use of the continuous vent principle, and they greatly reduce the number of joints, the latter feature being of itself a great gain to the plumbing system. Scattered at various points throughout this work these fittings may be found, but there are others which it will be of benefit to consider in this chapter.

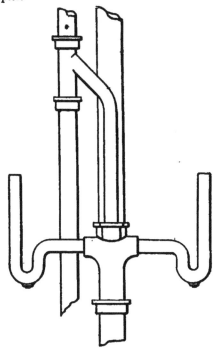

Fig. 175.—Use of Vented Cross.

In Fig. 174, for instance, is shown a fitting which illustrates the advantages to be gained from modern fittings. In this one waste fitting there is opportunity for the waste connection of water-closet and bath, and vent connection for each. The vent fitting of Fig. 174 not only does a large amount of venting with few joints and small amount of labor, but also provides a waste entrance for the lavatory.

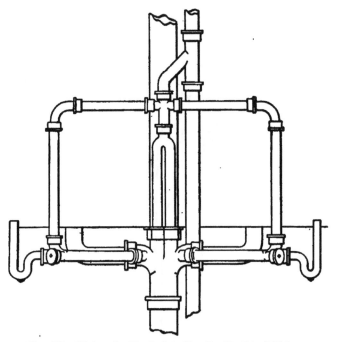

Fig. 176.—Fittings for Use in Installing Double Set of Fixtures.

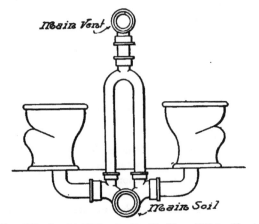

Fig. 177.—Special Fitting for Double Line of Water-Closets.

These same advantages appear also in the fittings of Fig. 175. This waste fitting, by the way, may be used for two lavatories or two bath tubs. Fig. 176 also shows a number of fittings whose use is valuable when two sets of fixtures are called for back to back, for instance, where two bath rooms on the same floor are on opposite sides of the partition.

The fitting shown in Fig. 177 also does its work, both waste

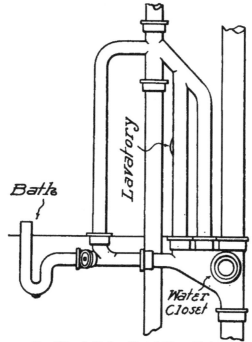

FIG. 178.—A Modern Vented Waste Fitting.

and vent, with few joints, and enables the work to be installed compactly and to the best possible advantage. Figs. 178 and 179 show fittings similar in character to those of Fig. 174, but of somewhat different design, to meet different conditions.

The additional vent hub on the waste fitting of Fig. 179 is for receiving the foot of the main vent stack. The fittings shown in

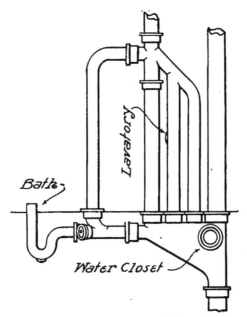

Fig. 179.—Another Modern Vented Waste Fitting.

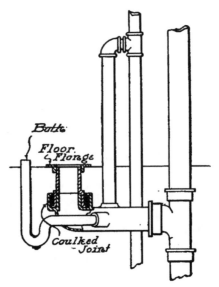

Fig. 180.—A Modern Type of Cast-Iron Water-Closet Bend.

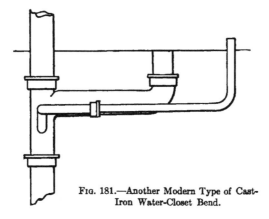

Fig. 181.—Another Modern Type of Cast-Iron Water-Closet Bend.

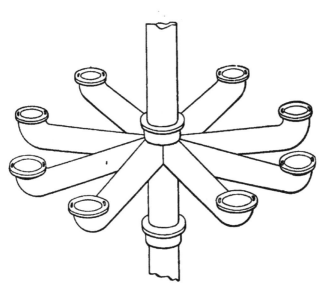

Fig. 182.—A Waste Fitting for Water-Closets Set in a Group at the Center of the Toilet Room.

these several illustrations are only a very few of the endless number of such fittings now on the market. Each one of them may be obtained with various modifications in design, until there is hardly a plumbing condition that is not perfectly covered by some one or more of these special fittings.

There is another class of fittings which have appeared only within a comparatively short time, which also are excellent in their way. We refer to the various cast-iron closet bends with their various handy features. In Figs. 180 and 181 two types of these fittings are shown. There are various other fittings of similar character, each one of them capable of being cast in a number of different modified forms, so that this class of fitting also, is capable of handling a great variety of working conditions. An especially clever fitting is to be seen in Fig. 182. This fitting is for use when a group of water-closets is to be installed in the center of the toilet room, away from any wall or partition. When it is considered what an amount of work, joints and fittings it would require to serve eight water-closets if put in under these conditions with ordinary fittings, the value of this fitting is seen. In fact, the work could not often be done if common fittings were to be used.

It is true also of many of the other special fittings, that by means of them work can sometimes be installed which could not possibly be installed with common fittings.

The description and illustration of these fittings give but a faint conception of the great number that are to be found on the market, but they will serve to show what great advantages come from their use, as indicated earlier in this chapter, and to indicate also the great saving in labor that they effect.

CHAPTER XVIII

PLUMBING FOR RESIDENCES, DWELLINGS, ETC.

THE subject of residence plumbing is one of the important branches of plumbing construction, quite different in many respects from such lines of work as the plumbing for public buildings, factories, etc., and indeed more or less different in many of its details, from the plumbing of apartment buildings.

The residence bath room especially, is a distinct feature in plumbing construction, upon which almost any amount of expense

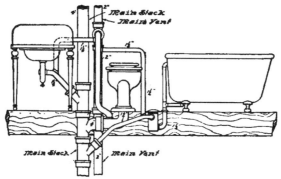

FIG. 183.—Connections for Bath Room. Separate Entrance into Stack for Each Fixture.

may be lavished, and in the appointments of which much taste may be displayed.

In Fig. 183 is shown an arrangement for the waste connections of the bath room, which is a good one, inasmuch as it provides a separate waste entrance into the stack for each of the fixtures. In addition to the three ordinary bath-room fixtures, there are several others which may often be found in the more extensive residences.

Among these are the sitz bath and foot bath, illustrations of which are given in Figs. 184 and 185. Their connections are very similar to those of the bath tub.

The child's pedestal bath, and the bidet are fixtures now used to some extent in residence bath rooms.

A fixture which adds much to the comforts of the bath room, is the shower bath. While the public shower bath is generally quite a costly and complicated affair, the residence shower bath commonly used, is simple and easy to install.

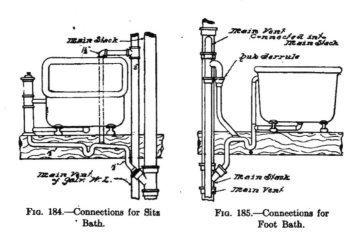

FIG. 184.—Connections for Sitz Bath.

FIG. 185.—Connections for Foot Bath.

The connections for the fixture, which is known as a receptor, are shown in Fig. 186.

The slop sink, the connections for which appear in Fig. 187, and the pantry sink, as shown in Fig. 188, are necessary to the complete equipment of the modern residence.

A method of connecting laundry tubs is shown in Fig. 189, the only objection to this method being the fact that with the trap at the end of the line of tubs, it leaves a considerable length of exposed waste, to throw out odors through the waste openings of the several tubs. The laundry tubs are sometimes located in the kitchen, particularly in the case of flats and apartment houses, in which case the connections of Fig. 190 are good.

This allows both kitchen sink and laundry tubs to secure separate waste entrance into the drainage system.

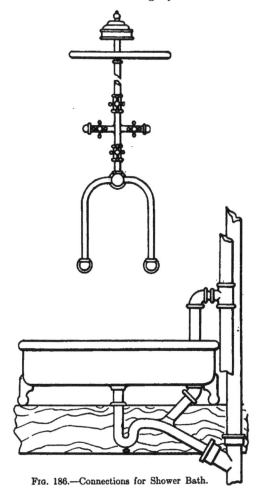

Fig. 186.—Connections for Shower Bath.

These two fixtures should never be connected into one trap, a practice which is often followed, but which is to be condemned under all conditions.

The connection of the refrigerator is also an important matter, inasmuch as the contamination of food through unsanitary connections is necessarily a source of great danger to the health of the inmates.

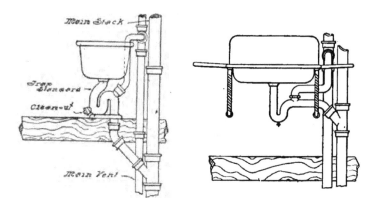

FIG. 187.—Connections for Slop Sink.   FIG. 188.—Connections for Pantry Sink.

Fig. 191 shows an entirely wrong method of connection for the refrigerator, but nevertheless, this and other similarly unsanitary connections are often made.

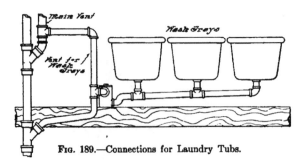

FIG. 189.—Connections for Laundry Tubs.

The proper method may be seen in Fig. 192. The drip pan should be trapped, and dripped into a drip sink which should be connected to the drainage system in the same manner as any other plumbing fixture. Under these conditions the refrigerator is not only protected by two traps, but there are two breaks be-

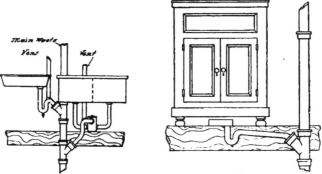

FIG. 190.—Connections for Kitchen Sink and Laundry Tubs.

FIG. 191.—Wrong Connections for Refrigerator.

tween the drainage system and the refrigerator, one between the two traps, and another between the refrigerator and its drip pan. It is advisable to have the refrigerator trap drip into the sink

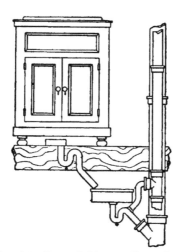

FIG. 192.—Proper Refrigerator Connections.

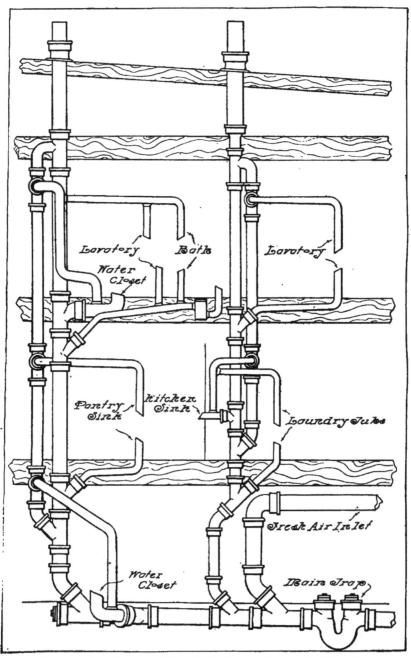

Lavatory

Bath

Lavatory

Water
Closet

Pantry
Sink

Kitchen
Sink

Laundry Tubs

Fresh Air Inlet

Water
Closet

Main Trap

FIG. 193.—Plumbing for Residence in Readiness to Receive the Water Test.

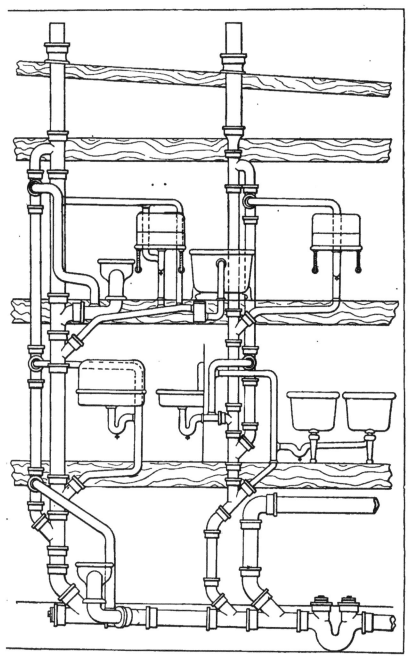

FIG. 194.—Plumbing System for Residence, Showing the Work of Fig. 193 Completed.

in the manner shown, rather than to have the openings of the two traps in line with each other vertically.

With these connections and intelligent use and precaution, there should be no reason why the refrigerator should not waste into the drainage system with as much safety as any other fixture.

The foregoing gives an idea of the details of connections for the different fixtures commonly found in residences.

In Fig. 193 is shown an elevation of the complete plumbing system for a residence, after the roughing has been completed, and the work is ready to receive the water test. This system is constructed according to the practice which is generally followed in most sections of the country. It is capable of improvement, however, by the application of continuous venting in place of the crown venting shown. The same system after it has reached completion, with all fixtures in position, is seen in Fig. 194.

CHAPTER XIX

PLUMBING FOR SCHOOLS, HOTELS, FACTORIES, STABLES, ETC.

THE plumbing systems for schools, factories, etc., and for such buildings as apartments, are very much more complex than those for residences and small dwelling houses, and call for the solution of problems of a considerably different nature. In this larger work, especially in the toilet rooms of schools, hotels, and various other public buildings, long lines of fixtures must be provided for, and upon such work much judgment and skill may be displayed.

This is true, for instance, in the connections for lines of lavatories. The old method of performing this work was according

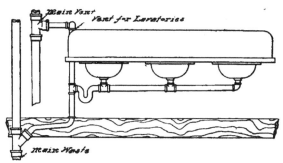

FIG. 195.—Poor Method of Connecting Line of Lavatories into One Trap.

to Fig. 195, in which a single trap is made to serve the entire line. This is obviously a poor method.

Whenever the trap stops up, as it is almost sure to do sooner or later, not one only, but the entire number of lavatories is rendered useless, until the stoppage is removed. Another objectionable feature is the fact that foul waste pipe running the entire length of the line of lavatories is constantly throwing its impure

216

odors into the room through the several lavatory outlets. An improvement over this method is shown in Fig. 196, these connections

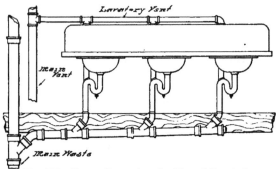

FIG. 196.—Proper Connections for Line of Lavatories.

giving each lavatory separate entrance into the main waste line, with opportunity for a cleanout in the end of it, by means of

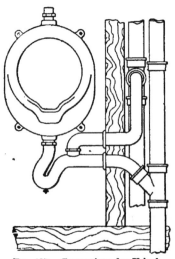

FIG. 197.—Connections for Urinal.

which any stoppage on the main may be removed. The chief objection to this method, however, is the great possibility of the

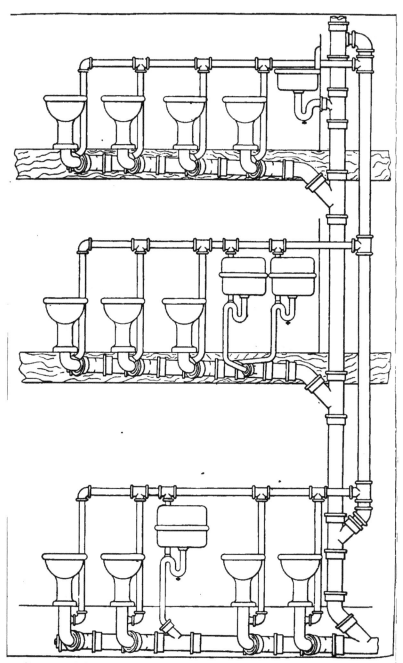

Fɪɢ. 198.—Ordinary Method of Venting for Toilet Rooms of Schools, Factories, Etc.

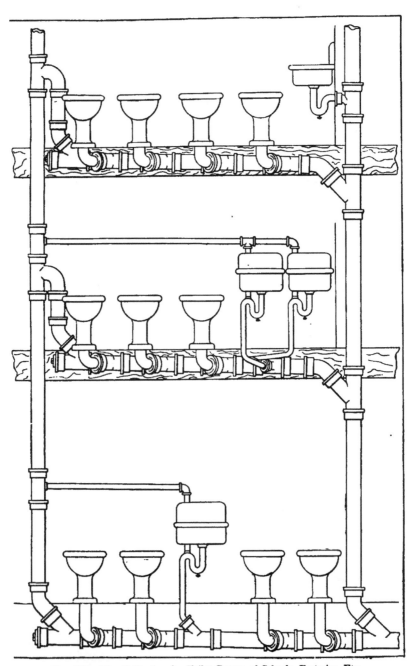

Fig. 199.—Circuit Venting for Toilet Rooms of Schools, Factories, Etc.

stoppage of the vent openings into the traps. This feature, as shown elsewhere in this chapter, may be very successfully overcome by the use of continuous venting. In another chapter, also, may be seen an illustration of a line of lavatories connected up with continuous vents. Not only is their use a great improvement from a sanitary standpoint, but ofttimes it results in great economy in the expense for labor and material, especially when two lines of lavatories or sinks back up to each other. Lines of urinals may often be connected to advantage in this same way. Although sometimes used on residence work, the urinal is a fixture found principally in large buildings of a public or semipublic nature. The common type of urinal and its connections are to be seen in Fig. 197. The subject of urinals, by the way, is considered at length by the author in his " Modern Plumbing Illustrated."

For public work, the massive porcelain urinals now in use are excellent, inasmuch as they are very cleanly, a feature greatly to be desired in urinals, which as ordinarily constructed and installed, are the most objectionable of all fixtures.

The pedestal urinal is one of the modern forms of urinal which is also very desirable.

In Fig. 198 is shown an elevation of the plumbing of toilet rooms for such buildings as hotels, schoolhouses, factories, etc., installed according to the approved methods in vogue in most cities at the present day. In Fig. 199 is shown an elevation of the same system installed with circuit vents, which subject is considered elsewhere in this work.

In many cases public toilet rooms may be served to better advantage by the circuit-vent system than by that shown in Fig. 198. It will often be found to decrease both the complication and the expense of the work. When there is but one toilet room, and it is desired to provide the water-closets with a circuit vent, the work may be performed according to Fig. 200, the vent in this case being known as a loop vent, from the manner in which it loops over the line of fixtures.

Very often, especially in public buildings, owing to the style of building construction, trap vents must be run to a point above the ceiling, and then horizontally into the main vent line, as seen in Fig. 201. The latter illustration shows the work put in under

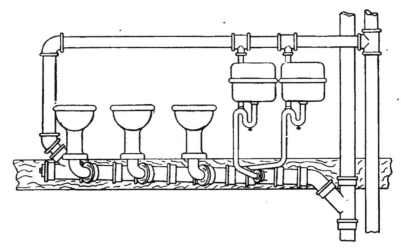

Fig. 200.—The Loop Vent.

the Durham system, which has come into extensive use in public-building work, notwithstanding the serious objections to its employment.

In the matter of ventilation for public toilet rooms, the local

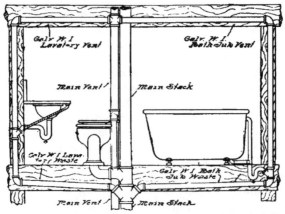

Fig. 201.—Bath-Room Connections, Durham System; Galvanized Wrought-Iron Wastes and Vents.

vent does good service when the service required of it is not too great. On large work, however, a method often followed is shown in Fig. 202, the foul air being drawn out through foul-air ducts, and fresh air forced in through fresh-air ducts.

Wash sinks for school and factory use and for similar pur-

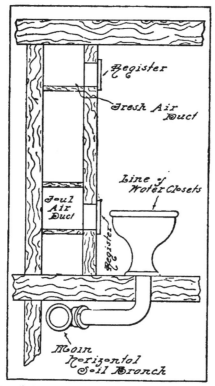

Fig. 202.—Ventilation of Line of Water-Closets in Public Toilet Room.

poses, are a subject of importance. For this purpose there are several good makes that may be obtained, among them those shown in Fig. 203, which represents a single line.

In Fig. 204 an end view of a double line of these sinks is given, and in Fig. 205 a top or plan view of the double line.

From the latter, it will be seen that the battery is made up of separate sinks, which are so made that they may be butted up to each other, enabling the installing of batteries of any desired length.

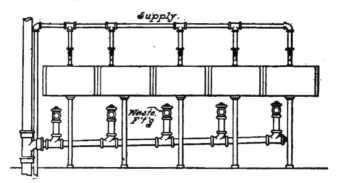

FIG. 203.—Wash Sinks for Schools, Factories, etc.

Such sinks are often placed at the center of the wash room, in which position the venting of the many traps and the running of the main vent would often be a difficult and awkward matter.

Therefore, in those cities where it is allowable to use non-

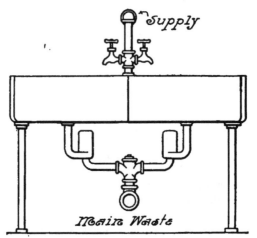

FIG. 204.—End View of Double Line of Wash Sinks.

siphonable traps without vents, the connections shown in Figs. 203 and 204 may be used to great advantage. This gives each fixture a separate waste entrance and a cleanout, with a cleanout at the

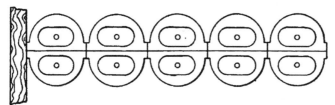

FIG. 205.—Plan View of Double Line of Wash Sinks.

end of the line of main waste pipe. Above the line of sinks, as shown, a line of supply is run, with outlets for each fixture, which are supported on the fixture itself. This line of supply answers also for holding towels, etc.

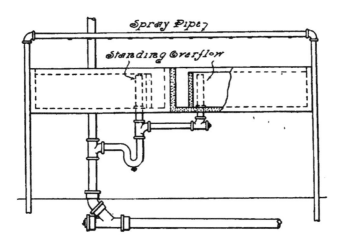

FIG. 206.—Factory Wash Sink.

If there is no difficulty in running vents, the continuous-vent principle may be employed on these fixtures. To carry this out, the work should be installed as in Figs. 203 and 204, but half-S traps used instead of other styles.

Another excellent form of factory wash sink is that shown in elevation in Fig. 206 and in plan in Fig. 207.

The sink is made in sections, generally of slate, and may be installed in any length by using a sufficient number of sections.

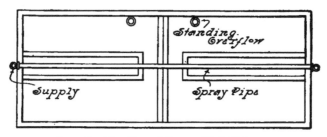

FIG. 207.—Plan View of Factory Wash Sink.

The novel feature of this sink is its center compartment. Into this falls the water from the spray pipe which runs above the center of the sink. From the center compartment the water constantly overflows into the main body of the sink. This arrange-

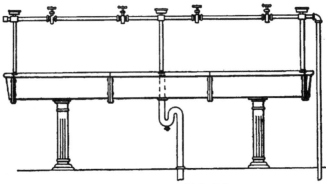

FIG. 208.—Sectional Wash Sink.

ment keeps the inner compartment always filled with clear water for washing the face, a great objection in most factory sinks being the absence of any such convenience. A standing overflow is provided for each sink section.

Another form of sectional sink is shown in Figs. 208 and 209. It is of cast iron, and the sections are bolted together to give any required length of sink.

The supply is carried through the length of the sink, and directly over its center, with a bibb taken out at intervals. The supply pipe is supported on brackets which are bolted to the sink, each bracket being supplied with a soap dish.

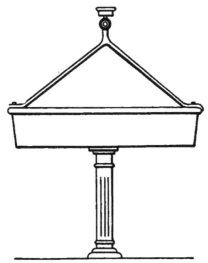

FIG. 209.—End View of Sectional Wash Sink.

The matter of drinking fountains is of importance in school work and in other public buildings.

Connections for the common form of drinking fountain are given in Fig. 210, concerning which there is no special novelty. Over this form of fountain, which necessitates the use of the same drinking cup by all that use the fixture, there has been great improvement in recent years.

The improved drinking fountain is shown in two forms in Figs. 211 and 212.

In these fixtures, the supply is connected directly to one or more bubbling cups.

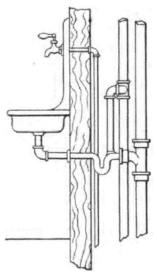

FIG. 210.—Common Form of Drinking Fountain.

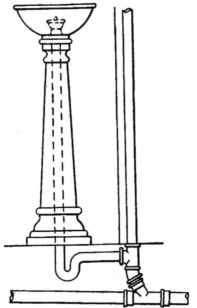

FIG. 211.—A Sanitary Pedestal Drinking Fountain.

By pressing down on the rim of the cup, the water is made to spurt or bubble up to any desirable height, according to the adjustment. This enables the water to be drunk without the use of a drinking cup, which is naturally a very much more sanitary method.

Such fountains as these are extensively used for all public purposes, both indoors and out of doors.

In public toilet-room work, it is often required to operate water-closet flush tanks automatically. A very good method is one adopted by several of the best manufacturers, in operating the

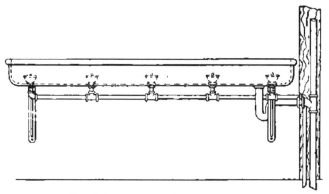

FIG. 212.—A Sanitary Drinking Fountain.

flush by means of levers attached to the seat in such a manner that when it is released these levers trip the flush valve in the tank. Another method is similar, but operated by the opening of the door to the water-closet compartment.

Flushing valves have in the last few years been rapidly coming into use on public work, thereby doing away entirely with flush tanks. In many cases the best method of handling public water-closets and urinals is by means of an automatic flushing system, which thoroughly flushes these fixtures at intervals of a few moments. The great objection to this course is the fact that foul matter entering the water-closets and urinals must often have to remain several minutes before it is flushed out. Therefore, on such work it is wise to have a very strong system of ventilation.

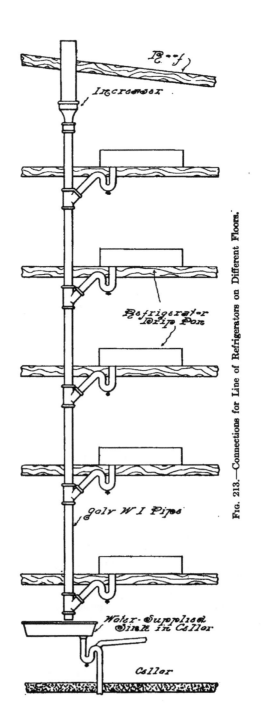

FIG. 213.—Connections for Line of Refrigerators on Different Floors.

In " Modern Plumbing Illustrated," by the author, the subjects of flushing valves and automatic flushing are illustrated and considered exhaustively.

The use of lines of refrigerators in large buildings, especially

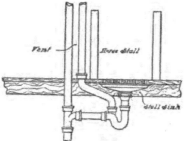

FIG. 214.—Plumbing for Horse Stall.

in apartment buildings, is a matter which may properly receive attention in this chapter.

In the chapter on residence plumbing, the connections for a single refrigerator are shown, but when a line of two or more refrigerators is to be connected with the drainage system, the

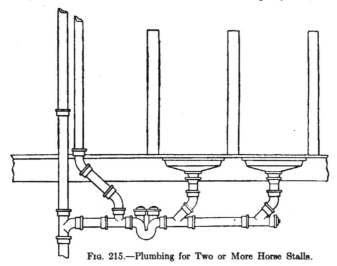

FIG. 215.—Plumbing for Two or More Horse Stalls.

method shown in Fig. 213 is generally adopted. The drip sink for such a line is usually set in the cellar, and should be trapped and vented in the same manner as any kitchen sink.

In addition to public buildings, such as schools, hotels, factories, etc., even stables now receive careful attention as to their sanitary arrangements, with the result that their sanitary conditions have in recent years been greatly improved. Although liable

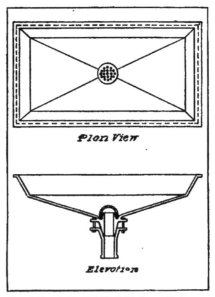

Plan View

Elevation

FIG. 216.—A Special Stall Drainage Sink.

to be somewhat overlooked, the plumbing of the stable should be as carefully attended to as that of the residence, for in our cities the stables of private residences and of business houses, public stables, engine-house stables, etc., are located largely in populous districts, where they may easily become public nuisances.

Naturally the most important feature in this line of work is the drainage arrangements for the horse stall, the most approved method of performing this work being shown for a single stall in Fig. 214, and for two stalls in Fig. 215.

The stall sink is shown in detail in Fig. 216, and is of cast iron, with a 2-inch outlet. The location of this drainage sink in the stall is shown in Fig. 217. For box stalls a similarly constructed square sink is used, a plan of which is given in Fig. 218.

The connections for the two stall sinks of Fig. 215 are preferable to the connections of Fig. 214. In the first place, while the outlet of the sink in Fig. 214 is connected directly into the trap, thus depriving the trap of its cleanouts, the connections as made in Fig. 215 will allow the use of two cleanouts on the trap and a third cleanout in the end of the horizontal line of waste. In

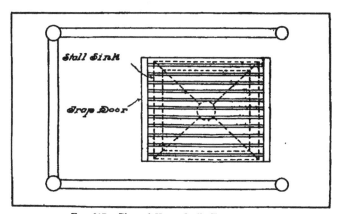

FIG. 217.—Plan of Horse Stall, Showing Sink.

order to allow two trap cleanouts to be used, the vent is connected to a tee placed next to the trap.

It is not desirable to allow one trap to serve more than two stalls, for the reason that under such conditions a long line of foul waste pipe will throw its odors out into the stable through the different stall outlets.

Floor drainage is another important feature in the plumbing of stables.

In another chapter will be found the subject of floor and yard drains. Such drains would be required in the carriage wash room, in the harness wash room, in the stable, etc. In Fig. 219 is shown an excellent form of construction for such drains. It is known

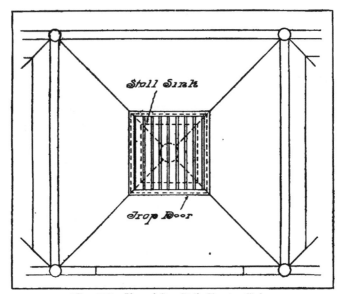

Fig. 218.—Plan of Box Stall, Showing Sink.

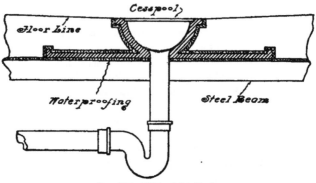

Fig. 219.—Watertight Drain.

as the F. D. C. drain. The drain is of the ordinary bell cesspool type, but cast with a broad flange, 30 inches in diameter. The drain is set in hot asphalt, which appears in Fig. 219 as the dotted section surrounding the cesspool and flange. The asphalt is waterproof, and its use does away entirely with leakage down the waste pipe, a nuisance often encountered in this work. In Fig. 220 are shown the connections for a horse trough, another necessary feature in stable plumbing. The horse trough should be provided with a standing overflow, in order to prevent the overflow of water onto the stable floor.

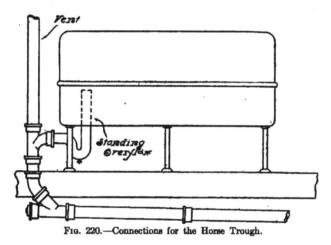

Fig. 220.—Connections for the Horse Trough.

In Fig. 221, the several connections of stable fixtures which have already been shown in detail, are assembled in one illustration, which shows the plumbing for a stable occupying two floors. In large city stables several floors are often used.

In addition to the fixtures and connections shown, most well-equipped stables are provided with toilet arrangements, with bath and toilet for hostlers, etc.

Whenever such plumbing is installed in a stable, it should be put in under the same restrictions and regulations as if the same work were to be installed in a residence.

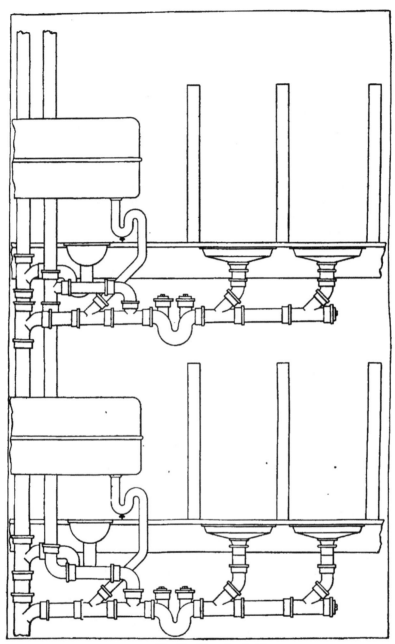

Fig. 221.—The Plumbing of a Stable.

CHAPTER XX

MODERN METHODS AND DEVICES IN COUNTRY PLUMBING

HIGH-GRADE country plumbing is at the present day a far different matter than it was years ago, both as regards methods employed and apparatus used.

One of the greatest steps in advance for plumbing systems which cannot discharge their sewage into a public sewage system, is to be found in the adoption of the septic tank and automatic sewage siphon, as shown in Fig. 222.

Briefly, the septic tank comprises several chambers, including the inlet or grit chamber, one or more settling chambers, and the discharge chamber, in which the automatic sewage siphon is located.

These chambers should be air-tight and light-tight. The septic action depends upon a certain class of bacteria which exist in sewage, and act upon it in the several chambers in such a manner as to reduce in a short time all vegetable and animal matter to liquid form.

This action renders the sewage purer in each successive chamber, until the discharge chamber is reached, when it has been sufficiently freed of all solid matter, to be forced by the automatic sewage siphon out into the underground system, for final disposal into the soil. The automatic sewage siphon acts only when the sewage has risen to a certain height in the discharge chamber.

One of the greatest objections to the use of the septic tank, especially for residences, is that considerable expense is attached to its construction. With the idea of obviating this feature, there has been placed on the market, siphoning apparatus and necessary fittings for use in connection with large sizes of glazed sewer pipe and fittings used to form the several chambers of the septic tank, as shown in Fig. 223. Twenty-four-inch pipe and fittings are gen-

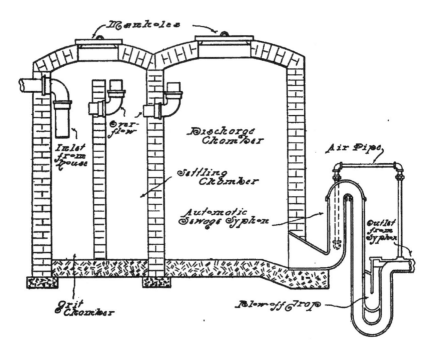

Fig. 222.—Septic Tank and Automatic Sewage Siphon.

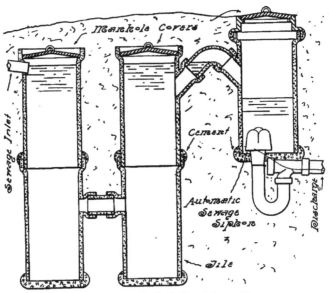

Fig. 223.—Septic Tank of Glazed Sewer Pipe.

crally used for this purpose. · It will be seen that for small work, such as for most residences, the use of this material will save a large amount of expense that would otherwise be entailed for brick work, etc., and the pipe can usually be bought of local firms.

The use of septic tanks may be very much extended, to handle large bodies of sewage, by the use of two or more automatic siphons, as illustrated in Fig. 224. The outlet connections of such siphons are made in such a manner that the discharge chamber of the septic tank may empty first into one and then into another of

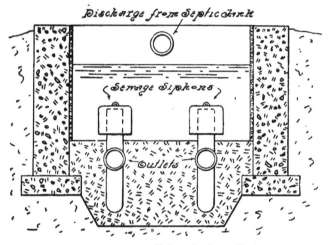

Fig. 224.—Sewage Siphons for Large Work.

several lines of underground pipe or into several different filter beds. In order to secure continuous and efficient filtration, it is always necessary to give the filtering material periods of inaction, so that oxygen may have an opportunity to pass into it, to insure the action of the bacteria. The intermittent working of these multiple siphons allows this advantage to be gained.

The sewage siphon is also used to advantage in the intermittent flushing of sewers, but as that subject is one with which the plumber would scarcely have to deal, it is hardly necessary to consider it.

The country districts have without doubt gained fully as much from improved methods and apparatus for procuring water supply, as from the advances made in the disposal of sewage.

One of the chief difficulties regarding country water supply, is the matter of obtaining a pressure. Until the introduction of the pneumatic system of water supply, dependence was made on the house tank for pressure. The action of the pneumatic system is

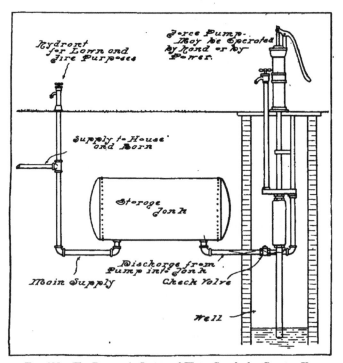

Fig. 225.—The Pneumatic System of Water Supply for Country Use.

so effective, however, and its construction and installation of so simple a nature, that the attic tank is fast being superseded, as a device that is entirely out of date. Hand or power pumping may be used in connection with it. Pressure is derived from the compressed air at the top of the storage tank. Fig. 225 shows a pneumatic supply system with the storage tank located underground

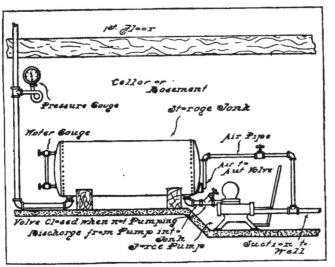

FIG. 226.—The Pneumatic System of Water Supply for Country Use.

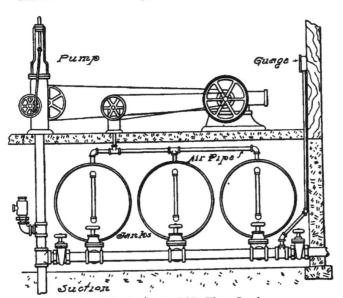

FIG. 227.—Pneumatic Public Water Supply.

and the pumping done by hand, while in Fig. 226 is seen a similar
system operated by means of a power pump, in which the tank is
located in the basement. This system is capable of being extended
to such a degree that by means of it public pressure supplies for
towns and villages of considerable size may be provided.

The general plan of such a public supply system is illustrated
in Fig. 227.

From this it will be seen that the capacity of the plant may be

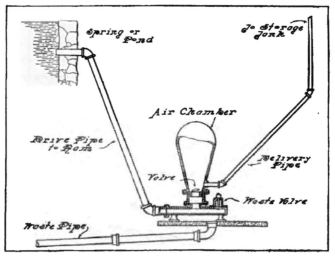

FIG. 228.—The Hydraulic Ram and Its Connection.

increased by adding additional tank capacity and greater pumping
capacity.

Another piece of apparatus much used in country work, which
has been greatly improved, is the hydraulic ram.

The common hydraulic ram shown in Fig. 228 is the type most
generally in use. In order to insure the most efficient action of
the hydraulic ram, the drive pipe, which delivers water to the ram,
from the source of supply, should be as direct as possible. Occasionally, the relative locations of the ram and its source are such
that it is difficult to run the drive pipe as directly as possible.

A method of surmounting this difficulty is seen in Fig. 229.
This consists in the use of a standpipe, open at the top, connected
with the drive pipe at or near the point where the latter changes
its direction.   The water will stand in this pipe when the ram has
been connected, at the same level as the water in the spring.   It
is the standpipe, then, that operates the drive rather than the
spring, its advantage being in making the drive more direct.

Under some conditions it may be more advantageous to use a
tank instead of a standpipe, the result being the same.

In Fig. 230 is shown a full-page illustration of a system of

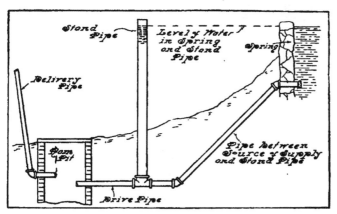

Fig. 229.—Method of Obtaining Direct Drive for Hydraulic Ram.

plumbing, drainage, and supply, for a small country home.   No
venting is shown, the fixtures having separate entrances into the
stack, and so planned that there will be the least possible danger
from siphonage.

This illustrates the common, and it may be called the old-style
method of providing a pressure supply.   The reader can see clearly
the advantages that would be gained in this work by the use of the
modern apparatus previously described.

It has not been the aim of the author in this chapter to give
anything but a brief description of the several devices described
and illustrated.

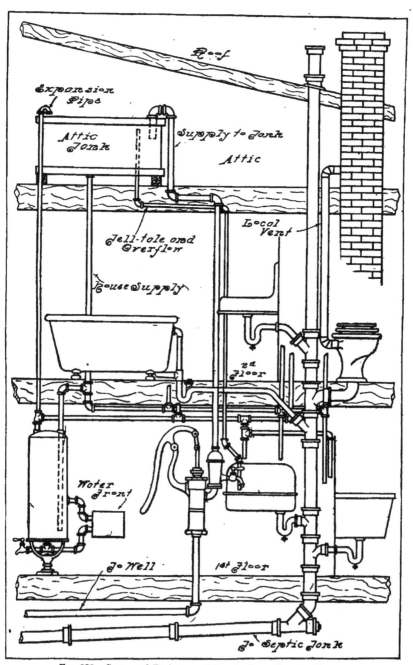

FIG. 230.—System of Drainage and Supply for a Country House.

However, a comprehensive treatment of each of these subjects, both from a theoretical and from a practical standpoint, will be found in the author's work entitled "Modern Plumbing Illustrated."

It may be added, by the way, that the subject of cesspools and the disposal of country sewage onto filter beds and into underground irrigating systems will be found elsewhere in this work.

The water lift, a device which is generally looked upon as one which has an application only to city work, is coming more and more into use in connection with country plumbing systems, and in many instances it will be found of great advantage. The action and description of the water lift will be found elsewhere in this work. Briefly, however, its action may be said to be that of the steam engine with water pressure as the motive power instead of steam pressure.

Fig. 231 shows an application of the water lift to the country plumbing system. In the absence of any street pressure, the water lift is operated by tank pressure. As the water used in running the water lift is of small amount, the demand on the tank is not great.

By means of the use of a compression tank, the lift delivers water to the fixtures under pressure. The tank operates by the compression of the air within it, and its proper position is at some point between the fixtures and the lift.

By means of the bibb on the suction pipe, the air in the tank may be renewed at any time. By opening the bibb slightly, air will be drawn in through it as the lift draws on the suction.

The cross-connection on the lift, as shown in the illustration, will allow the supply to fixtures of water from the tank whenever the well or cistern supply becomes exhausted. The use of the water lift in connection with country work is of special advantage when the supply of soft water is limited, and it is desired to use the hard well water as far as possible, or when it is desired to supply the house with soft water from cisterns and operate the lift with hard water pumped into the attic tank.

---

* "Modern Plumbing Illustrated," by R. M. Starbuck, is published by The Norman W. Henley Publishing Co., 132 Nassau Street, New York. Price $4.

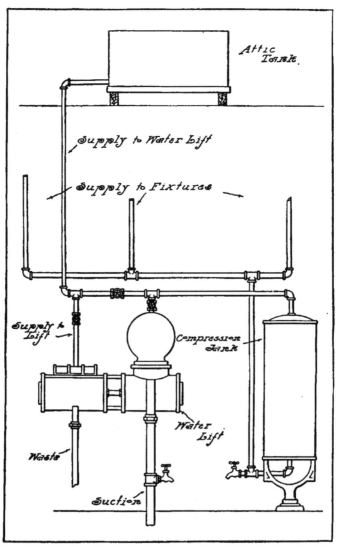

Fig. 231.—The Use of the Water Lift in Connection with the Country Plumbing System.

CHAPTER XXI

FILTRATION OF SEWAGE AND WATER SUPPLY

THE subject of filtration, and the action, construction, and connection of filters should be thoroughly understood by the plumber and by the architect as well.

At first thought this subject may seem to be somewhat outside of the plumber's province, but this is not true, for it is a matter which is very often associated with the procuring of a pure water supply, and also with the proper disposal of sewage. The filtration of water supplies is a matter more especially pertaining to city work, while the filtration of sewage, as taken up in this work, applies chiefly to country work, or at least to those plumbing systems which have not the advantage of disposal into a public sewage system.

Filtration depends upon the action of certain forms of bacteria, which attack the impurities of the water or sewage, reducing them to other and purer forms. In the purification of drinking water, the action is ordinarily performed by bacteria which exist in countless numbers in sand, charcoal, stone, and various other porous substances. This form of bacteria depends entirely upon the presence of oxygen for the performance of their work. In the purification of sewage, however, it must first come under the action of an entirely different class of bacteria, which exist in vast numbers in the sewage itself, and which multiply enormously in tanks or other receptacles for sewage, when arranged in proper manner.

These bacteria have the ability to reduce animal and vegetable matter to liquids. These liquids are then further purified in the manner described above, the two purifying processes enabling the transformation of sewage into water of such purity that it may be used as drinking water with perfect safety.

In the purification of water supplies there are two methods of filtration, that by pressure and that by gravity. The former clarifies the water and renders it suitable for most commercial purposes and for all household purposes, except as drinking water.

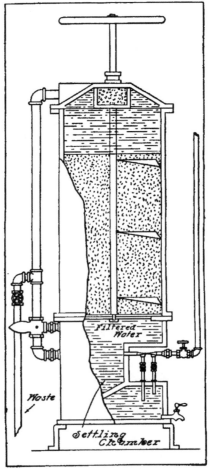

FIG. 232.—Domestic Filter.

Filters used for commercial and municipal purposes are in general of two classes, sand filters and mechanical filters, and for domestic purposes the same classes of filters are used, constructed in somewhat modified forms.

In Fig. 232 is shown a pressure filter for domestic purposes, depending upon the use of sand. Running through the center of the cylinder is a shaft provided with projecting arms. In cleaning the filtering material, the revolving of the arms breaks up the mass, thus enabling foreign substances, sediment, etc., to free themselves, and then be washed out through the waste by a reverse flow of water.

Another form of pressure filter is to be seen in Fig. 233, bone black in this case being the filtering medium.

Fig. 234 shows still another form of pressure filter, the filtering material used being sand and charcoal, mixed in with which is a quantity of stilts of irregular shape and made of burnt fire clay. In cleaning this filter, a reverse flow of water forces these stilts through the mass of filtering material, breaking it up into small particles, and freeing foreign substances, which pass off through the waste. Thus it will be seen, that in pressure filters, of which there are a great variety on the market, various forms of filtering substances are made use of, as well as various methods of cleaning, the latter being of great importance to the proper action of any filter. The value of various filtering materials and cleaning methods, and systems in use for delivering filtered water supplies in buildings, is taken up by the author in a previous work entitled "Modern Plumbing Illustrated," on page 217.

A general idea of the connections for a pressure filter for use in residences, manufacturing plants, etc., may be obtained from Fig. 235.

While the pressure filter is of importance under many conditions, and is of special value in large city buildings, certain kinds of manufacturing establishments, etc., it does not generally purify impure water sufficiently to insure safety in its use as drinking water.

As the country grows and increases in population, the subject of obtaining pure water supplies constantly demands greater and closer attention, for as our population spreads out and occupies more territory, the danger of the contamination of once pure supplies of water continually increases.

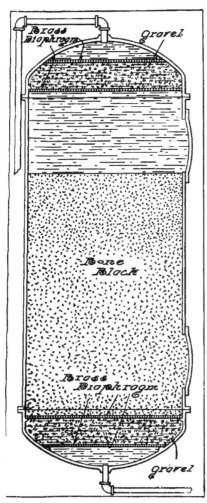

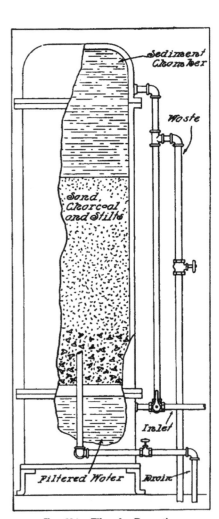

FIG. 233.—Pressure Filter; Use of
Bone Black.

FIG. 234.—Filter for Domestic or
Commercial Use.

The filtration of city water supplies by means of public filtration plants has been of untold benefit to the residents of many cities, but the danger from the use of contaminated water is not entirely overcome by this means, for inefficiency, carelessness, and

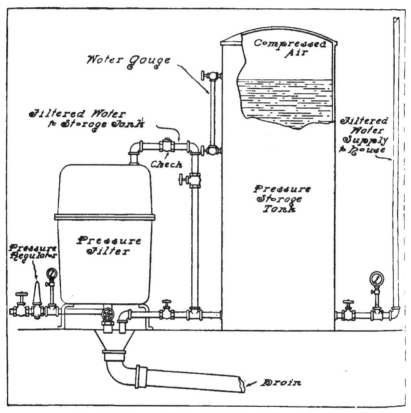

FIG. 235.—Pressure Filtering System for Residence Use, etc.

accident in the operation of such plants may easily endanger the health of an entire city.

That there is cause for extreme caution in procuring and maintaining a pure supply of water may be seen when it is considered that many of our most dreaded diseases are often directly traceable to the use of contaminated water.

Typhoid fever and diphtheria are chief among these diseases, and the former especially is in a great majority of cases due to impurities in the water supply.

Many cases may be recalled of epidemics caused by a single case of pollution.   For instance, several years ago, 1,200 cases of typhoid fever were traced to the use of an outhouse by a typhoid patient, the drainage from this house having made its way into a water course which served as the source of supply for the section in question.   It may be said that even perfect filtration, that is, as near perfect as it is practicable to make it, does not entirely safeguard the users against the typhoid germ, as a small percentage, at least, always pass through the filter.

The danger, however, is reduced to a minimum when efficient filtration is provided.   It may be said that distilled or boiled water is the only absolutely safe water for drinking purposes, though under most conditions neither of these processes is necessary if other proper precautions are taken.

Until recent years, it was generally considered that running water in traveling a few miles became purified through natural causes, such as oxidation, aëration, sedimentation, etc.   To a certain extent this is true, but as the water travels, it is constantly taking up new impurities, so that purification in this manner should not be depended upon to any extent.

Owing to the porosity of sand and the consequent existence in it of the bacteria necessary to filtration, this is the material mostly used in filtration plants, especially for large work.   That the action of filtration is dependent upon the presence of bacteria, is proved by the fact that whenever substances known to be injurious to them are allowed to enter the water, purification always ceases, either entirely or in part.   The sand filter or filter bed, as it is generally known, usually consists of several beds, such as shown in Fig. 236.   At the bottom of the bed, in a mass of broken stone and gravel, is laid a drain with open joints, into which the filtered water passes, and through which it is carried into a tight drain and thence to the storage point.

Above the broken stone and gravel is laid a bed of sand, which by the way, should not be of such depth that air may not readily pass through to supply and give life to the bacteria. The impure water is discharged onto the bed and allowed to percolate through the sand, gravel, and stone, this being the action of filtration. As the water passes through and divides between the particles of filtering material, it is open to the action of the bacteria which exist there.

It will be noted that in this method of filtration, there is no pressure upon the water forcing it through the filter, but that it

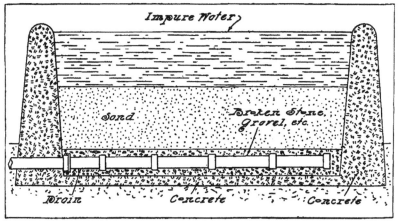

FIG. 236.—Sand Filter Bed.

acts entirely by its own gravity or weight. While the amount of water that may be filtered by this means is comparatively small when compared with the output of mechanical filters, it is nevertheless the most thorough in its work of any of the various forms of filters if properly taken care of.

Experience shows that for clarifying water supplies that are muddy and full of matter held in suspension, mechanical filtration accomplishes better work than sand filtration, and that the latter is the more efficient in the purification of water containing organic substances, such as the water of supplies contaminated by sewage.

Muddy water destroys the action of the sand filter by filling the pores. Therefore the sand filter to be efficient, must be periodically cleaned, which in large work is accomplished by mechanical means.

In the use of sand filters, it is excellent practice to first carry the water to be purified into a settling basin or reservoir, where the action of sedimentation may first clear the water of much of its mechanical impurity before it is discharged upon the filter beds. The general arrangement of filter beds and settling basins may be seen in Fig. 237.

The gravity principle is also applied to the domestic filter and to good advantage, producing a filter which comes very much

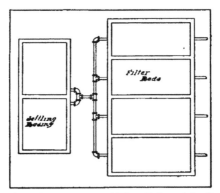

Fig. 237.—General Arrangement of Filter Beds and Settling Basins.

nearer to freeing the water of germ impurities and making it suitable for drinking purposes, than a pressure filter can possibly do.

There are several gravity filters on the market, any one of which does excellent work, so long as it is given proper attention and cleaned at frequent intervals.

The great trouble with filters used for domestic purposes, however, is that they are not properly attended to, under which conditions they may become a menace rather than the safeguard that they are intended to be.

In Fig. 238 is shown a filter working under gravity, it being one of the most popular and efficient forms of the gravity type. Water is delivered to the tank through a ball cock.

From the tank it filters through several porous porcelain tubes filled with bone black. From the tubes the filtered water enters

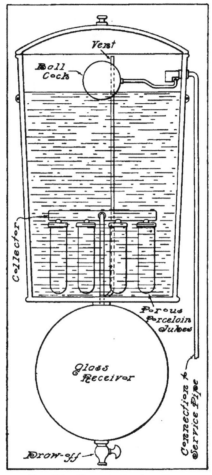

Fig. 238.—Domestic Gravity Filter.

a collector which delivers it into a glass globe, from which it may be drawn. Ice coolers of a similar nature are also made, in which the water is filtered, but in such a way that the ice does not come in contact with it, even in its impure state. This same principle is sometimes applied to the filtration of water supplies for hotels,

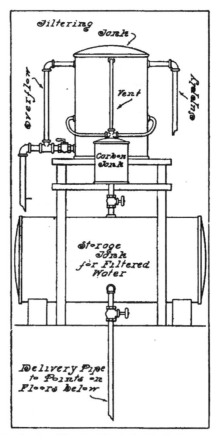

FIG. 239.—Gravity Filter for Hospitals, Hotels, Restaurants, etc.

hospitals, restaurants, etc. One method of constructing such a gravity filter is to be seen in Fig. 239, in which the tubes, which are of considerable number, are placed in the filtering tank and the filtered water carried from them to a carbon tank, where it is

filtered a second time, then delivered to a storage tank, from which
it is carried to the points at which it is to be used.

The matter of filtration is of great importance also, in the dis-

Fig. 240.—The Leeching Cesspool.

posal of sewage in country districts or wherever public sewage systems are lacking. Unless disposed of by discharging it upon the
surface, sewage in country districts is more often handled by cesspools than by any other method. The common cesspool shown in

Fig. 240 is well known to the reader, while the septic cesspool of
Fig. 241 may possibly be new to him. The latter while retaining
the solid matter that enters it, allows the liquids to leech away into

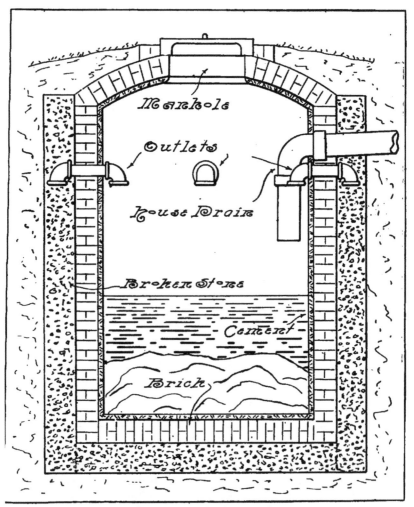

FIG. 241.—The Septic Cesspool.

the broken stone or gravel surrounding the cesspool. This particular type of cesspool is excellent when the soil is heavy or damp.

Another method of sewage disposal, in which the matter of filtration bears an important part is to be seen in Fig. 242.

Elsewhere in this work the subject of septic tanks in connection with automatic sewage siphons is taken up.

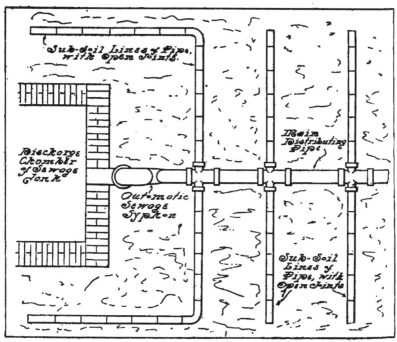

FIG. 242.—Sub-Soil System of Disposal of Sewage from Septic Tank.

These sewage siphons generally discharge the liquid sewage into an underground system of loose-jointed tile, so arranged as to allow the sewage to discharge over a large area and leech away into the surrounding soil.

The subject of cesspools, septic tanks, sewage siphons, sub-soil irrigation, and kindred subjects are treated in a comprehensive manner by the author in his work "Modern Plumbing Illustrated."

Sometimes it happens that the soil is of such nature that the sewage cannot be disposed of underground. Under these condi-

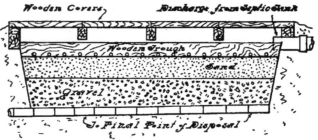

Fig. 243.—Side View of Sewage Filter Bed.

tions the sewage filter bed, shown in Figs. 243 and 244, may be used to advantage.

The partially purified waste is discharged by the automatic sewage siphon from the septic tank into wooden troughs, running the full length of the filter bed, and provided with outlets at fre-

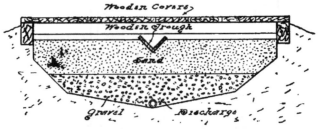

Fig. 244.—End View of Sewage Filter Bed.

quent intervals, through which the sewage escapes. When the liquids have filtered through the sand and gravel, they reach the under-drain in a pure state, and from this point may be disposed of in any way that is most practicable.

The subject of filtration should also include consideration of rain water and cistern filters. Rain water is considered the purest natural water that we have, and in its use for household purposes, it is necessary to clarify it rather than to actually filter it, for whatever impurities it possesses are generally of a mechanical nature, and held in suspension rather than in solution. Its impurities are gathered to a very slight extent in falling, and afterwards, in its passage to cisterns, it gathers such matter as leaves, twigs, dust, etc.

In the upper illustration of Fig. 245 is shown the construction of a very successful and easily·constructed filter for use in clarifying rain water before it enters the cistern.

The method of extracting the impurities of the water before it reaches the cistern, is better than the plan of filtering the water after it has reached it, as it leaves the latter in a much cleaner condition, and less frequent cleaning of the cistern becomes necessary.

In the filter referred to brick or stone is used, the entire interior being made waterproof by means of a cement lining.

A partition divides the filter into two compartments, the inlet chamber and the outlet chamber, this partition terminating sufficiently above the bottom to allow a free flow of water from one compartment to the other.

At the bottom of the inlet chamber fine gravel is filled in to a depth of 8 or 10 inches, above which is laid a layer of coarse gravel to a depth of 6 or 7 inches. Above the coarse gravel broken stone is filled in and the whole topped with a flooring of brick laid with loose joints.

The brick covering is used for holding back the coarsest substances entering with the water, such as sticks and leaves.

In the outlet chamber nothing is used but fine gravel, topped with brick, the latter being used to prevent the washing out of the gravel.

The discharge from the filter to the cistern should terminate an inch or two above the bricks.

The lower illustration in Fig. 245 shows another form of cistern filter operating on somewhat different lines.

In this case, the filter is built inside the cistern in the form of a cylindrical chamber, extending from the bottom of the cistern to a point near its top, the space at the top allowing the entrance of air. This chamber should be from 24 to 30 inches in diameter,

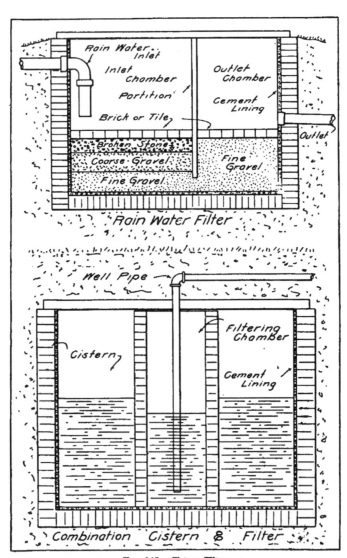

Rain Water Filter

Combination Cistern & Filter

Fig. 245.—Cistern Filters.

of brick laid in Portland cement. The water in the cistern filters slowly through the brick work of the cylindrical chamber.

It is considered that filtration through stone or brick, while slow, is very thorough. The slow rate of filtration is offset by the large area of filtering surface which the brick filtering chamber presents. The cistern should be lined throughout with Portland cement. Fig. 246 gives a very good method of construction for

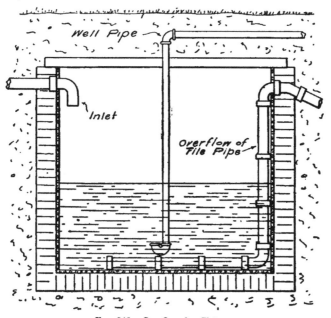

FIG. 246.—Overflow for Cistern.

a cistern overflow. The overflow is made of tile pipe, and as shown, it is laid along the bottom of the cistern and carried up to the level desired for the overflow, and there connected to the outlet. This form of overflow will carry off much of the sediment and filth accumulating in the cistern, thereby rendering it necessary to make less frequent cleanings of the cistern.

The same illustration shows a good method in connection with

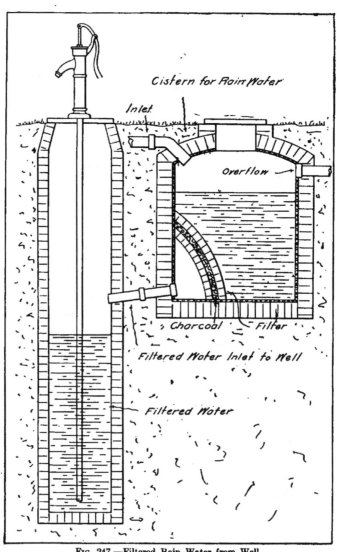

Cistern for Rain Water

Inlet

Overflow

Charcoal   Filter

Filtered Water Inlet to Well

Filtered Water

FIG. 247.—Filtered Rain Water from Well.

the well pipe of a cistern in the use of a return bend on the end of the pipe.

A straight pipe ending close to the bottom of the cistern will suck up sediment, while in the use of the return bend the suction draws the water into the pipe in a downward direction.

In Fig. 247 is shown another combination of cistern and filter which may often be used to advantage, especially in locations where rain water must be depended upon as a drinking supply at certain seasons of the year, or at all times. The illustration shows a common cistern, into which is built a filter having an arched surface, and constructed of two courses of brick, with a space of 2 or 3 inches between them. This space is filled with charcoal, which is an excellent filtering material.

In connection with the cistern and filter, a well is used, made as deep as practicable, into which the filtered water is discharged from the filtering chamber. The well is made waterproof. This method allows pure drinking water to be pumped, of the same cool temperature as ordinary well water.

CHAPTER XXII

HOT AND COLD WATER SUPPLY

THE work of the plumber is divided into two distinct lines—drainage and supply.

In nearly all city work, the drainage system must be installed according to plumbing ordinances established for the purpose of securing uniformly sanitary work.

The supply system, however, in most cases is not thus protected by municipal ordinances, although in some of the more progressive cities it is now safeguarded in the same manner as the drainage system.

There was a time when nearly all supply piping was of lead. To-day, however, the use of this material has been very largely displaced by the use of brass and galvanized wrought iron. It may be stated, however, that in some sections lead pipe is still used almost entirely for supply work, generally in such cases, owing to the chemical properties of the water supply.

Some waters will attack lead pipe more seriously than wrought iron, while the reverse may be true of other waters.

Thus, in some sections galvanized piping will fill with rust and sediment in a very few years, while over the surface of lead pipe a sort of protective coating will form, which will allow its continued use for an almost unlimited length of time. The author has known of instances where wrought-iron pipes and galvanized boilers could be used only four or five years before being made entirely unfit for use, the pipes becoming almost completely filled and the boiler rusted through.

On the other hand, he has seen galvanized supply piping taken out that has been in use for twenty to thirty years, which was very nearly as clear as when first installed.

When pipe is to be laid underground, and the quality of the water will possibly permit, it should be lead rather than wrought iron, as the former has a much longer term of life when subjected to the corrosive influences incident to the moisture of the ground.

For this reason, service pipes, even though of wrought iron, are usually connected to water mains by means of lead connecting pieces. Such connections are to be seen in Fig. 248. The upper

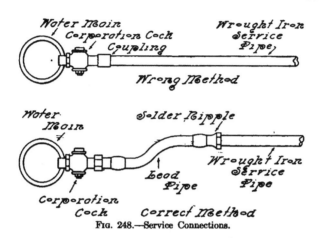

Fig. 248.—Service Connections.

connection made without lead is wrong, for it is very rigid, and liable to be broken off, whereas the lead connection will give sufficiently to take up any such strain.

From the lead connection the service pipe is carried to the

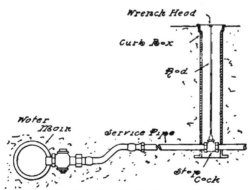

Fig. 249.—Shut-off on Service Pipe and Curb Box.

curb, where a service stopcock is usually located. It being necessary to close this stopcock from the street, a curb box, as it is called, is usually made use of, as shown in Fig. 249.

The curb box is so made that it may be varied in length to suit different depths at which the stopcock is located.

The bottom of the box is slotted so that it may set down over the pipe, resting on the earth beneath the pipe. To the stopcock is connected a rod which extends to the top of the box passing through the cover of the box and ending in a five-sided head. To open or close the cock, a socket wrench, made to fit this head, is used. A five-sided head is used instead of a square or hexagonal

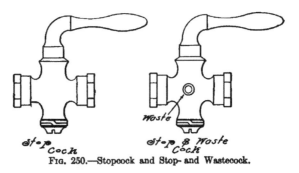

Fig. 250.—Stopcock and Stop- and Wastecock.

head, in order that only those connected with the water department and supplied with a special wrench may be able to operate the stopcock.

From the curb, the service pipe is carried through the foundation wall of the house. Just inside the foundation, the main supply pipe should be provided with a stop- and wastecock. In Fig. 250 is shown an illustration of the plain stopcock, also an illustration of the stop- and wastecock.

In the latter a small round waste opening will be observed. When the handle is turned to close this cock, the water in the piping, which is shut off by the closing of the cock, wastes out through the waste opening. By means of a small lead pipe, connected to the waste opening, this water may be conveyed if desired, to some open fixture, instead of being allowed to waste onto the cellar bottom or into the ground. The use of the stop- and wastecock is a very important matter in many places where water, if allowed to stand in the piping, is liable to freeze and burst the pipe. For this reason, the main stopcock on a main house supply, should be a stop- and wastecock, in order that the entire supply piping may be drained, a very important matter if the house is to remain vacant during cold weather. This cock should always be placed in a position which will be easily accessible in the event of an emergency. It should also be fully protected against frost, so that the cock itself and the pipe beyond it may not freeze. In warm cellars, precautions of this nature are often unnecessary.

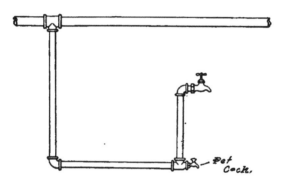

Fig. 251.—Deep Trap in Water Piping.

If necessary, however, the cock may be protected by means of boxing, hair felt, etc. The plumber in running his water piping should always be sure to run it so that no traps may be formed which will not drain off through the main stop- and wastecock.

For instance, in Fig. 251 the deep trap formed by running the branch down from the overhead line, and then up to the fixture, forms a trap which cannot be drained through the main stop- and wastecock.

If any pipe must of necessity be run in this manner, a pet cock or faucet should be placed so that when required this part of the piping may be drained. The running of pipes in this way is quite a common error, being often found on the hot-water piping especially. In order that the pipes may be thoroughly drained, they should always pitch down in the direction of flow toward the main stop- and wastecock.

Before proceeding further with the piping inside the house, there is the hydrant to be considered, which is shown in Fig. 252. The hydrant cock or shut-off is of special design as shown, and should be of the waste pattern, in order that all water in the vertical pipe may drain into the ground when the cock is closed.

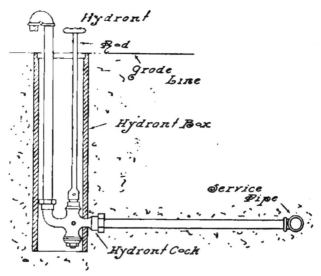

FIG. 252.—Hydrant Connections.

A rod carried to the surface is operated to open and close the hydrant cock.

On high-grade work, it is often customary to lead the main supply pipe directly to a keyboard. Such work is shown in Fig. 253. The main line of supply is run directly to the keyboard, from which every cold-water supply pipe in the house is taken. Each line is provided with a stop- and wastecock, and the waste from each cock connected into a main waste which should be carried to some open fixture into which it may drain. Laundry tubs, which are often located in the basement or cellar, are sometimes used for this purpose. The ends of the header should be provided with tees rather than elbows, in order that any future line may be easily taken off. The end tees should be plugged.

When lead supply pipe is used, the keyboard may be made a very neat thing, as much skill may be put into its construction. The keyboard shown is designed for the cold-water supply. An

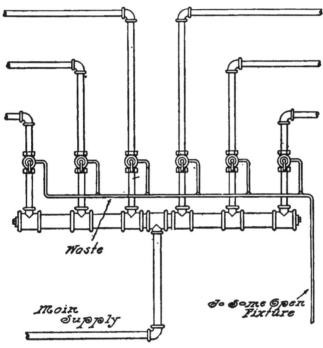

Fig. 253.—Keyboard.

additional keyboard may be used for the hot-water supplies, and a third one for the circulation or return pipes. On very nice work, polished brass supply pipe is used to a large extent. When brass is used, a very neat system can be obtained by the use of keyboards and by bending the pipe instead of using elbows and offsets. When a header is used for the hot-water pipes, the hot-water pipe from the boiler is carried direct to the keyboard, and from that point delivered to the several lines. When a circulation or return header is used, it should be connected into the return opening of the range or heater. In order to derive full benefit from the use of the keyboard, each valve should be tagged with the fixtures and room that it supplies. Very neat nickel-plated tags, with the proper words stamped on them, are now made for this special purpose.

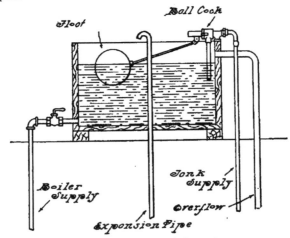

FIG. 254.—Attic Tank and Connections.

Keyboards make the work very systematic, and rob the supply of much of its mystery to the inmates. Whenever any defect or trouble with the piping arises, they may go at once to the keyboard and shut off the proper valve, avoiding the loss of time in hunting for the proper valve which is necessary in ordinary work. The loss of this time in the event of a serious break, often means great damage to the property from escaping water. Keyboard work is necessarily somewhat more expensive than ordinary work, but its value should commend it to much greater use than it has. If the keyboard is not used and the tank system of supply is used, the supply should be run to the attic tank, which with its connections is shown in Fig. 254.

There are two systems of supply in common use, the pressure system and the tank system. In the pressure system, the range boiler and all fixtures are supplied with water under street pressure. In the tank system, a tank is located in the attic, above all fixtures, this tank being supplied from the house main through a ball cock.

Years ago the attic tank was of large size, and used as a storage for water, often holding several hundred gallons. From this tank the entire supply for the house was delivered, including the range boiler and all fixtures.

In the use of the present tank, however, it is designed chiefly to supply the range boiler, the cold-water supply to fixtures being under street pressure. In the tank system as at present used, then, the hot-water supply is under tank pressure, while the cold-water supply, with the exception of the boiler, is under street pressure. As water is drawn from the hot-water piping at any fixture, an equal amount enters the attic tank through the ball cock, thus keeping a uniform supply of water in the tank.

There are certain advantages to be gained by the use of the tank system. In the first place, the pressure of water in the tank system is always uniform, whereas the street pressure varies greatly from many causes, such as a greater use of water at certain times of the day than at others. The pressure of the tank system being always uniform, the wear and tear on piping and valves is at a lower rate than in the use of the pressure system.

Lighter boilers may be used on the tank system also. The attic tank as now used is of far smaller capacity than the old-style attic storage tank. It is usually of about 50 to 60 gallons' capacity, lined with copper, and set up from the floor on pieces of joist. A very convenient size of tank is 2 feet in length, by 16 inches wide, by 15 inches deep. This is a small-sized tank, but cuts the copper to advantage.

The tank is generally supplied through a top supply ball cock. The supply to the boiler is taken from the bottom of the tank and should be provided with a stopcock close to the tank, as shown, in order that the supply to the boiler may be shut off from this point. In the case of several apartments, a single attic tank of larger size may be used, with separate supplies taken out for the different

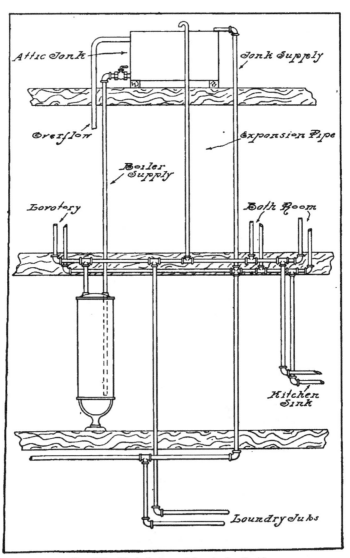

Fig. 255.—Tank System of Supply for Residence

apartments. An overflow should be run to some open fixture. It is often convenient to run this pipe into the flush tank of the water-closet in the bath room on the floor below. In the use of the pressure system no special provision need be made for expansion, as the expansion due to the hot water will be through the piping into the street main, and thence back to the reservoir. In the tank system, however, special means must be provided to take care of the expansion.

This provision consists in running a pipe from the highest point in the hot-water piping up and over the tank. Through this pipe any expansion of the hot water may vent itself into the tank. If several separate lines are fed from the same tank, a separate expansion pipe should be provided for each line. In some cases, a lead safe is placed under the attic tank, and a drip carried down, usually to the cellar or basement, to carry off any leakage from the tank. In general, however, this is not considered necessary.

In Fig. 255 is shown a tank system of supply for a residence, as ordinarily put in, and in Fig. 256 a pressure system of supply for a two-flat house.

In the pressure system, separate lines of supply are carried up to each kitchen boiler, with branches to the kitchen fixtures, and also separate lines to each bath room, each line being provided with its own stop- and wastecock.

In shutting off a supply system and allowing the water standing in the pipes to drain out through the waste of the stop- and wastecock, it will be found that by simply opening the cock, the desired result cannot be obtained. It will be necessary to open a faucet at the highest fixture in order to drain out the whole line. If a faucet on a lower floor is opened, the pipe will simply drain out up to that level. In other words, in order to allow the water to flow out of a pipe, it is necessary to have atmospheric pressure act upon the top of the column of water to be drained out. In order to completely drain the piping, it is often necessary to open faucets at certain of the fixtures. For instance, in Fig. 240, to drain the water in the pipes running to the kitchen fixtures, it will be necessary to open a faucet on these lines.

In the case of the pressure system, it is necessary to provide against the siphonage of the contents of the range boiler.

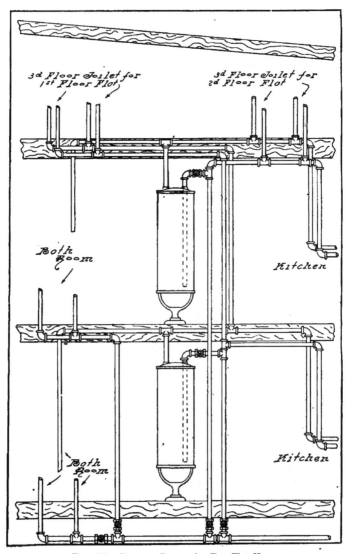

FIG. 256.—Pressure System for Two-Flat House.

The boiler tube, shown by dotted lines in Fig. 256, dips down into the boiler to a point near the bottom, the supply to the boiler being much longer than the tube, and terminating at a point much lower than the level of the boiler. Now the siphon has a short arm and a long arm, the latter ending at a point much below the short arm. Therefore it will be seen that the boiler tube and boiler supply in connection with the house main and service pipe reaching to the street main forms a perfect siphon apparatus, and a break in the house main or in the street main might allow the water in the pipe leading to the boiler to waste back and siphon out the entire contents of the boiler. If a break should occur in the night, for instance, this result might easily occur. The siphon-

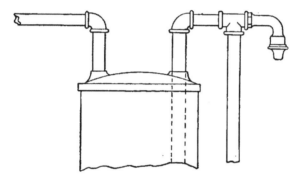

Fig. 257.—Use of the Vacuum Valve.

age of the contents of the boiler will leave a more or less perfect vacuum in the boiler, which might result in its collapse, this being especially true of certain makes of copper boilers.

In the case of the boiler supplied from the attic tank, this danger is entirely lacking, owing to the location of the source of supply above the boiler rather than below it. There are two methods of preventing the siphonage of range boilers. It may be done by drilling a hole in the boiler tube at the top of the boiler. This, however, is open to the objection that rust and sediment will in time fill the hole and render it useless for the purpose for which it is designed.

A better and surer method is shown in Fig. 257, a vacuum valve being used for the purpose of preventing siphonage. This valve should be placed on the supply to the boiler at the point where it turns from the vertical line to the boiler. It is necessary that this valve should be located at the highest point of the siphon, just as it is necessary to vent the trap from its crown, for the reason that in order to prevent the operation of the siphon, air must be admitted at its crown. The operation of the vacuum valve is the following: In the event of a break on the supply pipe, the contents of the boiler start to siphon out, owing to the creation at the top of the boiler of a partial vacuum. The instant a vacuum is created on the inner side of the vacuum valve, atmospheric pres-

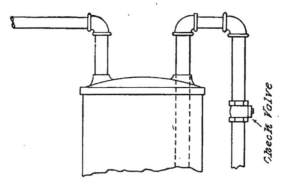

FIG. 258.—Wrong Use of Check Valve to Prevent Siphonage.

sure opens it, and air enters, thus effectually breaking the siphonic action. At other times, the pressure of the water against the valve keeps it closed.

The vacuum valve should be set to point downward, as shown, in order that any passage of water out of it may fall upon the floor rather than upon the walls or ceiling. It is a good plan to have the valve, if possible, located over the sink, so that any leakage from it may enter the sink instead of falling upon the floor. The only disadvantage in the use of the vacuum valve is that if it has not operated for a considerable length of time it may stick and refuse to work.

A dangerous method of preventing siphonage by the use of a check valve on the boiler supply is shown in Fig. 258. Ignorant workmen sometimes place it on this line, with the idea that as soon as the water in the boiler attempts to flow in the opposite direction to its natural flow, the check valve will close and prevent siphonage. It will certainly perform this duty, but in its use it acts in another way, which is very unsafe. Under normal conditions, it closes the supply pipe against expansion, and as the expansion of the boiler is naturally through the supply pipe, the use of the check valve at any point upon it prevents the natural expansion of the water as it heats. This means that the boiler is in danger of bursting.

The collapsing of range boilers and explosion of water fronts may occur from several different causes. If the connections between the range and the boiler on a pressure system should be frozen, there would be serious danger of an explosion.

If the pipes were thus frozen, expansion would be cut off and steam would be generated, resulting in the explosion of the boiler if the range fire should be started under the circumstances. If the supply to the boiler on a tank system, and the expansion pipe should be frozen, a fire built in the range would be liable to burst the boiler, especially as tank boilers are not constructed to withstand such high pressures as pressure boilers. Even though the boiler were full of water, with the boiler supply frozen, the contents of the boiler would not flow to the water front, for the reason that the frozen section of the pipe would prevent the action of atmospheric pressure from above on the water in the boiler.

It is well in the winter season, whenever the range fire is allowed to go out at night, to open faucets before building the kitchen fire, in order to make sure that the pressure is on and no freeze-up has occurred during the night. The workman, in making repairs to the piping on pressure work, such as repairing faucets, etc., when the range fire is going, should open a hot-water faucet as soon as the boiler valve is closed, in order that any expansion may have a vent.

When the cold-water supply for any reason is shut off from the water front, and the latter becomes very hot, the moment water is allowed to enter it again steam will be generated the instant the cold water comes in contact with the hot surface of the water front, the expansive force of the steam being very great, and in danger of bursting the water front, unless there is a vent for it. For this reason it is a dangerous matter to use valves on the range connection. They are sometimes used in multiple connections, and also sometimes on the ordinary single range connection, as a matter of convenience. It will be seen that the use of such valves would allow the water front to be cleaned out without drawing off the boiler, and in sections where the water is full of lime and the water front must be cleaned from time to time, it is very convenient to use these valves. Their use is accompanied with danger, however. For instance, the valves may be forgotten when the water front is put back, and there is liable to be enough moisture present to form steam, which without outlet is liable to be a dangerous factor. Then, again, one valve may be opened and the other through carelessness allowed to remain closed. The choking of water pipes with deposits of lime, rust, and sediment is another cause of water-front explosions.

In addition to the collapsing of boilers due to the siphonage of the contents of the boiler, there is another way in which the same result may occur. To produce a collapse of the boiler, it is necessary to create a vacuum inside it, the collapse being just opposite in action to the bursting of the boiler. Therefore, anything causing a vacuum to be formed within the boiler, will result in its collapse, if the boiler is not strong enough to withstand the strain. It is comparatively common to find the boiler collapsed, owing to the ignorance of the inmates. For instance, the supply to the boiler may be found frozen in the morning after the range fire has been started. To obtain water for the use of the household, it may be drawn out of the sediment cock. Meanwhile the water front is heating the boiler and filling it with steam. When the pipe supplying the boiler thaws out, the cold water rushes in, instantly condenses the steam, thus causing a vacuum, and the boiler collapses if not sufficiently strong to withstand the outside pressure. The collapse occurs, owing to the fact that when the vacuum exists inside there is no pressure to hold the sides of the boiler out, and they are crushed in by atmospheric pressure, which is approximately 15 lbs. to the square inch. It is very rarely that a galvanized wrought iron boiler collapses, as it is of sufficient strength to withstand the pressure of atmosphere against a vacuum. It is not an uncommon occurrence for copper boilers, however, to suffer from this cause, unless strengthened inside. A collapsed copper boiler may often be forced back by turning on the pressure, and sometimes this can be done so effectively that almost no trace is left on the sides of the boiler of its collapse. A collapsed boiler should never be struck with a mallet or hammer, however, as the marks and indentations thus made will not be taken out when the boiler is forced back into shape. If the pressure is insufficient to

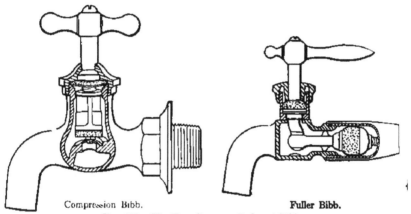

Compression Bibb.　　　　　　Fuller Bibb.

Fig. 259.—The Two Common Styles of Bibbs.

force the boiler into its original shape, the head must be taken off and the side forced out from the inside. The use of safety valves on range boilers is seldom seen, and their use is not necessary if the boiler is properly provided for.

⊹ There are three kinds of bibbs or faucets used in connection with the water supply: compression work, Fuller work, and self-closing work, the two first named being most common. From a glance at the compression and Fuller faucets shown in Fig. 259, it will be seen that the latter works with a cam motion, and that when the faucet is closed, it is closed very quickly, whereas, in order to close the compression faucet, the handle must be turned

several times, and a much longer time thus taken in shutting off
the water. Water, as is well known, is almost incompressible, and
will not compress sufficiently to take up a sudden shock. Therefore, in the use of Fuller work, much trouble is caused due to the
rattling of pipes when faucets are closed, a feature entirely lacking in compression work. Therefore, even though Fuller work is
more expensive than compression, and used very extensively on
high-grade work, compression work will in general be found to
give much more satisfactory results. Not only is the hammering
of pipes disagreeable, but such action is necessarily harmful to
pipes and valves.

Self-closing work closes very quickly also, and is open to the

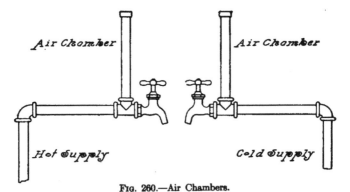

Fig. 260.—Air Chambers.

same objection as Fuller work. When the pressure of the supply
is very heavy, this trouble is a serious one. The only way to proceed against the trouble is to use air chambers. Air, unlike water,
is very compressible, and easily takes up the shock occasioned by
the closing of valves.

In Fig. 260 is shown the customary method of providing air
chambers at the different fixtures. This method consists in turning upward with the supply pipe a distance of a foot or so. Whenever either of the faucets shown in Fig. 260 is closed, or faucets
or valves in other parts of the house are closed, the resulting shock
is taken up in these air chambers, hammering and vibrations being
thus prevented.

Sometimes air chambers are formed by continuing the supply pipe past the faucet horizontally, without turning the pipe up. The last-named method is a very poor one, however, for the water soon carries out the air with it and the air chamber becomes water-logged and absolutely useless. The air chambers shown in Fig. 260 will in time also become water-logged, and when once in this condition cannot be renewed with air by drawing off the water in the piping, as the water in the air chambers will not pass out of them, owing to the fact that there is no air pressure at their

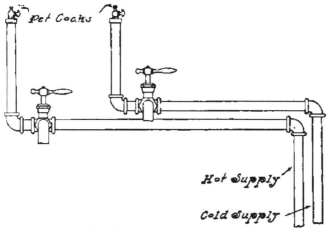

Fig. 261.—Use of Pet Cocks on Air Chambers.

upper ends to force the water out. The method shown in Fig. 260 is a very common one for providing air chambers on the supply system, but is in reality a poor method, as the water will gradually absorb the air and carry it off through the faucet in minute parti-cles, and in time, as stated above, absolutely destroy the air cham-ber. The method shown in Fig. 261 would present a means of renewing the air in these air chambers, and thus overcoming the difficulty above mentioned, but is a device seldom made use of, for some unknown reason. The illustration referred to shows a pet cock used at the upper end of each air chamber. When the pipes begin to hammer, it shows that the air chambers have become water-logged, in which event it is necessary simply to close the main stop- and wastecock, allowing the pipes to be drained. When the pressure has been shut off, open the pet cocks until the water has run out of them, when they may be again closed. In this way, by the use of pet cocks, it is an easy matter to renew the air chambers at each fixture in the house. The method is sometimes adopted of using a single large air chamber on the main supply pipe, allowing this device to perform its work for the entire house. In Fig. 262 is shown a desirable method of constructing and connecting such an air chamber. A short branch

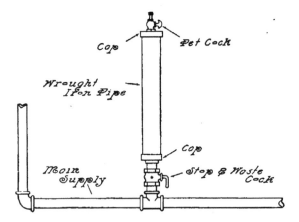

FIG. 262.—Air Chamber on Main Supply Pipe.

may be taken from the main supply, into the bottom of the pipe forming the air chamber, and between the chamber and the main, a stop- and wastecock should be placed.

The chamber may be made of 2-, 3- or 4-inch galvanized wrought-iron pipe, capped at the upper end, and tapped to receive a pet cock. The joints should be made absolutely air tight. When this air chamber becomes water-logged, it is a simple matter to close the stop- and wastecock and open the pet cock, thus allowing the water standing in it to drain out through the waste. After the chamber has been entirely drained, close the pet cock and open the stop- and wastecock, and it is again ready to perform its duties. If the stop- and wastecock is not used on the branch to the air chamber, it will be necessary in draining it to close the stop- and wastecock on the main supply, thus shutting off the entire building.

On many supply systems, the use of a water-pressure regulator is accompanied by good results. It makes the valves and pipes safe from the dangers due to high pressure, prevents hammering and vibrations of pipes, and avoids the splashing of water when drawn under high pressure. When used on pressure work a relief valve attached, allows for the expansion, and in the case of a

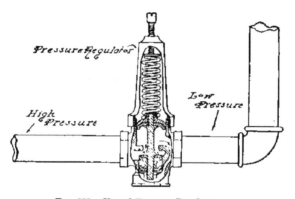

FIG. 263.—Use of Pressure Regulator.

break in the main, the regulator remains closed, thus preventing the siphonage of the boiler. The action of the pressure regulator is automatic, and when once set needs no further attention. The regulator shown in Fig. 263, works by means of a spring which is compressed, the spring being put under any desired tension by screwing down on the set-screw at the top.

A few remarks are necessary concerning the running of water pipes.

They should always be so run that no sags or dipping of the pipe may occur and thus form a trap which cannot be drained. When piping in which sags exist, must be drained in cold weather in the event that the house is to be vacant, it is impossible to drain the traps thus formed, and their contents often freeze and burst the pipe, whereas the owner has assured himself of protection against this trouble by having the system properly drained.

Pipes should never be run against cold cellar walls, or other walls that may at any time be exposed to frost. When it is necessary to so run them, however, they may be protected by covering them with hair felt or other similar material, or by boxing them. Several concentric boxes with 1-inch air spaces between them provide excellent protection to pipes against extreme cold. It is often

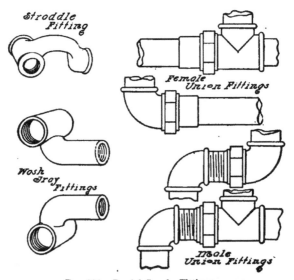

FIG. 264.—Special Supply Fittings.

a good plan to run the main supply pipe through the cellar underground as far as possible, this course not only preventing freezing, but keeping the water cooler than when run overhead.

The "sweating" of exposed water piping is a matter which causes much trouble. It is caused by the formation of condensation on the surface of the pipes, the moisture forming in sufficient quantity to flow along the pipes and drip off. The reason for this trouble is that in warm places the moisture of the air condenses against the sides of the cold pipe. It may be overcome by covering such pipes. It sometimes occurs between floors, the moisture dripping down onto the ceiling below. In this case, a sheet metal gutter run under the pipe and pitched toward one end, and dripping into a drip pipe effectually remedies the difficulty. Such a drip may be carried into an open cellar fixture. There are several special supply fittings which are of excellent service, a few of which are shown in Fig. 264.

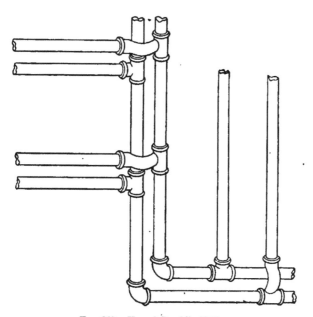

Fig. 265.—Use of Straddle Fittings.

The straddle fitting is a most valuable fitting for use on parallel lines of hot- and cold-water pipe. In many places throughout the house the hot- and cold-water pipes will be found running side by side, and in the use of ordinary fittings it is usually a very awkward undertaking to cross over one of these pipes with a branch from the other. The straddle fitting, as its form shows, is designed for this special purpose. The curved part of the fitting is of sufficient radius to entirely clear the pipe which it must cross.

The use of the straddle fitting is shown in Fig. 265, from which it will be seen that a fitting of this style not only adds greatly to the appearance of the work, but saves labor and the use of a number of fittings.

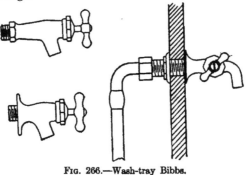

FIG. 266.—Wash-tray Bibbs.

Regarding the running of the hot- and cold-water pipes side by side, when so run horizontally the hot water should ordinarily be run above the cold water, as the heat radiated from the hot water

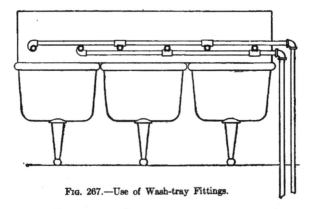

FIG. 267.—Use of Wash-tray Fittings.

will affect the cold water to a greater degree if the latter is run above. The male and female union elbows and tees shown in Fig. 264 represent another valuable type of fitting. It will be clear that fittings of this type are of great value where the work is close, and there is not sufficient room in which to use a tee or elbow and a union.

In Fig. 266 are shown several different styles of wash-tray bibbs. In the use of the ordinary faucets on wash trays, with the handle upright, there is often difficulty, owing to the projection of the bibb handles so high up as to prevent the use of covers on the trays.

The wash-tray fittings to be seen in Fig. 267 are fittings which allow neat work to be installed in connection with wash trays. By means of them, the wash-tray bibbs may be kept on a straight line, as shown in Fig. 267. In the use of ordinary tees and elbows, the bibbs are on two horizontal lines, the hot-water bibbs being on a line above the cold-water bibbs. The wash-tray elbows and tees are each made in two styles, one to be used on the upper line, throwing the bibb opening down, and the other to be used on the lower line, to throw the bibb opening up.

CHAPTER XXIII

RANGE BOILERS—THEORY OF CIRCULATION

THE subject of cold-water supply, which has already been considered, is a comparatively simple matter. On the other hand, the subject of hot-water supply involves numerous difficulties which do not enter into the former branch of work. Indeed, the proper installation of the hot-water supply system is often a most perplexing problem, one demanding a knowledge of the theory which underlies the action of hot water, and the application also of knowledge which comes by experience. In this branch of plumbing construction, more than in any other, practical experience counts for a great deal. It is the employment of a knowledge of the theory of the subject in combination with the practical knowledge that comes by experience, that produces the perfect system of hot-water supply.

Many a system of hot-water supply produces results which, to the person unacquainted with the subject, would seem to be all that is required of it, whereas, if the same system had been properly constructed, it would have been able to do better work, and a greater amount of it. A great deal of the supply work that is installed, is like all other construction work—it will answer the purpose, while at the same time it is not capable of performing its work as it should be performed. As in the case of the drainage and vent systems, the perfect operation of the hot-water supply system depends very largely on the observance of the small points which, to the uninitiated, would often appear to be of small consequence. By the observance of these small points, one workman will install a system which will produce excellent results, while another workman, careless in observing these same points, will construct a like system from which only poor or fair results are to be obtained.

The principle of circulation underlies all hot-water supply

work, as well as all heating systems, whether hot water, steam, or hot air, and a thorough understanding of this principle is necessary to an understanding of either subject. For the purpose of this explanation, it is necessary to understand something of what is known as the molecular theory. According to this theory, all bodies, regardless of their composition, are made up of molecules or particles, these particles being so minute, and of such numbers, that they cannot be estimated. These particles are in constant motion or vibration, the path which each molecule traverses being so small as to be immeasurable. When heat is applied to some bodies, metals, for instance, these particles are set in more violent vibration, and the result, as is well known, is the expansion of the body. If heat continues to be applied of sufficient intensity, the vibrations of the molecules become so rapid and so violent that they refuse to hold together, and separate from the main body, that is, the body melts. Thus it will be seen that by means of the molecular theory, the action of expansion and contraction, the melting of metals and many other phenomena may be explained. Indeed, it is by means of this theory that innumerable actions and operations may be explained.

The molecular theory may be applied much more extensively than the above, but the simple statement as given, will be sufficient for the present purpose. As a means of illustration, suppose that a block of ice be subjected to heat. In its original form, the ice is a solid, compact mass. As the heat is applied, however, according to the above explanation, the particles or molecules of the ice begin to vibrate more rapidly, finally refusing to hold together longer, and the ice melts and forms water. If heat continues to be applied to the water its temperature rises and its molecules expand. The vibration of these molecules finally reaches such a stage that it is stronger than atmospheric pressure, and in their expanded state, being lighter than the air, they rise into the air in the form of steam. Thus, by the application of heat, the original block of ice has been changed to water, which is a fluid, and the water in turn has been changed to steam, which is a vapor. Each of these actions is an example of the action of circulation.

Now, when this same principle is applied to the range boiler, as shown in Fig. 268, the action is the following:

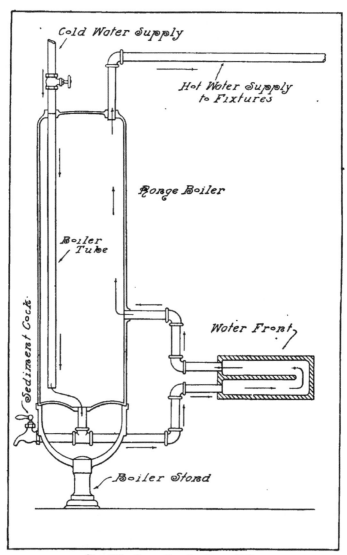

Fig. 268.—Connections for Range Boiler.

Cold water enters the water front of the range, from the boiler, and in passing through the water front is heated. When heated, as already seen, the particles of water become expanded, and therefore lighter than the colder particles, with the result that they rise, as indicated in the illustration by arrow heads.

After entering the boiler, the heated water will continue to rise to the highest possible point, or until it has become cooled.

Because of the tendency of hot water to rise, the hottest water will be found at the top of the boiler. While such is the action of hot water, a reverse action occurs in the case of cold water. The particles of cold water being unexpanded, are much heavier than those of the hot water, and their natural tendency is to fall to the lowest points. Therefore, the coldest water will be found at the bottom of the range boiler. In order, also, that this natural tendency may be favored as far as possible, the supply of cold water to the range boiler is carried through a pipe directly to the bottom of the boiler, instead of being connected to the top.

Inasmuch, also, as the storage of hot water is at the top of the boiler, rather than at the bottom, the pipe supplying fixtures with hot water should always be connected at the top of the boiler. A connection at any other point would give entirely unsatisfactory results.

The construction of a successful hot-water supply system, then, depends upon the running of pipes of proper sizes in such a manner as to provide the easiest and most natural path for the hot water. Having now seen that the hot-water supply depends upon the circulation of hot water, it will be readily understood that the same principle underlies certain other actions. For instance, hot-water heating also depends upon the circulation of hot water; steam-heating upon the circulation of steam; hot-air heating upon the circulation of air, and ventilation upon the circulation of air. The action of the local vent, moreover, depends upon the circulation of hot air.

The hot-water boiler in common use, such as shown in Fig. 268, has four openings, two at the top, one at the bottom, and one on the side. Into the latter, the hot water or flow pipe from the water front is connected. The connection shown in Fig. 268 is made under favorable conditions, the water front being at such height that a good rise can be obtained between the range and boiler, the range being located in close proximity to the boiler. The latter is a condition always to be desired, but not always to be obtained.

With a short range connection, there is less loss from friction of pipe and fittings, and less loss of heat than would result in the use of a long flow pipe.

In the use of a long flow pipe there is also much greater

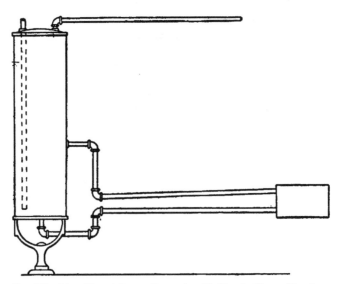

FIG. 269.—Flow Pipe of Range Connection Pitching in Wrong Direction.

danger of a dip or sag in the pipe, and greater danger that it will pitch in the wrong direction. The tendency of hot water being upward, the greatest care should be taken that the flow pipe from the range pitches upward at all points.

The connection shown in Fig. 269 will at once be seen to be a very poor piece of work, from which satisfactory results cannot possibly be expected.

It is a very common error, however, to run the flow with a pitch in the wrong direction. The best practice in the construction of range connections, calls for the use of 45-degree elbows. Their use is shown in the illustration of Fig. 270. The advantage gained is due to a decrease in the friction of the water in passing through a pipe so provided. The path for the hot water made by the flow pipe of Fig. 270, is clearly much more smooth than it would be if the bends were made abruptly by means of the common 90-degree bends or elbows.

In constructing the range connection, provision should always be made for drawing off the contents of the boiler without the necessity of disconnecting any part of the connection. This is

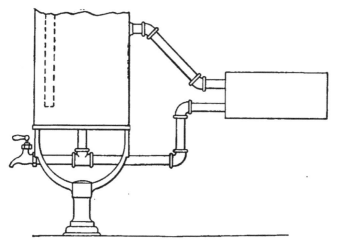

FIG. 270.—Use of 45 Degree Elbows on Range Connections.

accomplished by the use of a sediment cock, as shown in Fig. 268. A common bibb is generally used for this purpose, and it should be located at the lowest point in the range connection, in order that all the water in the boiler and in the range piping may be drawn off. In order to make the water flow out of the boiler, it is necessary to exert atmospheric pressure upon the contents of the boiler, and this is generally done by opening a bibb on a floor above the boiler, or by disconnecting one of the boiler couplings at the top of the boiler. The objection to the use of the sediment cock as the only means of draining the boiler, is that the water must be disposed of by drawing it off into pails, which is naturally a long and tedious undertaking.

In Fig. 271 is shown a method of draining the boiler into a convenient fixture trap, usually that of the kitchen sink. This method consists in running a wrought-iron or lead waste from the cold-water range pipe, and providing the connection with a stop-cock. When the stopcock is opened, the contents of the boiler

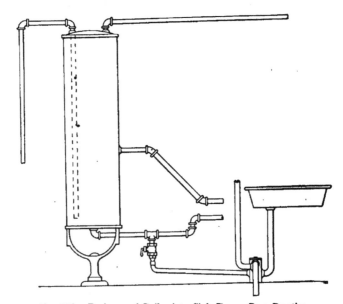

Fig. 271.—Drainage of Boiler into Sink Trap,—Poor Practice.

quickly pass off into the drainage system, through the trap to which the draw-off pipe is connected.

This method, however, is not to be considered good practice, as by means of it, direct connection is made between the water supply and drainage systems. These two systems should not be directly connected in this instance or in any other instance. The connection of the boiler waste into the kitchen sink trap is a very common one on old-style work, but is in general practice but little at the present time. Another somewhat similar method of drain-

ing the range boiler is that of Fig. 272, in which the connection
is made into the drainage system, the waste pipe being served by
its own trap. This is open to the same objections that apply to the
work of Fig. 271.

The proper method of providing drainage for the range boiler
is to be seen in Fig. 273. In this case, the boiler waste is con-

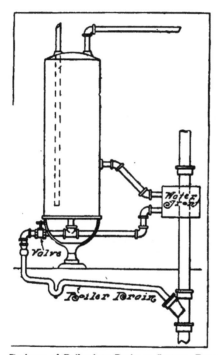

Fig. 272.—Drainage of Boiler into Drainage System—Poor Practice.

ducted into an open fixture, the laundry tubs in the basement.
Such a method, while providing fully for the drainage of the
boiler, avoids direct connection into the drainage system. There
often collects in the bottom of the range boiler a very heavy body
of rust and sediment, which also often collects in the range connection, sometimes almost entirely filling it. The water front

becomes filled with sediment very often also. When the latter occurs, the water front must be taken out and cleaned. A very effective method of doing this work is to heat the water front over a hot fire.. If possible to heat it over a forge the work can be done most effectively and easily. This dries the sediment, and

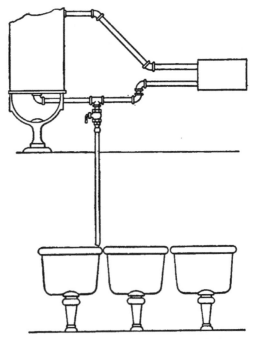

Fig. 273.—Proper Drainage of the Range Boiler.

that which does not crack and flake off can usually be dislodged by means of a rod or by hammering the casting.

Special devices of merit are on the market, by means of which the sediment may be drawn off direct, without drawing off the contents of the boiler. In these devices, the water is taken into the cold-water range pipe from a point above the top of the collection of sediment.

In some sections of the country, very little trouble is experi-

enced from rust and sediment, while in others, mucn trouble is
experienced. Every possible precaution should be taken against
the filling up of the boiler connections and water front with sediment, as it results in checking the free circulation of the water.
In addition, the presence of rust and sediment produces a discol-
ored water, unfit for kitchen, laundry, or toilet purposes. Another
evil, encountered in some sections, is the depositing of lime in the
pipes and in the water front. Special devices for the prevention
of this trouble are also on the market, and for them, satisfactory
results are claimed.

In the proper action of the range boiler many points are to
be considered. As already stated, it is very essential that the flow
pipe should be properly graded between the range and boiler, never
being allowed to dip or sag. Another feature, which is too often
overlooked, is the maintenance of a good fire in the range. If the
body of coal in the fire box is thin, or full of ashes, it cannot be
expected that the water front will properly perform its work. In
order that it may do its best work a live fire should be maintained.
Very often, the cause of poor heating is due to the use of coal of
too large a size. Under such conditions the air spaces between
the coals is of such an amount as to have a cooling effect upon the
fire, and to prevent good contact of the body of live coals against
the water front. The troubles just named produce similar results
in heating systems. It very often happens that people enter com-
plaint to the plumber that boiler work which he has installed is
not properly constructed, and is not giving good service, whereas
the sole cause of such results is the poor management of the range
fire. This is true to such an extent, that the workman of experience, when called upon to pass judgment on such work, will generally, after an inspection of the range connections, look at the
range fire, as the most probable cause of the trouble.

Another source of poor results in range-boiler work is the
wrong proportion of heating surface in the water front as related
to the size of the boiler to be heated. The heating surface may be
too great for the size of the boiler, or it may be too small. If too
small, the water will not heat properly, and if too great, it will
overheat, boil and form steam, causing the kicking and hammering so often to be heard in range boilers. Such results are not

only of great annoyance to the inmates of the house, but are injurious to the boiler and piping. Obstructions in the range connection must be avoided. These obstructions might result from collections of rust and scale in the connection, especially if of iron pipe, from lime deposits, from union gaskets that had worked into the pipe, and from other causes. An obstruction, if serious, generally causes the overheating of the water, the consequent formation of steam, with the same results as mentioned above.

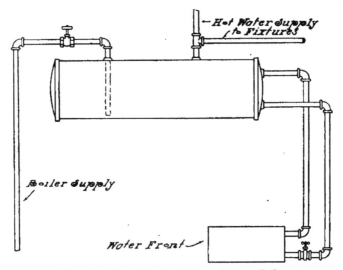

Fig. 274.—Connections for Horizontal Range Boiler.

Range connections of too small pipe should not be used, as under such conditions the evils of overheating the water passing through the water front may arise. If iron pipe is to be used, nothing smaller than ¾-inch pipe should be considered for the range connection, as smaller sizes will more readily fill up. If brass or lead connections are used, it is safe under some conditions to use ⅝- or even ½-inch pipe. Even in their use, however, it is far better practice to make the range connection of nothing smaller than ¾-inch pipe.

Thus far, mention has been made only of the vertical boiler.

The horizontal range boiler is also much used, though not to the extent on small work that the vertical boiler is. The principles governing the installation and operation of horizontal boilers are in no way different from the principles already given relating to vertical range boiler work.

In Fig. 274 is shown a common method of making horizontal range boiler connections. The cold-water supply to the boiler is conducted through a boiler tube to the bottom of the boiler, as in

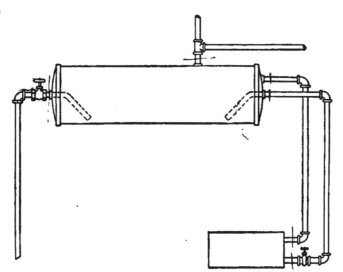

Fig. 275.—Connections for Horizontal Range Boiler.

the use of the vertical boiler. In this illustration, the flow pipe from the range is connected into the upper part of the end of the boiler, and the cold water out of the bottom. The hot-water connection to the fixtures is generally made as shown, at the same end of the boiler that the flow pipe from the range enters, as the water at this point is fully as hot as at any other point in the boiler.

In Fig. 275 another method of connecting the horizontal boiler is to be seen. In this case, the boiler supply is connected at the center of the end and carried to the bottom of the boiler by means of a bent boiler tube. The cold-water connection from the boiler to the range is made through the center opening of the opposite end, the water being taken from the bottom through a bent pipe, as shown. The flow pipe from the range and the flow pipe to the fixtures are connected as shown in the preceding illustration. The boiler supply should always be provided with a valve, located at an accessible point near the boiler.

In connection with the use of the supply valve, when used on the pressure boiler, the precaution should be taken of opening a

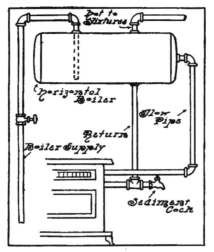

Fig. 276.—Connections for Horizontal Range Boiler.

hot-water faucet if the range fire is in action. The reason for this is that when the valve is closed, all opportunity for the expansion of the hot water is cut off, and the opening of a hot-water faucet is necessary to provide a vent for the expansion. It will be seen that with a heavy fire continuing to deliver hot water to a boiler on which there is no expansion, serious trouble is bound to occur if such conditions are allowed to exist for any length of time. A third method of connecting the horizontal range boiler, differing only in minor essentials from the two methods already mentioned, is illustrated in Fig. 276.

Fig. 277 illustrates a method of connecting the horizontal boiler which is often made use of, but which is open to objection. In the first place, it will be noted that the boiler supply is taken into the bottom of the boiler, at a point directly beneath the outlet of hot water to the fixtures. This means that a stream of cold water will be thrown directly up into the body of hot water, and into the entrance of the flow pipe from the boiler, which would naturally be detrimental to securing the best results from the boiler. Not only should the boiler supply be conducted to the bottom of the boiler, as indicated in the two preceding illustrations,

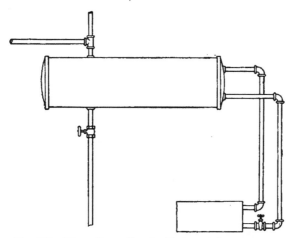

FIG. 277.—Wrong Connections for Horizontal Range Boiler.

but the hot-water supply pipe to fixtures should be taken out of the end of the boiler which is entered by the flow pipe from the range.

Fig. 278 represents another common method of connecting horizontal range boilers, which is open to objections similar to those named in connection with Fig. 277, though the errors are not so serious. As to the use of materials for range connections, lead, brass, and galvanized wrought iron are commonly employed. Probably galvanized wrought iron is most commonly in use. The selection of proper material for this work depends largely on the chemical properties of the water supply, as also, the selection of piping for the entire house supply system. Some waters act very rapidly on wrought-iron pipe, the action being so severe in many cases, that the range connections must be renewed at comparatively frequent intervals, if of this material. Under such conditions, the use of brass or lead is necessary.

Brass connections are perhaps the most satisfactory. Lead connections are more liable to sag and form traps, which, as already seen, results in unsatisfactory work. When lead is used

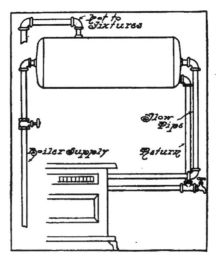

Fig. 278.—The Horizontal Range Boiler Improperly Connected.

on the range connections, it is necessary to use brass boiler connections and water-front couplings. A range and boiler thus connected are shown in Fig. 279. The brass connections make tight by means of ground joints, whereas, in the use of wrought iron, unions with gaskets, or right and left couplings must be used. In the use of lead pipe, wiped joints must be used to connect the pipe with the brass connections. Brass boiler couplings and water-front couplings are also often used in connection with work constructed of wrought iron or brass.

Several forms of boiler couplings are shown in Fig. 280. As seen from this illustration, they may be obtained in either the straight or bent pattern, for either lead or screwed pipe. Those designed for lead have plain ends, in order to allow solder joints to be wiped to them.

In Fig. 281 are seen several fittings for range boiler work, made either of brass or malleable iron. Water-back couplings are made in several styles, as seen in Fig. 282, for both lead and

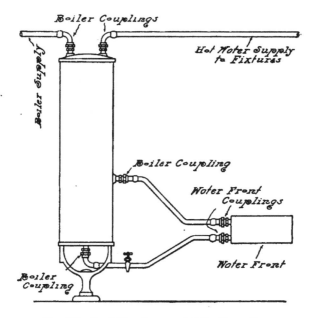

FIG. 279.—Lead Pipe Range and Boiler Connections.

screwed pipes. These also are made straight or bent, with short or long spuds. They may also be obtained with an inside thread on one end. In range boiler work, it will often be found that the flow pipe gives out more quickly than the cold-water connection. The reason for this is that there is much more expansion and contraction on the flow pipe, due to the fact that it carries hot water. The continual expanding and contracting of this pipe, as it alternately heats and cools, will in time weaken the pipe and its joints, and cause leakage. Even if the heat of the pipe is comparatively even, and the alternate expansion and contraction not great, it is a well-known fact that a heated pipe will not give as long service as a cold pipe.

In Fig. 283 is shown a special device for use in taking

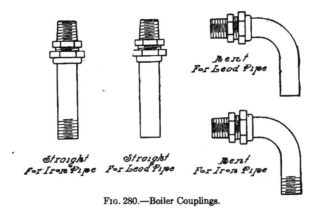

Straight
for Iron Pipe   *Straight*
For Lead Pipe   *Bent*
For Iron Pipe

FIG. 280.—Boiler Couplings.

range-connection measurements, known as the center-meter. The device consists of a number of small steel rods and several specially constructed joints. These joints are of aluminum, in the form of small cubes. Through each joint, two holes, slightly larger than the diameter of the steel rods, are drilled at right angles to each other. These two holes are so drilled that they

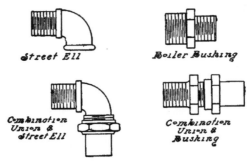

Street Ell   *Boiler Bushing*

Combination
Union &
Street Ell   *Combination*
Union &
Bushing

FIG. 281.—Malleable Iron Boiler Fittings.

break into each other slightly, at the point where they cross. By so constructing them, a single set-screw tightens both rods. Four of the rods shown in the illustration referred to, are provided with 1-inch pipe plugs. The center-meter is used in the following way: In measuring for the flow pipe, for instance, the two rods having plugs are screwed into the boiler opening and into the

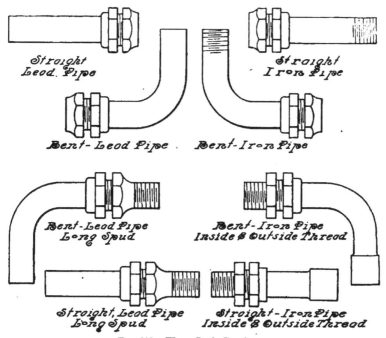

Fig. 282.—Water Back Couplings.

water-front opening. By means of the joints, the rods are then placed in the same position that the flow pipe will take. Measurements can now be taken from center to center, and from end to center, or, if desired, the device may be laid flat upon the floor, and the same measurements taken. The joints are also made with a third hole drilled at 45 degrees, thus enabling the workman to take 45-degree measurements. It is, of course, impracticable to provide steel rods long enough to use on long-range connections, and if provided, the plumber would find them awkward to carry. In the case of long connections, the rods may be built out as far as possible from the range and from the boiler, and the measurement for the long run of pipe taken in the usual manner between the two last measuring points. The use of this device will be found to save much annoyance to both workman and customer. In the event of wrong or incomplete measurements, it often becomes necessary for the plumber to return to the shop to get out

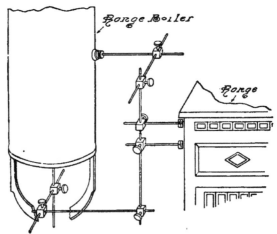

FIG 283. — Use of Center-Meter, a Device for Taking Range Connection Measurements.

additional pipe, which is usually much disliked by the customer. The center-meter, if used properly, cannot make these mistakes, even in the hands of an unskilled person.

In the running of hot-water pipes, there is often opportunity for the exercise of judgment. For instance, in Fig. 284 are shown two methods of running such pipes, one of them a correct method and the other incorrect. The tendency of hot water is always to rise. Therefore, the practice of carrying the pipe from the top of the boiler directly down to fixtures on the same floor as the boiler, and to fixtures below, does not afford a natural path

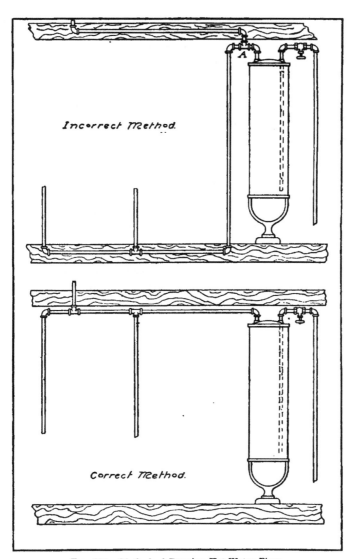

FIG. 284.—Method of Running Hot-Water Pipes.

for the hot water. It means that the hot water must take a downward and unnatural direction, rather than an upward, natural direction. This practice of running hot-water pipes is, nevertheless, a common one. In the instance of Fig. 284, where a connection is taken from the high point, to supply fixtures above the boiler, any accumulation of air will rise in this connection, and escape through the highest hot-water faucet, whenever it is opened. If it were not for this connection, however, there would be danger of the accumulation of air at the high point, which would interfere with the circulation, and very often cause the circulation to cease entirely.

The collection of air in high points in the hot-water pipes, is an evil which must always be avoided, as it is the means of endless trouble in both supply and heating systems. The correct method, shown in Fig. 284, consists in carrying the flow pipe from the boiler horizontally above the boiler, and dropping down with branches to the several fixtures. This method provides the more natural path for the hot water, and is in all ways the more satisfactory method of the two. Ordinarily the hot- and cold-water pipes are run parallel and close together. When so run, the hot-water pipe should be carried above the cold water. The reason for this is that as heat rises, the heat from the hot-water pipe will have less effect upon the cold-water pipe, if run above it.

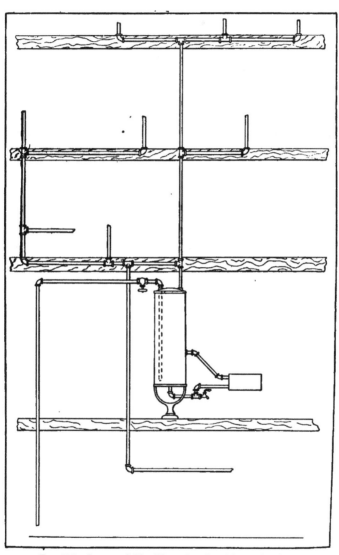

FIG 285.—System of Hot Water Supply without Circulation.

CHAPTER XXIV

CIRCULATING PIPES

In the running of hot-water piping on ordinary work the supply lines to fixtures are run as directly as possible to them, the different branches ending at the fixtures. This method is shown

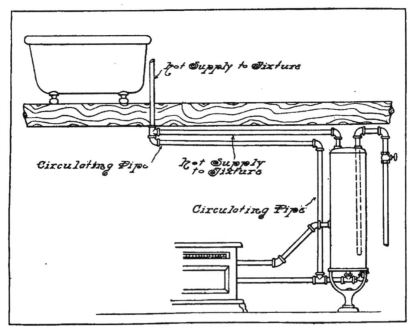

Fig. 286.—Circulation Applied to a Single Fixture.

in Fig. 285. There is great objection to this course many times, and for the following reason. Although the water in the piping is supposed to be hot, it cools very fast under certain conditions, and especially in branches at a distance from the boiler. In many

311

of these branches, particularly those which supply fixtures not in constant use, the hot-water pipe for a considerable distance from the fixture is generally filled with water that is either cold or nearly so. This means that before hot water can be drawn at the fixture, a considerable length of pipe filled with cold water must be drawn off before the water comes hot. Under all circumstances, this is an annoyance to the person using the fixture, and in many cases, where the supply of water is limited, this unnecessary waste of water cannot be afforded. When the public supply is metered, and must be paid for by the foot, such waste means unnecessarily high water bills.

A remedy for these troubles can generally be applied to nearly all the fixtures of the house, and while the remedy means the out, lay of a certain additional amount of money, under most conditions such outlay is an economy in the end. The remedy is the circulation pipe.

Fig. 286 shows the circulation pipe applied to a single fixture, and in Fig. 287 is shown a hot-water boiler providing hot water for the kitchen sink and the bath room, the system being supplied with a circulation pipe. This pipe is nothing more than a return, connected to the flow pipe, and with the latter, forming a complete circuit from the water front back to the water front. The water in the circulation pipe being cooler than that in the flow pipe, falls back into the cold-water range pipe, to enter the water front and be again heated. Thus, the upward tendency of the hot water in the flow pipe from the boiler, and the downward tendency of the cold water in the circulation pipe, produces a continuous circulation of hot water through any line of pipe to which the circulation pipe is connected.

When the hot-water supply line is provided in this manner with a circulation pipe, as in Fig. 286, only a very small amount of cold water in the branch to the fixture must be drawn off before the water will run hot. Branches may be taken off the flow pipe at any point, and run up to fixtures above or carried down to fixtures below. As the work is constructed in Fig. 287, the kitchen sink does not have full advantage of the circulation pipe, as its branch must drop down for a considerable distance to supply it.

The circulation pipe in this illustration might have been run

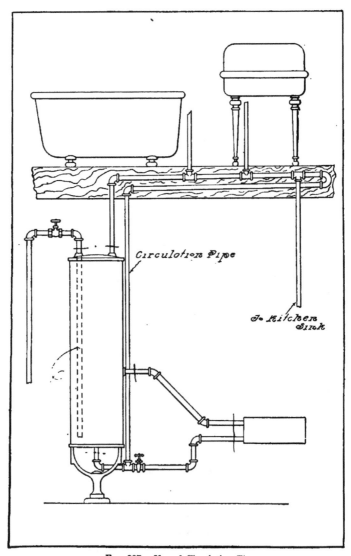

Circulation Pipe

To Kitchen Sink

FIG. 287.—Use of Circulation Pipe.

in another way to provide more fully for the kitchen sink. Instead of running the circulation back to the boiler, parallel with the flow pipe, it might have been dropped down to the sink, after passing the lavatory, and a branch to the sink taken out of the circulation pipe, the latter then being carried back and entered into the cold-water range pipe, as shown in Fig. 288.

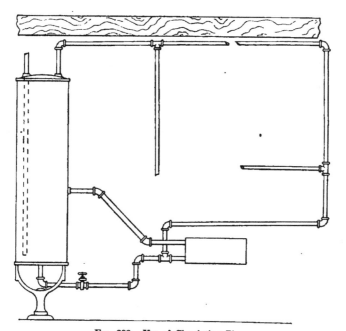

Fɪɢ. 288.—Use of Circulating Pipe.

In Fig. 289 is shown the same system of hot-water supply as that shown in Fig. 285, with the addition of circulation. As seen from the illustration, the hot-water supply to fixtures is carried directly to the top floor, where it turns and runs horizontally to the farthest fixture. From this point, the circulation pipe A is carried down and connected to the return of the range connection. If necessary, branches may be taken to fixtures from this circulation pipe, although it is not to be expected that water may be at

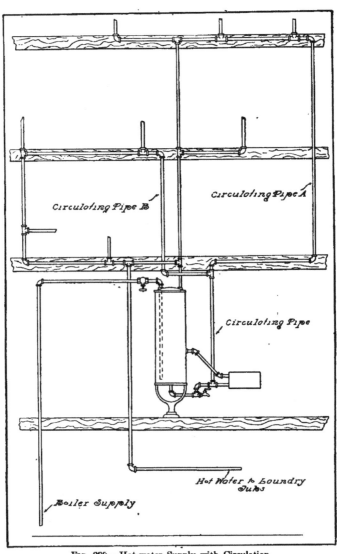

Circulating Pipe B

Circulating Pipe A

Circulating Pipe

Hot Water to Laundry Tubs

Boiler Supply

Fig. 289.—Hot-water Supply with Circulation.

once drawn as hot as branches taken off the flow pipe will deliver. Above the boiler a branch connection is taken out of the main flow pipe to serve fixtures in other parts of the house on the two floors above the boiler. After passing the last fixture on the third floor, the circulation pipe B is connected and carried down, being entered into the return or circulation pipe from the first line.

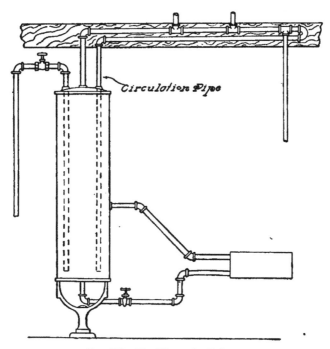

Fig. 290.—The Three-tube Boiler.

For fixtures below the boiler a branch is taken out of one of the flow lines and carried down to the desired points. Circulation cannot be provided for these fixtures because of their position as related to that of the boiler. Therefore, in obtaining hot water at the laundry tubs, it will generally be necessary to draw off the cold water standing in the greater part of the length of pipe running to this fixture. In connection with the work thus far illustrated, the return or circulation pipe has in each case been carried back into the return of the range connection. This is ordinarily the method followed. In the use of the three-tube boiler another and neater method may be employed. This method is shown in Fig. 290. In the three-tube boiler a second boiler tube may be used, which should run down to a point near the bottom of the boiler,

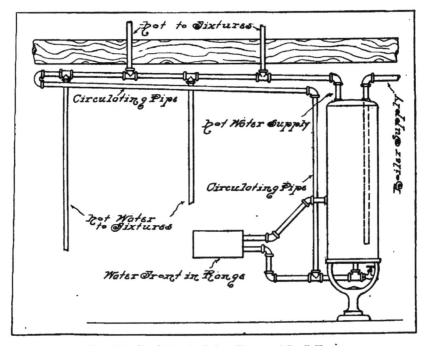

FIG. 291.—Circulation Applied to Fixtures of Small House.

as in the case of the boiler tube used on the boiler supply. To this second tube, the circulating pipe may be connected as shown, which results in returning the cooled water as well as by means of the connection into the return of the range connection. This illustration will also serve to show the manner in which circulation may be provided for fixtures on the same floor as the boiler. This is accomplished, generally, by running the flow pipe from the boiler horizontally, on the ceiling, above the points where the fixtures to be supplied are located, and dropping from this main flow pipe with branches to the several fixtures. From a point just beyond the branch to the farthest fixture a circulation pipe is carried back to the boiler and connected to the return of the range connection. This is the best that can be done toward securing circulation for fixtures thus located. Necessarily, the cold water must be drawn out of the branch from the main to the fixture before the water will come hot, but even so, the use of circulation under these circumstances will be found to be of benefit. Another method of providing circulation for fixtures on the same floor as the range boiler will be seen in Fig. 288. In this method, instead of running the circulation pipe back to the boiler, just below and parallel to the flow pipe, it is dropped down from the ceiling to a point considerably below, and then carried horizontally back to the range return.

In this method, branches to fixtures may be dropped down from the flow pipe on the ceiling, or taken out of the circulation pipe. While the use of circulation in connection with large hot-water supply systems is a matter of considerable additional expense, in applying it to many small systems, such as commonly found in small residences, cottage houses, etc., where the plumbing is usually centralized, it often means the use of only a very small amount of additional piping. This fact may be seen by reference to Fig. 291, in which circulation is applied to the fixtures of the entire house, by the running of a comparatively small length of pipe. In the foregoing illustrations, circulation has been shown in connection with direct pressure systems only. In Fig. 292 is shown a tank-pressure circulating system of hot-water supply for a residence. There is no material difference in the work, except the use of an expansion pipe on the tank-pressure system. Fig. 292 shows the range boiler heated by means of both kitchen range and gas range, a very common combination.

In Fig. 293 is illustrated a tank system of hot-water supply, without the use of circulating pipes. A comparison of the two illustrations should prove conclusively to the student the practical advantages of circulation and the great saving in water bills following its use.

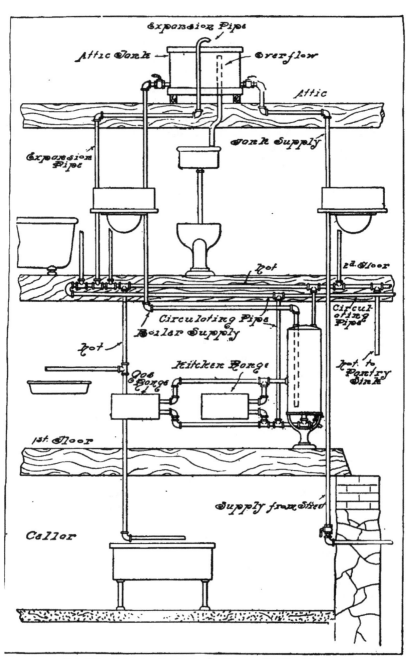

Fig. 292.—Hot-water Supply for Residence, with Circulation.

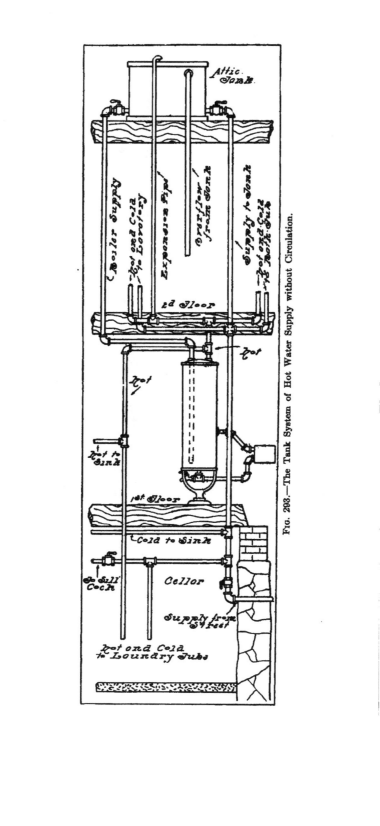

FIG. 263.—The Tank System of Hot Water Supply without Circulation.

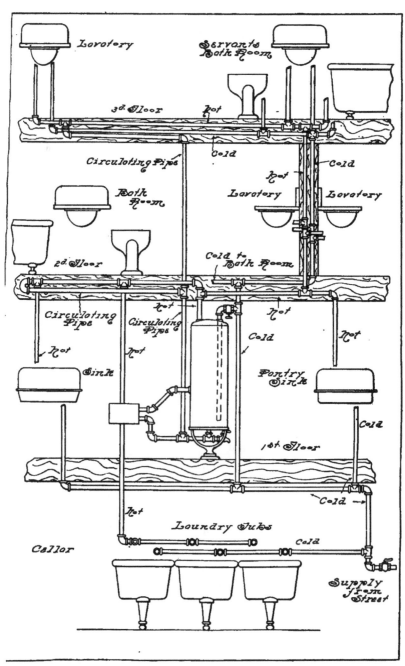

FIG. 294.—Pressure Hot and Cold Water Supply for Residence, with Circulation.

In Fig. 294 is illustrated a complete pressure hot- and cold-water supply system for a residence, with circulation, there being three separate lines of the latter. By many workmen the subject of circulation is not well understood, but a clear understanding of the subject is necessary, if satisfactory supply work is to be constructed. The subject of circulation must be considered at every point on the hot-water supply system, and as conditions are of such great variety, it will be readily understood that to be successful, the workman should be familiar enough with the subject to apply its principles under any and all conditions.

As previously stated, not only is this knowledge necessary, but practical experience in the installation of such work is of very great value. From the preceding consideration of the subject, it should now be clear that the use of the circulating system of hot-water supply is of very great advantage, and this is especially true of large work. It will be found that on large work, and on smaller systems as well, the saving in water bills will not be long in covering the additional first cost of installing circulation, and it goes without saying that such a system is far more convenient than the ordinary system of hot-water supply.

CHAPTER XXV

PROBLEMS IN RANGE BOILER WORK

WHILE the great majority of range-boiler connections are simple and straightforward, there are numerous instances, constantly arising in the experience of the plumber, which call for much ingenuity on his part, as well as a practical and theoretical knowledge of the subject of circulation.

These complex conditions in range boiler work, arise from the varied locations of range and boiler, relative to each other; from the unique requirements that the supply system must fulfill; from the use of more than one boiler; from the use of more than one source of heat; from the requirement that heat by radiation must be obtained from the hot-water supply system, and from numerous other causes. The successful solution of these complex connections that are continually being met by the plumber, present a field of work in which he can display his ignorance of anything out of the ordinary line of work, or in which, if able, he may display a knowledge of the principles of circulation which will gain for him the respect and confidence of his customers. In this chapter some of the problems in range connections, which are continually requiring solution, will be taken up. It should be stated, however, that the problems considered are really few in number as compared to the great variety of such problems which might be considered if space could be devoted to the subject.

Those which are considered, however, are of importance, and a thorough understanding of them will go far in helping to solve other problems in circulation. One of the more simple, but yet important connections, is that shown in Fig. 295, the use of which is to produce a quick supply of hot water. By means of the ordinary connection of the flow pipe, which enters the side of the boiler, hot water is stored in the boiler and from there delivered to the fixtures. When the fire is first built in the range, however, considerable time must elapse before the hot water delivered to the boiler can store itself in sufficient quantity to be of any service. Before hot water can be delivered to the fixtures from the boiler, the hot water entering the latter must heat up a large body of cold water standing in it. By means of the connection shown in Fig. 295, however, hot water can be delivered directly into the flow pipe from the boiler in a very short time after the range fire has been

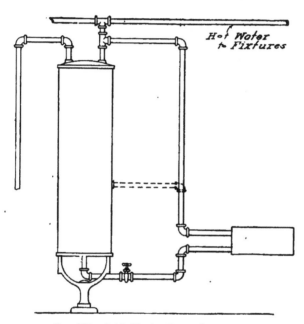

Fig. 295.—Quick-Heating Range Connection.

started. Not only is this advantage gained, but hot water will store itself in the boiler almost as readily when this connection is in use as when the side connection is made. As the water in the flow pipe cools slightly, it must inevitably fall back into the boiler to make room for the hotter water that is being constantly delivered to the flow pipe. It is in this way that storage of hot water goes on.

Under many conditions this form of connection is of special advantage. For instance, in many homes, the kitchen range fire is allowed to go out each night, and when it is rekindled the following morning, hot water will be required as quickly as possible to provide it at the kichen sink. It can be readily seen that in this case the quick heating connection will give far more satisfactory service than the side connection into the boiler.

Fig. 296 will show that this same connection can be provided

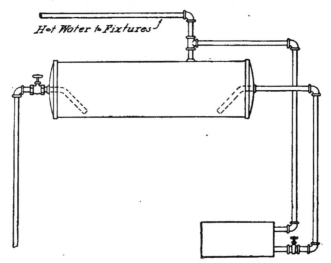

Fig. 296.—Quick-Heating Range Connection for Horizontal Boiler.

for the horizontal boiler equally as well as for the vertical boiler. A modification of the quick heating connection is often used, as shown by the dotted lines in Fig. 295. This form of connection consists in running the flow pipe from the range, up and into the flow pipe from the boiler, and taking a branch from this line into the side of the boiler. This plan can be used to advantage, as it gives a quick supply of hot water, and storage is made through each connection. Another means of obtaining a quick supply of hot water is by the use of a gas heater, as shown in Fig. 297.

Gas heaters are made in a great variety of styles, and by many manufacturers, and are used extensively, and to advantage. Many houses, apartment buildings, etc., are now being built with the kitchen heated by the house-heating system, and therefore requiring no coal range for heating purposes, the cooking being done on a gas range. Under these circumstances, the use of an auxiliary heater is of great advantage. It is usually provided with

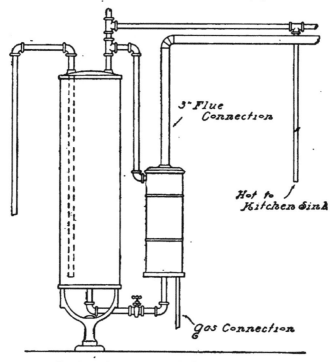

3" Flue Connection

Hot to Kitchen Sink

Gas Connection

FIG. 297.—Connections for Auxiliary Gas Heater.

a quick-heating connection, as shown in the illustration, from which hot water can be quickly obtained, without heating up the entire body of water in the boiler. Under almost any circumstances, the auxiliary gas heater may be used to advantage in the summer season, when it is undesirable to heat up the rooms of the house by running the kitchen range. The gas heater should be connected to the kitchen chimney by means of a 3-inch smoke pipe.   Instantaneous gas heaters may be used to advantage in bath rooms, without the use of a boiler for storage purposes.   As their name implies, some makes of these heaters will produce a supply of hot water almost instantaneously, making them very convenient for bath and lavatory purposes under various conditions.

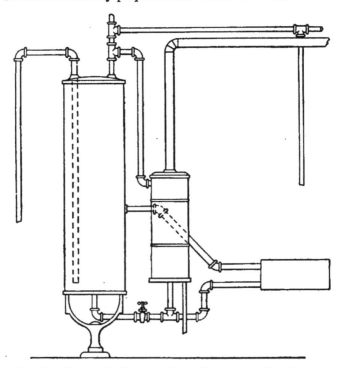

FIG. 298.—Range Boiler Heated by Kitchen Range and Auxiliary Heater.

In Fig. 298 is shown another very common scheme of connections, in which the gas heater is connected to deliver hot water quickly, and the kitchen range connected in the ordinary manner, the latter being depended on to produce a storage of hot water in the boiler.   The cold-water connection to the gas heater is taken out of the return to the range.   This combination of connections may also be used to advantage when the auxiliary gas heater and the gas range instead of the coal range are used. The gas range may be provided with a water front, and connected to the range boiler with as satisfactory results as the regular kitchen range. It is often required to connect a range boiler and range when the two are on opposite sides of a door. The correct method of performing the work is to be seen in Fig. 299. It is obvious that to connect the flow pipe from the range into the side of the boiler

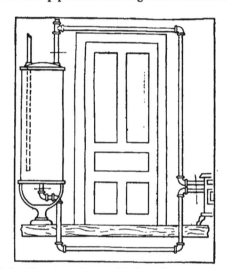

Fig. 299.—Boiler Heated by Range with Door Between. Correct Method.

in the ordinary manner, would be an impossibility, as it would have to pass across the doorway. Noting this fact, the uninformed workman will sometimes attempt to solve the difficulty by carrying the flow pipe down and under the floor, and then vertically into the side of the boiler, as in Fig. 300. This is clearly wrong. A trap is formed, and in order to carry hot water through it, it must be forced, for it will never circulate in the natural way. The correct method of Fig. 299 will avoid such difficulties, and will perform the required work in a proper manner. It will be observed that the proper solution of this problem is nothing more nor less than the use of a quick heating connection, fully described above. Another very similar problem is that in which the range and boiler are in adjoining rooms. The same means are employed in making proper connections, as will appear from Fig. 301.

The connection of the range boiler to a range on the floor below it, is a connection often called for, such a connection being shown in Fig. 302, from which it will be seen that no different principle is involved than in the work on an ordinary range connection. The location of the range boiler on the floor above the range often comes from the use of the former to heat a bath room, which it can

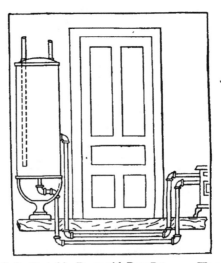

Fig. 300.—Boiler Heated by Range with Door Between. Wrong Method.

usually do very successfully. When the bath room is located adjacent to the kitchen, and on the same floor as the boiler, the latter may often be located in the bath room, and its heat used as a means of heating the room. These conditions often exist in flat houses.

One of the most common range-connection problems is that of heating a boiler from two ranges, one being on the same floor as the boiler, and the other on the floor below. The problem often appears also, where a laundry stove in the basement is to be utilized, or a coil in the furnace required to give additional heat to the boiler. Connections under these conditions should generally be made in such a manner that the boiler may not only be heated from both sources of heat, but also by either source alone. There are several methods by means of which this work may be successfully performed, four of which are shown in Figs. 303, 304, 305, and 306. It is well to state in this connection that on such problems as this one the use of valves to control the heating from the two sources of heat is not in general a wise course, as they must necessarily

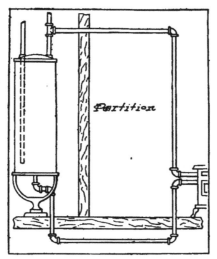

Fig. 301.—Boiler Heated by Range in Adjoining Room.

be controlled by people not familiar with such matters, and the wrong use of valves sometimes leads to disastrous results. While either of the four methods mentioned will accomplish the desired results, it is natural that there should be a preference in selecting the method to be used. Method No. 1, shown in Fig. 303, is perhaps the most natural and simplest, and therefore the method most commonly employed. It is true, however, that this method is not considered the most satisfactory. In the No. 1 connection the flow pipe from the upper range is connected into that from

the lower range, and there is danger that the flow of hot water
from the lower range will in a measure obstruct the free passage

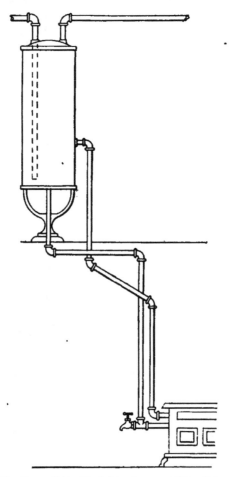

Fig. 302.—Range Boiler Heated by Range on Floor Below.

of hot water from the upper range. If the water issuing from the
lower range happens to be heated to a higher degree than that from

the upper one this trouble is increased, the result of such conditions not only being seen in decreased efficiency, but it is also liable to result in hammering, which is always a disagreeable feature.

Method No. 2, Fig. 304, avoids the difficulty found in No. 1,

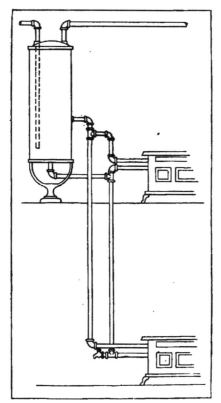

FIG. 303.—Range Boiler Heated by Two Ranges on Different Floors. Method No. 1.

the two circuits being entirely separate. The only arguments against No. 2 are that in order to use it a boiler must be used which is not commonly to be found, and that a somewhat greater amount of pipe is required, although the latter objection is comparatively insignificant.

The system shown in Fig. 305, method No. 3, is probably the most satisfactory of the four systems shown. This method provides a direct line of circulation, with no obstructions, and with the least possible amount of pipe, the latter feature having the

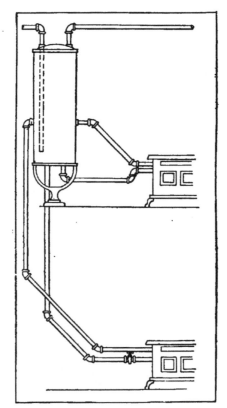

Fig. 304.—Range Boiler Heated by Two Ranges on Different Floors.
Method No. 2.

advantage of presenting the least amount of surface to cool the hot water in its passage to the boiler. When either range is not in operation there is nothing to prevent the heating of the boiler by the other. Method No. 4, Fig. 306, is also to be considered a very effective one, and is in many cases preferable even to No. 3. According to this method, the connection from one of the ranges should be a quick-heating connection. Either one of the ranges may be thus connected, according to circumstances.

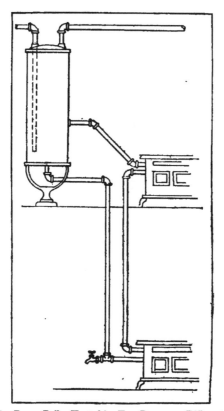

FIG. 305.—Range Boiler Heated by Two Ranges on Different Floors. Method No. 3.

Another problem, one with which the average plumber is generally unacquainted, consists in heating a range boiler on the floor below that on which the range is located. In considering this problem, it may be stated at the outset that the conditions are

entirely unnatural, for it means that hot water must flow downward from the range to the boiler, whereas the natural course is
an opposite one.   As a consequence, the heating of a boiler under
these conditions must not be expected to be accomplished with

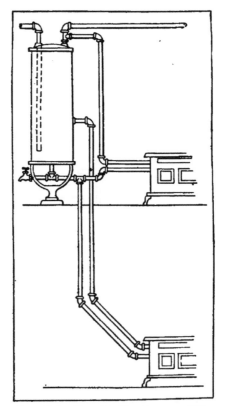

Fig. 306.—Range Boiler Heated by Two Ranges on Different Floors.
Method No. 4.

anything like the same degree of efficiency that is to be obtained
under natural conditions.

To obtain any results whatever, it is necessary on such work
as this to run the flow pipe vertically above the range, usually to

the ceiling, from which point it is then carried down to the top
of the boiler and connected, as appears in Fig. 307. If the flow
pipe can be run higher than to the ceiling—to the ceiling of the

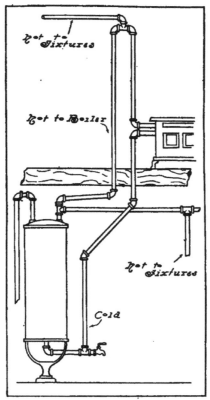

Fig. 307.—Heating of Range Boiler on Floor Below Range.

next floor above, for instance—the results obtained will be so
much the better.

In carrying the flow pipe vertically through the greater distance, it is given more opportunity to cool, and therefore falls to
the boiler more readily. A difference in temperature is necessary
in all circulation work. The greater vertical rise of the flow pipe

also gives a greater weight of water, which is essential in systems of this nature. By means of the method shown in Fig 307, a storage of hot water can usually be obtained, sufficient in amount if the demands upon the boiler are not too great. The chief

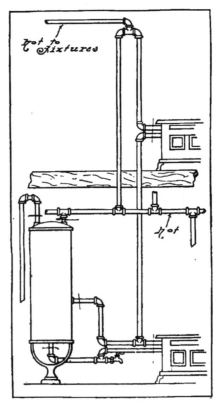

Fig. 308.—Boiler Heated by Range on Same Floor and Range on Floor Above.

difficulty in connection with the proper solution of this problem is the collection of air at the top of the loop. Unless provision is made to relieve this air, it will very quickly make the system inoperative.

If there are fixtures on the floor above the range, the remedy is easily applied by taking a supply pipe from the top of the loop to some fixture that is in common use, as, for instance, a bath-room lavatory.   If the system is under tank pressure, of course the expansion pipe from this high point will do the work. If, however, the system is under direct pressure, and there are no third-floor plumbing fixtures, the relief of the high point cannot be accomplished in a satisfactory manner.   The only thing that can be done under these circumstances is to place a pet cock at the high point, by means of which the air may be relieved when necessary by opening it by hand.   Since this method is not automatic, it is open to strong objection, and the only way in which it may reach any degree of satisfaction is to see to it that some one opens the valve at frequent stated intervals.   A drip pipe to the sink should be run from the pet cock.   Another way in which this problem sometimes presents itself is to be seen in Fig. 308, where not only a range above the boiler, but also a range on the same floor as the boiler is to be used.   This problem is not so common as the previous one, but sometimes occurs when the boiler must for some reason be located in the basement, and it is required to heat it from the laundry stove in the basement and the kitchen range on the first floor.   The best feature about these circumstances is that when the greatest amount of water is required— that is, for washing purposes—the laundry stove, which is connected in the ordinary manner, will be in operation, and will usually be able to provide amply, whereas it would be difficult often to get a sufficiently abundant supply from the upper range.   The work shown in Fig. 308 does not bring in any features different from those encountered in the preceding problem.

CHAPTER XXVI

HOT-WATER SUPPLY FOR OFFICE AND APARTMENT BUILDINGS, ETC.

THE principles governing hot-water supply are naturally the same, whether it be in relation to small residence work or to the more extensive systems of large buildings.

In the latter work there is not only a much larger quantity of water to heat and distribute to various parts of the building,

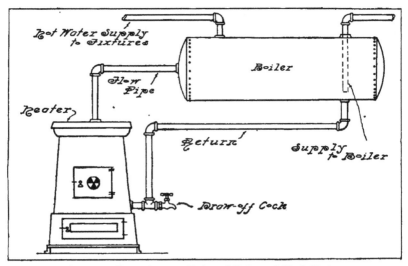

FIG. 309.—Connections for Horizontal Boiler and Tank Heater.

but, owing to the fact that there are often in these buildings hundreds of people making use of hot water, the perfect and continuous operation of the system becomes a necessity. This makes it necessary that the piping be run on correct principles, and that mains and branches be of sufficient capacity to properly perform

339

their work. On small hot-water systems a serious error may not prevent the furnishing of hot water after a certain fashion, serving only as a matter of inconvenience to a few, while the same error on large work would produce great inconvenience to a very large number of people.

Hot water is generally furnished to large buildings by a special heater, such as shown in Fig. 309, located in the cellar or basement and connected to a large hot-water tank, which may be of the horizontal type, as in the above-mentioned illustration, or of

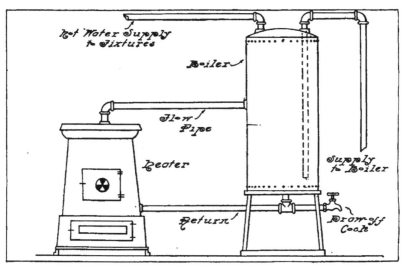

FIG. 310.—Connections for Vertical Boiler and Tank Heater.

the vertical type, as in Fig. 310. The horizontal tank hung from the cellar timbers is the more generally used of the two types, the principal reason being that it is less in the way than the vertical tank. As far as the connections between heater and tank are concerned, they are similar to those of the kitchen range and boiler, and therefore whatever has been stated concerning the latter applied to the former also.

In addition to the use of water heaters for tank heating, live and exhaust steam are also used, in connection with steam coils inside the hot-water tank, as in Fig. 311. An advantage gained by this method is that during the winter season, when the heating plant is in operation, the tank may be heated by means of the coils without using the tank heater, while during the summer months the latter may be used.

Coils are often used to provide additional heating surface, when sufficient hot water cannot be secured by use of the tank heater alone.

The proper method of supporting horizontal boilers is shown in Fig. 312. This consists in the use of heavy, wrought-iron

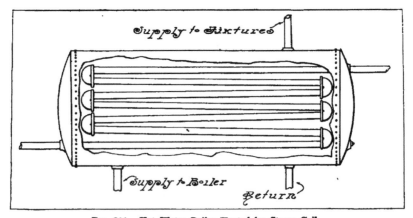

FIG. 311.—Hot Water Boiler Heated by Steam Coil.

hangers at each end of the boiler. These hangers pass around the boiler, taking the weight of it, and being securely fastened to the cellar timbers.

In Fig. 313 is shown a hot-water supply system for a large building, working under tank pressure. A tank system has the advantage of delivering water under a constant pressure, while the direct-pressure system varies considerably.

A varying pressure is not only an annoyance, but it is hard on the valves and piping. As explained in another chapter, the direct-pressure boiler is liable to siphonage, while the boiler working under tank pressure is not.

The main flow pipe in Fig. 313 is carried directly to the highest point, and thence horizontally to a second vertical line of fixtures, dropping down from this point and returning to the heater, thus forming a complete circuit.

It will be seen that the piping constantly rises to the high point where the expansion pipe is connected. When the water has traveled thus far from the heater it has begun to cool, and falls through the second vertical line back to the boiler, but being

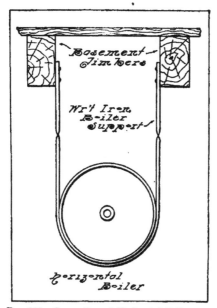

FIG. 312.—Supporting of Horizontal Boiler.

sufficiently hot to supply the fixtures on this line with hot water. The rising of the hot water and falling of the cooler water continues without interruption so long as the water is being heated, and constitutes what is known as circulation.

The expansion pipe from the high point is a necessity on the tank system of supply, not only to vent the system in case the water becomes overheated, but to relieve it of air, thus preventing

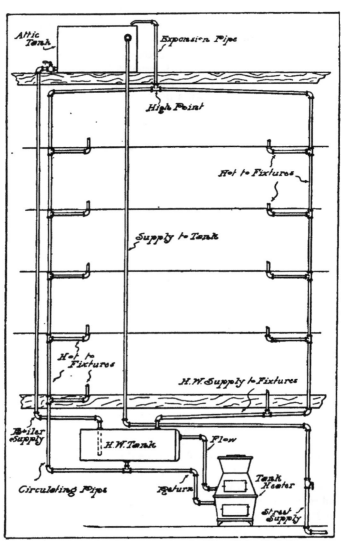

FIG. 313.—Hot Water Supply for Large Building Under Tank Pressure.

air-lock, which is often the cause of the inability of the hot-water system to work properly. The attic tank is generally supplied by direct pressure. When the direct pressure is not sufficiently high in the case of high buildings, the water lift is often made use of. A description of the water lift and its action, as well as descriptions of several systems on which it is used, may be found in the following chapter.

In Fig. 314 a system of hot-water supply known as the overhead system is shown, in some respects similar to the work illustrated in the preceding figure.

This system in the present case is under direct pressure. The overhead supply system is similar in principle to the overhead heating system, and wherever it is possible to install it, may be depended upon to give fully as good results as any other system.

When such a system is under direct pressure, the expansion takes place back through the supply pipe to the boiler and thence through the street mains to the source of supply. Owing to this fact, it is not generally necessary to run an expansion pipe if it were not for venting the system of air. Such a pipe, as seen in Fig. 314, is generally connected to an expansion tank, and an overflow from the tank onto the roof.

In the overhead system, as in the system of Fig. 313, the main flow pipe runs as directly as possible to the top floor, and then is run horizontally, drop risers being taken out wherever required, these pipes entering a main return in the basement, which carries the return water back to the boiler, the drop risers thus doing the work of flow and return. This system probably provides more evenly heated water than most other systems of supply.

A third hot-water supply system for large buildings is shown in Fig. 315, this system differing considerably from those already shown. The main flow pipe is carried from the boiler to such points as vertical risers are to be supplied, the main pitching upward from the boiler. These risers should connect at the top into a main horizontal line, to which a main vertical return connects, through which the water is carried back to the boiler. An automatic air valve should be placed at the highest point on the piping, to relieve the system of air-lock. On each vertical line, as shown, there should be a valve, by means of which the circulation of hot

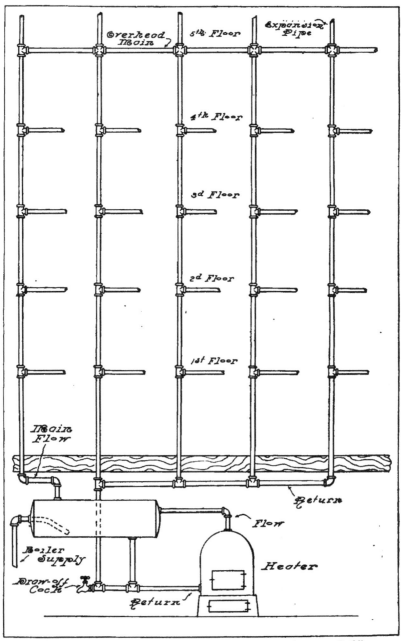

Fig. 314.—Overhead System of Hot Water Supply for Office or Apartment Building.

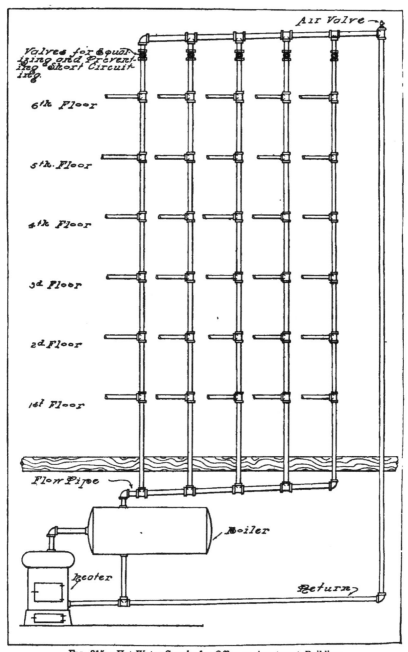

FIG. 315.—Hot-Water Supply for Office or Apartment Building.

water may be equalized, in order to prevent different parts of the system from taking too large a share of hot water, to the detriment of other parts of the system.

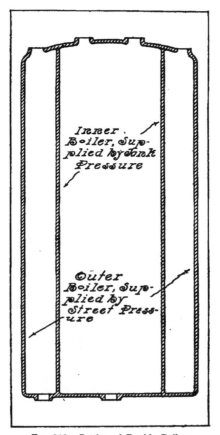

Fig. 316.—Section of Double Boiler.

In selecting the proper system of hot-water supply for a large building, as much judgment is needed as in the selection of the proper system of heating.

While one system under certain circumstances and conditions

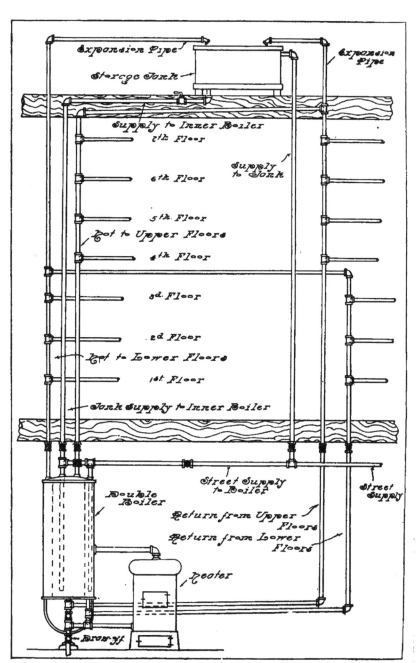

Fig. 317.—Hot Water Supply from Double Boiler.

will perform excellent service, another will fail entirely. If the plumber is well grounded in the principles of circulation, and a man of practical experience, he will usually be able to determine what system of supply under the given conditions will give the best results.

The double boiler is a device which finds an important application in the hot-water supply systems of many high buildings in the large cities. It is very seldom used, however, in any but the largest cities.

In Fig. 316 is shown a sectional view of the double boiler,

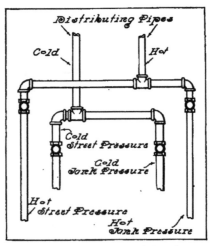

Fig. 318.—Simple Form of Cut-off.

from which it will be seen that it consists of two boilers, one inside the other. The outer boiler is heated in the usual manner, and the inner boiler is heated by contact with the heated water of the outer boiler. The outer boiler is under direct pressure, and the inner boiler under tank pressure. It will be readily considered that in high buildings, running up many stories, the upper floors are sometimes above the height at which water under city pressure can reach. Even though this condition is not permanent, it often happens that during certain times of day the pressure which at other times is sufficient is so reduced that it cannot force water to the higher floors. It is under these conditions that the double boiler is made use of, as shown in Fig. 317.

The inner boiler supplies hot water to the upper floors under tank pressure, and the outer boiler supplies the lower floors under street pressure.

The attic storage tank must generally be supplied by means of a pump or water lift.

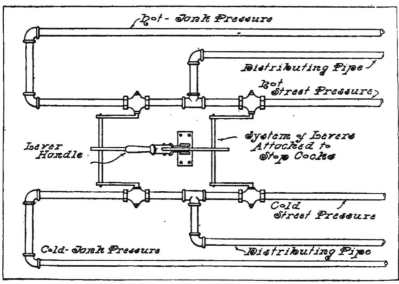

FIG. 319.—Automatic Cut-off.

The cross connection between the two boilers allows both to be fed with street pressure when the latter is high enough to reach the upper floors. At night when the pressure is high, this course may be adopted, thus saving the expense of pumping to the tank.

In Fig. 318 is shown a simple form of cut-off, a device often employed on double boiler work for the purpose of delivering into the distributing pipes a supply of water under either tank pressure or direct pressure, as the case may be.

The successful operation of this cut-off is entirely dependent on the attention and caution of the attendant in the opening and closing of the proper valves, and the occasional lack of care has resulted in casting this device away for automatic cut-offs, such as the one of Fig. 319.

In the latter, each of the four valves is rigidly attached to a system of levers, operated by a handle, the throwing of which either opens or closes the proper valves, thus obviating any mistakes.

The same work that is accomplished by the double boiler may be performed by two single boilers connected in the proper manner, as seen in Fig. 320.

In order to run the two boilers under different pressures the water front of each must be entirely separate from that of the other. Separate coils in the same heater may be used for this purpose. Special heaters having two separate heating surfaces may also be used. The general connections for this system are quite similar to those of Fig. 317. One boiler supplies the upper floors, and is therefore under tank pressure, while the other supplies the lower floors under street pressure.

It may be stated that double-boiler work is taken up by the author in his work entitled "Modern Plumbing Illustrated."

A very common difficulty that is encountered in many sections of the country, especially in the West, is the accumulation of lime in the range connections and piping. This trouble is serious enough in connection with the procuring of hot-water supplies for residences and dwellings, but in the case of larger work, such as public or semipublic buildings, its existence results in much greater annoyance.

In some localities the only natural supply of water that can be obtained is hard water, strongly impregnated with lime, which it takes up in its passage through the soil. The depositing of lime takes place principally in hot-water pipes, although it also occurs in the cold-water pipes. When the lime has once begun to accumulate on the interior of a pipe, the accumulation increases rapidly, and often in a comparatively short time the pipe will become entirely filled. This condition is not only a source of much annoyance, but a source also of danger.

Many attempts have been made to clear pipes thus filled with various substances, but even though sometimes partially successful, such a cure does not produce permanent results. It is usu-

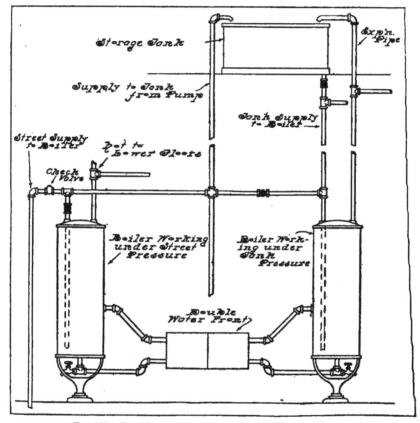

Fig. 320.—Two Single Boilers Doing Work of Double Boiler.

ally more satisfactory to replace the filled pipe with new pipe rather than to attempt to clean out the lime deposit.

Acids act on such deposits, as also caustic soda, but they constitute a harsh remedy, capable of doing harm as well as effecting the desired remedy.

Special patented devices for attachment to the range connection may be procured, which are claimed to prevent the choking of the pipes with lime.

It would seem, however, that these various devices and recipes were not along the proper lines, and that a much better plan would be to prevent the entrance of the impregnated water into the range connection, where most of the trouble from accumulation of lime occurs. Fig. 321 illustrates a method of this nature. According to this plan, two attic tanks are used, a small tank for rain water and larger tank for the hard water of the natural supply. It will be noted that no range boiler is used.

A down supply line from the rain-water tank is connected directly to the water front, the flow pipe from which is carried up to the hard-water tank and connected to a heating coil located in the latter. After passing through this coil, the water passes back to the rain-water tank. This constitutes a complete system of circulation for the heating of the contents of the hard-water tank by means of the coil, the work being done by water free from lime, and thus avoiding the deposit of lime in the range connections. From the hard-water storage tank a line of hot-water supply is taken down to the various fixtures. It is an excellent plan to place blocks of limestone on the heating coil in the hard-water storage tank, as the lime in the water will deposit on such blocks in preference to the piping or sides of the tank. The use of these blocks will therefore aid greatly in keeping the tank and piping free of lime. If limestone is not at hand, oyster or clam shells will do the work. Shells placed in a tea kettle in which hard water is used will prevent the accumulation of lime inside.

While the method just described is the most effective one that has yet been suggested, there are two objections connected with its use that should be mentioned. In the first place, if the hard-water storage tank is open it cannot be made to heat to so high a temperature as the range boiler, owing to the escape of heat from the exposed surface. In the second place, more or less steam must inevitably escape into the air, and in many cases this feature would be objectionable. Without doubt, however, the tank could in most cases be heated to a sufficiently high temperature for all ordinary purposes.

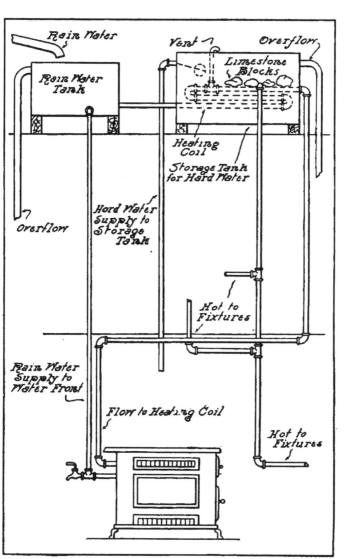

Rain Water

Vent

Overflow

Rain Water
Tank

Limestone
Blocks

Heating
Coil

Storage Tank
for Hard Water

Overflow

Hard Water
Supply to
Storage
Tank

Hot to
Fixtures

Rain Water
Supply to
Water Front

Flow to Heating Coil

Hot to
Fixtures

FIG. 321.—Method of Preventing Deposit of Lime in Range Connections.

There is no reason, however, why this tank cannot be sealed over, with a vent taken through the roof, which would in a large measure free it of its objectionable features.

Another method of preventing lime deposit is to use a range boiler having a coil, the water front being connected direct to the coil, but not otherwise connected to the boiler. The water front should be supplied with rain water, and from the high point on the flow pipe an expansion pipe should be carried to the tank.

CHAPTER XXVII

THE WATER LIFT AND ITS APPLICATIONS

As generally considered, the water lift finds its principal application in city work, but may also be used to great advantage in the country, and in connection with institutions, manufacturing plants, etc., that have their own private systems of water supply. In Fig. 322 is to be seen a sectional view of a successful type of

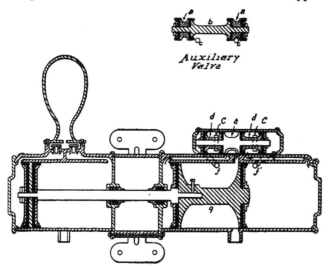

Fig. 322.—Sectional View of Water Lift and Auxiliary Valve.

water lift, and of its auxiliary valve. Owing to the position of the auxiliary valve, it is impossible to show it in a sectional view of the water lift, and therefore it is shown in a separate view.

Fig. 323 shows the connections for the water lift more clearly than the sectional view does. The water lift is operated by water .pressure, and its action may be compared to that of the steam engine, water pressure taking the place of steam. Fig. 323 shows that there are four pipes connecting with the water lift, including the connection with the water supply, the suction pipe into the body of water to be lifted, the discharge pipe from the lift to supply the fixtures, and the waste. The latter should never be connected directly into the drainage system, but may be indirectly connected. The water pressure which operates the lift, first passes into the auxiliary valve chamber, and into the space marked b, at

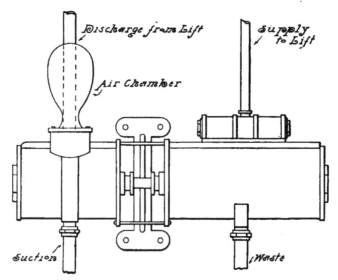

FIG. 323.—Connections for Water Lift.

either end of which is a leather cup. The main and auxiliary valves are separated by a wall, and connecting them are two openings c, c, cut through this wall. These passages connecting between the two valves are never closed, and consequently water always fills the chambers b and d, d. The chamber g is always in exhaust through the waste connection on the driving cylinder of the lift. As shown in Fig. 322, the pressure of the water on the piston head g has forced it to the left end of the driving cylinder. This pressure has been exerted by water entering on the rear of the piston-head from the chamber d, through the port, as shown by the arrows. Chamber g is now exhausting into the exhaust chamber connecting with the waste, through the port in front of the piston head, which is connected to that chamber by the chamber e in the main valve. The construction and arrangement of valves is such that this exhaust takes place alternately, at either end of the driving piston. Having thus shown the manner in which pressure water is admitted to the driving cylinder, and exhausted from it, the operation of the valves should be considered. The two valves, main and auxiliary, are set parallel to each other. A small opening is made into the driving cylinder from the auxiliary valve chamber, and at each end of it, as shown by f and f. In the chamber b of the auxiliary valve, are two passages, c, c, which connect into the space in the cylinder of the main valve, which is between the valve head and the cylinder head. The arrangement is such that one of the passages c, is alternately connected with the chamber b, the water of which is under pressure, while the other passage c is alternately connected with the exhaust passage a. In traveling to the left, the driving piston has uncovered the passageway f, and the pressure water enters the chamber of the auxiliary valve at its right end, thereby forcing the auxiliary valve to the left end of its cylinder. The other end of the cylinder is exhausting through f into the exhaust chamber g in the driving cylinder. When the auxiliary valve has traveled to the left, water under pressure passes from b through c into the space formed between the main valve and cylinder heads.

The pressure exerted on the main valve at its left end shifts it over to the right, and water under pressure from the chamber d at the left, passes into the driving cylinder at its left end, by way of the port leading into it. The driving piston is then forced to the right, uncovering f, and producing a series of operations similar to those just described. When the auxiliary valve shifts the pressure to either end of the main valve, the opposite end will be exhausting, and when the main piston brings the pressure on either end of the auxiliary valve, the other end will be exhausting. Because of this action, neither of the two valves meets with any resistance, and pressure water is against the main valve throughout its stroke. This makes it impossible for the lift to become centered. In the illustration Fig. 323, the cylinder at the right is known as the driving cylinder, and that at the left as the suction cylinder. There is no connection whatever, between the two cylinders. Rigidly connected to the same piston rod, are the driving piston and the suction piston, each working in its own cylinder. The suction pipe is connected at the center of the suc-

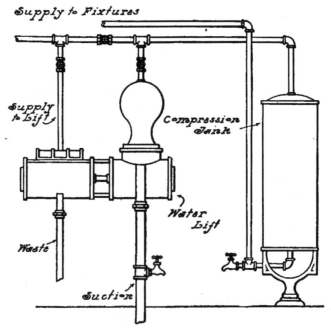

FIG. 324.—Water Lift Used on Direct Pressure System.

tion cylinder, and as the piston passes its entrance, a vacuum is created, which draws the water to be lifted, into the suction cylinder, from which, on the next stroke of the piston, it is forced up into the discharge pipe, two check valves holding the water as it is forced up. The air chamber prevents any shock due to the pumping.

There are various ways and various systems in which the water lift may be applied. Perhaps the simplest and most common system on which it is used, is the one shown in Fig. 324. This is called the direct-pressure system. It may be operated in city or town work by means of the public water supply, and in country work by means of attic or windmill storage tanks. In this system, the water lift under street pressure, pumps filtered water or soft water, as the case may be, directly into the pipes supplying the fixtures.

An important part of this system is the compression tank. When water is pumped into the tank, it compresses the air in it, and whenever water is drawn at any fixture, the compressed air forces it out under pressure. Whenever the air in the tank becomes

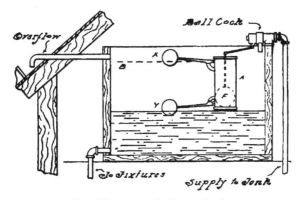

FIG. 325.—Automatic Storage Tank.

exhausted, it may be renewed by opening slightly the bibb on the suction pipe. Owing to the vacuum produced by the piston in the suction chamber, air will be drawn in and be delivered into the tank. In order that air may not be carried out more than possible when the tank is drawn upon, the supply to the fixtures from the tank is taken out of the latter at the bottom. The discharge from the lift into the compression tank is connected into the top of the latter. The use of the tank gives a steady stream and reduces the shock and hammering of pumping. By operating the valves on the cross-connection between lift and compression tank, water from the city mains may be delivered to the fixtures direct in the event

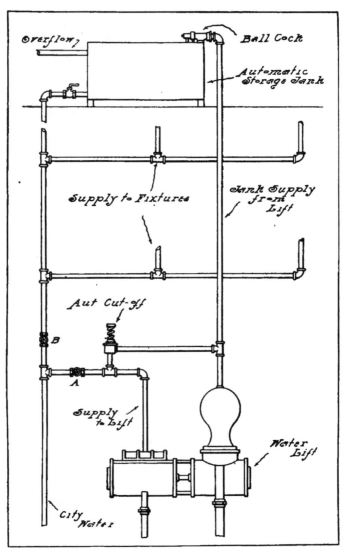

Fig. 326.—Water Lift Used on Automatic Storage Tank System.

that the soft or filtered water supply becomes exhausted. The water lift is now extensively used in connection with the automatic storage-tank system, which is often made use of in supplying soft or filtered water in large quantity. This system is shown in Fig. 324, and in Fig. 325 a sectional view of the automatic storage tank, the action of the latter being as follows:

This tank is supplied by the water lift through a ball cock whose float works in a cylinder A, of small size, placed inside the storage tank. Two other floats, X and Y are connected by a lever seating arrangement to two openings into the top and bottom of the cylinder F. Whenever the water falls below the level slightly above C, the float Y falls and opens the lower opening, through which the water in A escapes, causing the float F to drop, this action causing the ball cock to open, and also relieving the pressure on the cut-off shown in Fig. 326. The lift then starts into operation, forcing water up into the tank until the water reaches the level B. When this level is reached the float X is raised, thus opening the upper inlet into A, filling the latter with water, and raising the float F, which shuts off the ball cock.

The pressure of the water in the pipe between the lift and the tank is sufficient when the ball cock closes to close the automatic cut-off, which results in cutting off the water pressure from the lift. The water lift remains inactive until enough water has been drawn from the tank to bring the water level down to C again. By the use of the valves A and B, water from the city mains may be delivered to the fixtures when the regular supply is for any reason cut off. A modification of this system is often found in high city buildings in which the public water supply is not of sufficiently high pressure to supply the upper floors. In this system the lower floors are supplied by city pressure in the ordinary manner, while the upper floors are supplied from the automatic storage tank in connection with the water lift. It will be seen that under these conditions, the city pressure being the operating power and also the supply that is to be pumped, the supply to the lift and the suction must each be connected to the public water supply system. There are several other systems of supply, to which the water lift may be applied, which might be illustrated and described, if space permitted.

The advantages of the water lift are many, among them being the fact that its operation is automatic, requiring no attendant and little attention; it uses comparatively little water in operating; the action of the lift is comparatively noiseless, and there is little wear and tear on the working parts.

CHAPTER XXVIII

MULTIPLE CONNECTIONS FOR HOT-WATER BOILERS— RADIATORS AND COILS HEATED BY RANGE BOILERS

WHILE the large majority of range connections are very simple, involving no novel features, very often conditions and requirements arise which alter the matter entirely, often producing very difficult problems. Among the problems constantly arising, are those which require the connection to the same boiler of two or more ranges, coils, or heaters, and the supply from the hot-water system of heat for radiators and coils. When these multiple connections are used on the kitchen range, the conditions are generally such that the range alone furnishes sufficient heating capacity for the boiler, the additional heating capacity being needed only during the colder months.

These facts necessitate the making of connections in such a way that the boiler may be heated properly by the several heating surfaces together, or by either of them alone. A combination such as mentioned above which is often demanded, is to be seen in Fig. 327, in which a coil radiator on the floor above the range boiler is required to be heated, this additional service making it necessary to connect a coil in the furnace to give additional heat when the heating coil is being used. The best method under the circumstances, is to carry the flow pipe from the furnace coil directly to the top of the heating coil. This method delivers the water to the radiator before it has cooled to any extent, and gives the heating coil more power than other methods of connection would. A vent on the coil is necessary to prevent it from becoming air bound.

The return from the coil is carried into the return from the range boiler to the range, and a connection made from this pipe into the return of the furnace coil.

There is nothing about the connection described to interfere in any way with the regular work of the boiler in supplying hot water to the fixtures of the house.

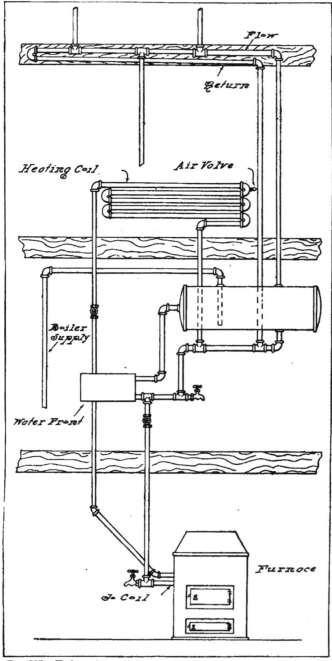

Fig. 327.—Horizontal Boiler Heated by Furnace Coil and Coal Range—
Boiler Heats Coil on Floor Above.

Valves on the flow and return of the furnace coil will enable the cutting out of the coil from the rest of the system when the furnace is no longer in use.

Another common requirement is the heating of a radiator by the hot-water supply, when the only heating surface is that of the

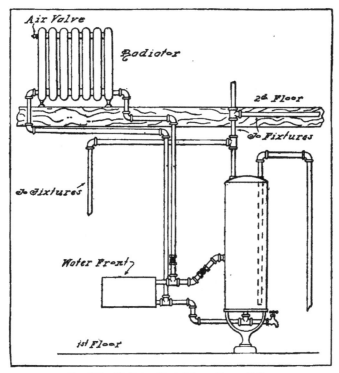

FIG. 328.—Radiator Heated from Range Boiler.

range. The great objection to this is that too much is often expected of such a connection, and also that it becomes a detriment sometimes to the regular work of the boiler. A small boiler heated by a small range should not be expected to provide both a hot-water supply and radiation.

A connection of this nature is to be seen in Fig. 328. A feed pipe for the radiator is taken from the range connection and carried to the radiator, which should be provided with an air valve, the return being taken into the return of the range connection. Valves are placed on the flow pipes to boiler and to radiator, the latter being located at the radiator if more desirable. The use of

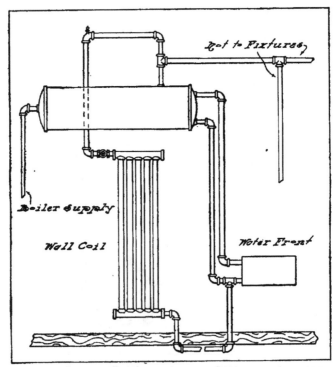

Fig. 329.—Wall Coil and Fixtures of Apartment Supplied by Horizontal Boiler.

these valves allows the heat of the range to be thrown either to the boiler or to the radiator, as the case may be.

For instance, if the demand for hot water is heavy, the radiator may be turned off for the time being. It must be seen to, however, that each of the two valves is not closed at the same time. In this connection it may be stated that valves should be used to as small an extent as possible on hot-water supply work, as their wrong use is sometimes attended with serious consequences.

Small rooms, such as bath rooms, small bedrooms, etc., which

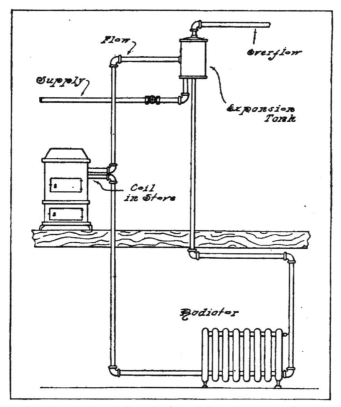

Fig. 330.—Heating Radiator by Stove Coil on Floor Below Stove.

would require only a few feet of radiation may often be successfully heated in this way.

Another familiar problem is that requiring the heating of a radiator or coil on the same floor as the range and boiler. Such an arrangement is shown in Fig. 329. To heat the coil, the flow pipe from the boiler is carried up and then directly down into the

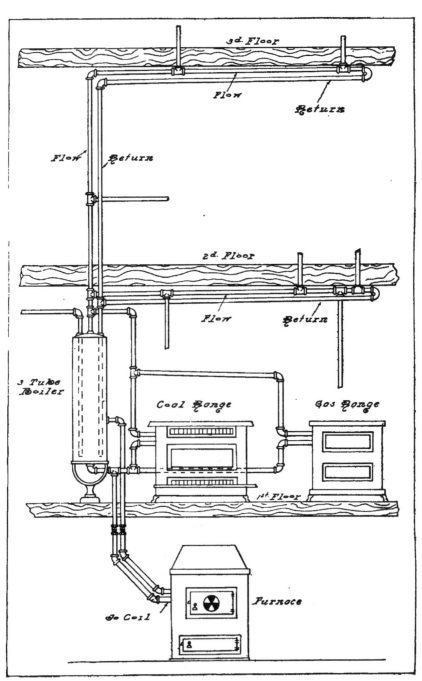

FIG. 331.—Range Boiler Heated by Furnace Coil, Gas Range and Coal Range.

top of the coil or radiator, a valve being placed on the pipe. The return is connected from the bottom of the coil or radiator into the return of the range connection. It is necessary to relieve this connection of air by means of an air valve at its high point. In the case of a supply system under tank pressure, the expansion pipe would perform this duty.

A more uncommon connection is shown in Fig. 330, in which a radiator is to be heated by a stove coil, without use of the hot-water supply system, and with the radiator on the floor below the stove. This radiator may be heated by running the flow pipe from the stove as high as possible, and connecting it into an expansion tank provided with an overflow. From the bottom of the expansion tank a feed pipe into the bottom of the radiator is taken, and the return end of the radiator connected back to the return of the coil. The water in the tank must stand above the opening of the flow pipe into it, and should be turned on from time to time to make up for any loss that may have been sustained.

The heating of a radiator under these adverse conditions is due to the weight of water rather than to circulation, and can be made to give fair results with a good heating surface in the stove.

The range boiler is very often fed from two or more different sources, such, for instance, as kitchen range, furnace coil, laundry heaters, gas ranges, etc. Such a combination is seen in Fig. 331 in which the boiler is heated by a coal range, gas range, and furnace coil. Either one of these sources of heat may be used independently of the others.

The connections of the flow pipes from the two ranges are so made as to produce quick heating of the boiler, while the flow pipe from the furnace coil enters the boiler at the side in the usual manner. The boiler shown in Fig. 331 is of the three-tube pattern, which allows the circulating pipe to be carried to the bottom of the boiler.

CHAPTER XXIX

THEORY FOR THE PLUMBER

In order to be successful in his work, the plumber of to-day must have at his command not only a knowledge of the practical requirements of his trade, but also a knowledge of the theory that underlies it. Every action that takes place in the drainage or supply system depends in some way upon some natural law, as also the action of various devices employed on the plumbing system.

It will be evident then that a knowledge of certain of these actions, and the laws governing them, is necessary to the plumber, in order that he may be able to understand and solve the various problems that are constantly arising in his work. Possibly to a greater extent than in almost any other trade the efficiency of the plumber consists largely in his ability to avoid trouble and to successfully get out of trouble that he already finds himself in.

Of the various phenomena to be considered, that of atmospheric pressure is perhaps of first importance. The atmosphere may be considered as a very light fluid, of certain depth, surrounding the earth. Although of small density, the weight of the atmosphere, which is computed to be about 45 miles in depth at the sea level, is very appreciable. Experiment has demonstrated that at sea level, the pressure of the atmosphere amounts to about 14.7 pounds per square inch. In ordinary computations, atmospheric pressure is considered as 15 pounds per square inch. Now in a square foot of surface, there are 144 square inches. Therefore, the pressure of the atmosphere on each square foot amounts to about 2160 pounds, or over a ton. This will serve to indicate what an immense pressure the atmosphere is capable of exerting.

That this pressure does not result in crushing everything that it comes in contact with, is due to the fact that the same pressure is exerted from all sides, thus equalizing the effect. Thus in the case of the human body, atmospheric pressure is exerted from without and from within, the two forces balancing each other and producing no results. If, however, a vacuum is formed on one side of an object, and atmospheric pressure is exerted on the other side, the obvious result is the crushing in of the object.

The action of atmospheric pressure, combined with the formation of a vacuum or partial vacuum, is to be met in a variety of ways in the plumbing system, some of the more common instances being the following:

Whenever siphonage takes place, whether it is in connection with traps, or in connection with the range boiler, or the action of water-closets and various other fixtures, the action is due to the creation of a vacuum on one side, and the pressure of the atmosphere on the other. This also underlies the action of pumps. In the siphonage of a trap, a vacuum must necessarily have first been formed on the sewer side of the trap seal. When this condition has been fulfilled, there is nothing to oppose the atmospheric pressure exerted on the house side of the seal, and the result is that the contents of the trap is forced out by the pressure of the atmosphere. It will be understood, by the way, that a vacuum is a portion of space from which the air has been exhausted.

The siphonage of boilers occurs in the same way as the siphonage of traps. In the case of the boiler, however, the vacuum is generally formed by the passage out of the pipe supplying the boiler of the water held in it, while the vacuum on the drainage system is often produced by the passage past the entrance of the trap of a body of waste, through the pipe into which the trap connects. In the operation of the pump, the action is as follows: As the piston of the pump is raised, it causes the formation of a vacuum in the suction pipe, and the action of atmospheric pressure on the surface of the water in the well forces the water up through the suction pipe. If the vacuum were perfect, and there was not the friction of the pipe to be considered, the water would rise in the suction pipe nearly 34 feet above the level of the water in the well. A more or less imperfect vacuum and the friction of pipe and fittings results in cutting down this distance considerably, depending on the conditions that exist in each case.

The same principle underlies the action of the vacuum valve as well as other devices used on the plumbing system. Under ordinary conditions, the vacuum valve remains closed, owing to the pressure of the water against the valve. When a vacuum occurs on the inner side of the valve, however, atmospheric pressure opens the valve, admitting air, and thus preventing the siphonage of the boiler. Various other examples might be mentioned, if necessary, of the effect of a vacuum and atmospheric pressure in connection with the plumbing system.

Atmospheric pressure is exerted not only downward, but in all directions. Hydrostatics is another subject which holds much interest for the plumber. Hydrostatics treats of the conditions of liquids in equilibrium, and of the pressures which they exert. One of the principles demonstrated in the study of this subject is that liquids are almost incompressible. This principle is made use of in the hydraulic ram. On the other hand, air is extremely compressible. The air chamber is often used on pumping and supply systems, the compressibility of air allowing the air chamber to take up any shock which may occur on the piping. When the air has become exhausted from the air chamber, however, and it has become filled with water, the latter being incompressible, the results of shocks through the pipes again become noticeable.

Another very important principle is the following: Pressure exerted anywhere upon a mass of liquid is transmitted undiminished in all directions, and acts with the same force on all equal surfaces, and in a direction at right angles to those surfaces. This principle may be demonstrated by means of the vessel shown in section in Fig. 332. In this vessel, the several openings are fitted with pistons of equal area. If pressure is exerted on the surface of the water in the vessel by means of a piston working through another opening, the six pistons shown will be pressed out in the direction of the arrows, a distance equal to that through which the additional piston is forced in. In any body of water, the pressure at any level is proportional to the depth, and the pressure is the same at all points on that level. The pressure of a column of water one square inch in area, and one foot high, is equivalent to .434 lbs. Therefore, to find the pressure of a column of water, multiply its head in feet, by .434. The pressure which the upper layers of a liquid exert on the lower layers, causes the latter to exert an equal reaction in an upward direction. This it will be seen, is a necessary consequence of the principle of transmission of pressure in all directions. This upward pressure is called the buoyancy of the liquid. The pressure exerted by a liquid, due to its weight, on any portion of the liquid, or on the sides of the vessel in which it is contained, depends on the depth and density of the liquid, but depends in no way upon the shape of the vessel or upon the quantity of the liquid. Another principle, which is well understood, is the fact that water will always strive to reach its own level. The

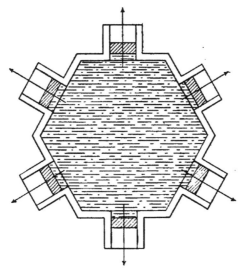

Fig. 332.—Direction of Pressure.

fact, however, that this principle underlies the action of the artesian well is probably not so well understood.

In Fig. 333 is shown an illustration from which the principle governing the artesian well, may be studied. Wherever this well is to be found, it will also be found that the strata composing the earth's surface is of two kinds, the one permeable to water, such as sand, gravel, etc., the other impermeable to water, such as clay. Let it be supposed, as shown in Fig. 333, that in a natural basin of greater or less extent, there are two impermeable layers, A B and C D, inclosing between them a permeable layer, E F. The rain water falling on the part of this permeable layer which comes to the surface, will filter down through it, and following the natural fall of the ground will collect in the hollow of the basin, from which it cannot escape, owing to the impermeable nature of the layers above and below it. The result is, that the space between the impermeable layers fills with water throughout its course.

If now a hole is bored from the surface, through the upper impermeable layer and into the water-bearing stratum, the water escaping, will endeavor to reach the level from which it has descended, the result being that it will gush out to a height depend-

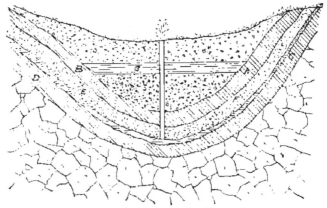

Fig. 333.—The Artesian Well.

ing on the difference between the levels at which the boring is made and the point at which this stratum comes to the surface. The water which feeds an artesian well often comes from a distance of sixty or seventy miles, and these wells are sometimes capable of delivering several hundreds of gallons of water per minute. In the action of the artesian well, it is not atmospheric pressure that forces the water up, but the pressure of the column of water between the well and the point where the water-bearing stratum comes to the surface.

Capillarity is a characteristic of liquids, which as seen in a preceding chapter, is often met with in connection with traps. While the phenomena of capillary action are numerous, there is only one feature of the subject which will directly interest the plumber. This feature is the fact that when a body in which very minute tubes or pores exist is immersed in water, the liquid will rise through these minute tubes to heights much above the level of the water itself. In order that this may happen, the substance immersed must be capable of being moistened by the water. The action is not due to any pressure or to action of the atmosphere, but to a sort of attractive force between the substance immersed and the liquid. If, for instance, a fine glass tube is thus immersed, the liquid will be seen to rise in it to a considerable height above

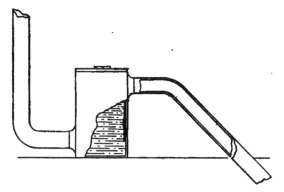

Fig. 334.—Destruction of Trap Seal by Capillary Action.

the level of the water. The application of this principle to plumbing, appears in the destruction of trap seals by capillary action.

In Fig. 334 is shown a trap into which a collection of lint, etc., dips. This material reaching from the trap seal into the outlet presents a danger to the trap seal much greater than would at first appear. By capillary action, the water in the trap is drawn up through this collection of lint, threads, etc., and deposited in the outlet a drop at a time. In the course of a comparatively short time the entire seal of the trap may be drawn out in this manner.

The friction of liquids is a matter which applies directly to supply work. In flowing over a surface, against the surface of a pipe, for instance, a liquid meets with more or less resistance, and in addition, there is a certain amount of friction between the molecules or particles of the water itself. This is called fluid friction. Fluid friction does not depend in any way upon the pressure of the liquid against the surface with which it comes in contact. It increases with the roughness of the surface and with the area of the surface, and within certain limits it increases with the velocity of the liquid.

Friction has greater effect in the case of small pipes than in large pipes. The reason for this is that in small pipes a larger proportion of the liquid comes in contact with the surface of the pipe than in large sizes. In long lines of pipe the friction may be of such an amount as to entirely cut off the flow of water.

Bends and other fittings add greatly to the friction in pipes. It is for this reason that changes in direction of pipes are often made by bending the pipe rather than by using bends or elbows.

The effects of heat present a subject which is also of very great interest to the plumber. The theory of heat now generally accepted, is that it is a form of motion. According to this theory, all bodies are made up of infinitely small particles or molecules, which are in constant motion. When heat is applied these vibrations increase, and expansion of the body results. If heat is continued, the expansion at last becomes so great that the particles will not hold together, the body loses its form and passes into the liquid state. If now heat is still further applied, by virtue of the continued expansion of its particles, the liquid mass will become transformed into a gas or vapor. When heat is withdrawn, the reverse action of contraction takes place.

Expansion and contraction of different metals varies considerably. In the calking of lead joints on cast-iron pipe this is to be seen. A metal or composition of metals has long been sought which in cooling will not contract so much as lead will, for as any workman well knows, when it cools, calking lead will draw away from both surfaces with which it is in contact. Type metal is about the only composition which answers this requirement, as its expansion and contraction are very slight. This metal, however, is not only too expensive for this purpose, but is too hard for calking.

It is because of the expansion of water when heated that

larger sizes must be used on flow pipes than on returns, and it is for the same reason that expansion tanks must be used.

It is due to the expansion and contraction of bodies that circulation takes place, whether it be circulation of water, steam, or air. As water becomes heated, the heated particles are in a more expanded state than the colder particles, and therefore are lighter. They therefore tend to rise, allowing the colder and heavier particles to fall and fill their places. The heating of air results in similar action.

Water is a substance which expands and contracts differently than any other substance. Other substances expand when heated and contract when cooled. At a certain definite temperature, however, water will expand whether heated or cooled. This temperature is 39.2° F., the temperature at which water is the heaviest. If this were not so, in freezing, water in the form of ice would be heavier than the water itself, and ice would be formed at the bottom of a body of water rather than at its surface.

Because of its ability to expand when heated to a high point, or cooled to a low point, water will burst the vessel in which it is contained under either condition; in the former case by freezing, and in the latter by the expansive force of steam. In freezing, the expansive force of water is very great, about 30,000 pounds to the square inch.

The boiling of liquids is a subject of interest. Boiling is the rapid production of elastic bubbles of vapor in the mass of a liquid. When water is heated at the lower part of a vessel the first bubbles are due to the disengagement of air which the water has absorbed. Small bubbles of vapor then begin to rise from the heated parts of the sides, but as they pass through the upper layers, the temperature of which is lower, they condense before reaching the surface. The formation and condensation of these first bubbles result in the singing noticed in water before it begins to boil. Finally, large bubbles rise and burst at the surface, and it is this action that constitutes boiling.

The temperature at which water will boil, that is, its boiling point, rises with the pressure. Therefore, water will boil more quickly at the top of a mountain than at its base, as atmospheric pressure at the top is less than at the bottom.

For any given pressure, boiling begins at a certain temperature, which for equal pressure, is always the same for the same liquid.

Regardless of the amount of heat that is applied, as soon as boiling commences, the temperature of the liquid remains stationary. Thus, water boils at 212° F. at sea level, and no matter how heavy a heat is being applied, the temperature of the water after it begins to boil remains at 212° F. This is a point worthy of remembrance, as there is a· general mistaken idea that the more heat is applied, even after water begins to boil, the higher the temperature of the water will be.

Water which contains matter in solution will not boil at as low a temperature as pure water. Thus, a water containing salt, or acid of any kind, will not boil at 212° F. Substances held mechanically by the water, however, such as sediment, sand, etc., do not affect the boiling point.

Evaporation is a subject in which the plumber has an interest, as evaporation is one of the most dangerous evils that the trap seal is subject to.

Evaporation is the slow passage of a liquid into the form of vapor. Whatever may be the temperature at which a vapor is formed, an absorption of heat always takes place. If, therefore, a liquid evaporates, and does not receive from other sources a quantity of heat equal to that which is given out in producing the vapor, its temperature sinks, and the cooling is greater in proportion as the evaporation is more rapid. Experiments have been made, showing that water may be frozen by means of rapid evaporation. Evaporation increases as the temperature increases, and as the exposed surface increases. Currents of air passing over the surface of a body of water also increase the rate of evaporation. The latter cause is the reason that the vent system increases the rate of evaporation of trap seals.

The vent system communicates with the outer air, and it is the currents of air passing through the piping that adds to this evil. The reverse action of evaporation is that of condensation. Condensation is the passage of a vapor into the liquid state. Warm vapors coming in contact with cold surfaces result in the condensation of the vapor. This action underlies the operation of distilling apparatus, the vapor of the liquid that is boiled being condensed again into the form of liquid. Condensation of vapors in the vent system necessitates the running of vent pipes in such a way that the condensation may not accumulate in the pipes, but will drain off into the drainage system. In summer time, the condensation accumulating on cold-water pipes is an evil often encountered.

Heat may be transmitted in two different ways, by conduction and by radiation. When a piece of metal is heated at one point this heat gradually spreads through the metal. When heat is transmitted through the mass of a body, from one particle to another, the body is said to be heated by conduction. Metals are excellent conductors of heat.

Heating by radiation is of more practical importance to the plumber, however, than heating by conduction. When a person stands at a little distance from a fire or other source of heat, he experiences the sensation of warmth. The heat in this case is not transmitted by conduction by the intervening air, but the rays of heat pass through without raising the temperature of the air. This heat is transmitted by radiation. That the heat is not due to the temperature of the air may be known from the fact that if a screen be interposed the sensation at once disappears, which would not be the case if the surrounding air had a high temperature. Therefore, it is seen that bodies may send out rays which excite heat, and which pass through the air without heating it.

Fusion is a subject connected with that of heat, which has been already slightly touched upon. Fusion is the passage of a solid into the liquid state. Most substances have the power of fusion. Exceptions are to be noted, however, in such substances as wood, paper, coal, etc., which instead of fusing, decompose under high temperatures. Many substances have long been considered impossible to fuse, but as it has become possible to produce higher temperatures, their number has steadily decreased. Such hard substances as rock crystal have been fused. Every fusible substance begins to fuse at a certain temperature, which is invariable for each substance if the pressure be the same. Regardless of the intensity of the heat applied, from the instant that fusion begins the temperature of the body ceases to rise, and remains constant until the fusion is complete.

Solidification is the reverse of fusion, it being the passage of a body from the liquid to the solid state. Every body, under the same pressure, solidifies at a fixed temperature, which is the same as that of fusion of the same substance. From the commencement to the end of solidification, the temperature of the substance remains the same.

In connection with this chapter, the subject of gravity, though not of the direct, practical importance to the reader that other subjects considered may be, should not be overlooked.

Briefly stated, gravity is the tendency of any body to fall toward the earth. When a gravity supply of water is spoken of, what is meant is that the supply is due not to any outside force, but simply to its tendency to fall. The same significance is attached to the gravity heating system. Weight is the common meaning of the term gravity. Thus, in the gravity supply system, water is delivered by gravity, that is, by virtue of its weight. In drainage work, the common system is known as the gravity system as distinguished from systems in which the drainage is forced along by special ejectors or pumps.

A few remarks concerning the properties of water will not be out of place. Water is composed of hydrogen and oxygen, two parts of the former to one of the latter. Water readily absorbs gases, this action occurring to the greatest extent when the pressure of the gas upon the water is greatest, and at low temperatures. The reason for this is that when under pressure and at low temperatures, the elastic force of the gas is less than under the reverse conditions. The absorption of gases by water renders it necessary to cover storage tanks for water when located in such positions as to be liable to such danger.

Water is hard or soft according to the relative amount of certain salts which are present in it. These salts are generally taken up by the water from the earth, the most common being those in which lime is present. A water containing these salts is said to be hard. Rain water, being free from salts of this nature, is soft, and in addition is the purest water obtainable. Rain water or any other pure water, however, often attacks certain metals more strongly than other more impure waters. This is due to the fact that the elements of which it is composed are more free to unite with other substances than water which already contains more or less matter of a chemical nature.

Air is composed of oxygen, nitrogen, and a small amount of carbonic-acid gas. The proportions are about one part of oxygen to four parts of nitrogen. Nitrogen is a poisonous element, very destructive to life. Upon the presence of oxygen all combustion and chemical action depends. While nitrogen is destructive of life, oxygen gives life, although the former is necessary to dilute the latter, for otherwise the process of oxidation would be so severe that life could not be maintained.

Other subjects might be taken up to advantage if space allowed, but for lack of that, the author has devoted himself entirely to those subjects which have a more or less practical application in the work of plumbing. Much other material, such as the subject of siphonage, will be found at different points, but which for various reasons are considered under other headings.

CHAPTER XXX

DRAWING FOR THE PLUMBER

It is not the purpose of this chapter to go extensively into the subject, but to give some of the necessary principles which will be of assistance along these lines. While it is not to be expected that the average workman in the plumbing trade is or can become a skilled draughtsman, the requirements of the times certainly demand that the plumber, if he is to make the most of his capabilities, must have a certain practical knowledge of the subject of drawing, as applied to his own trade. It is of inestimable value to the employing plumber and to the foreman on plumbing work, to be able to show intelligibly by means of a pencil sketch, for the benefit of workmen or customers, methods of connections, etc. Furthermore, in many cities of the country, boards of health now demand sketches of contemplated work, both on new and old construction, to be submitted before issuing a permit to perform the work. Again, in many cities, in order to secure a plumber's license, the applicant must be able to draw the connections for work as indicated by his examiners, and to be able to criticise intelligently drawings of plumbing construction of faulty nature. Journeymen plumbers' unions in many instances also require applicants for admission to pass an examination which includes the making and criticizing of plumbing drawings. These remarks will serve to show some of the reasons why ability to read and make drawings is a necessary part of the plumber's knowledge, and it may be truly stated that the necessity for such knowledge is steadily increasing.

The mechanical, architectural, and engineering draughtsman is compelled to go deeply into the subject, but the rudiments are sufficient as a foundation for the plumber, his greatest difficulty being in executing drawings neatly and in such a manner as to be readily understood.

The plumber really needs to be acquainted with only two views, these being known as the plan view and the elevation.

Experience shows that if he learns to properly distinguish between these two views, the plumber's greatest difficulty as a draughtsman will disappear, and that if he does not thoroughly master this principle, his drawings will in all probability be a confusion of plan and elevation, which it will often be impossible for another person to understand. A perspective view of plumbing connections, which, by the way, is a very difficult drawing to make, should very rarely be used by the plumber, although there is a strong temptation to make use of it.

Every object, if it is to be shown completely by drawings, will require two views, a plan and an elevation, although in showing plumbing work, one view will often, and probably usually show the work with sufficient clearness.

A plan view is a view obtained by looking down upon the object as it stands in its natural position. Thus a cellar plan or floor plan of a house is obtained by viewing the cellar or floor from a point above it. An elevation, on the other hand, is a view obtained by standing away from the object, and looking horizontally at it. Every object such as a house, would have four elevations, front, rear, and two side elevations. For the plumber's use, however, not more than two elevations, front and side, are ever needed, and in a great many cases only one elevation is required by him. He must know what the elevation of the house is, in order to know the distance between floors, the total height, etc., in figuring the amount of piping in vertical lines of pipe. He needs the plan view equally as much, to show him the horizontal lines of piping.

It will be clear then that a full knowledge of the work can be obtained only by means of at least one elevation, and the several plan views of the cellar and floors, and in estimating work, these drawings are always necessary. On the other hand, very often an elevation or a plan, as the case may be, will be sufficient. For instance, in showing the principles of certain work by means of a drawing, very often an elevation will show all that is necessary.

The idea of plan and elevation may be seen by reference to Fig. 335.

The first is a perspective view of a piece of pipe, and the other two views are the plan and elevation of the same piece of pipe.

The perspective view gives as much information concerning the object as the plan and elevation combined, that is, it shows the length, shows that it is cylindrical, and also the inside and outside diameters. On the other hand, the elevation shows only length and width, and gives no idea as to whether the object is square or round. In connection with the elevation, the plan is necessary, in order to show that the object is cylindrical instead of square, and

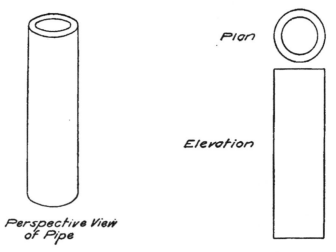

Plan

Elevation

Perspective View of Pipe

Fig. 335.—Perspective and Mechanical Views of an Object.

that it is a hollow cylinder and not solid. It may be asked, since the perspective in one view gives the entire information, while in the mechanical drawing two views are needed, why it is not better to use perspective views.

In the first place, it is very much more difficult and takes more time to make the perspective view of this piece of pipe than to make the two mechanical views. In the second place, in making a perspective view of a complicated system of piping and fixtures, the task would become so much more difficult than the making of the mechanical views, that the person not well versed in such work could not expect to do otherwise than produce a drawing which would be utterly impossible to understand.

Regarding the plan and elevation, it may be stated that if the pipe of Fig. 335 had been a square pipe, the elevation would not have been different, but the plan would have been a hollow square, rather than the circular view shown.

Another point that requires mention is the fact that if the pipe had laid upon its side instead of upon end, when the two views were made, the plan would then have been what the elevation now is, but shown lengthwise or horizontally, instead of vertically. The elevation in that case would be the same as the plan view now shows. If careful study is given to the foregoing simple principles, the subject of plan and elevation will be fairly well understood.

In looking over sketches drawn by workmen, it is especially noticeable that they invariably confuse plan and elevation in showing fixtures, such as sinks, lavatories, wash trays, water closets, etc. To give them a clearer idea of how these fixtures should be shown, Figs. 336 to 339 are given.

These several views are of common fixtures, and in most cases it is as well to show these simple forms of fixtures in drawings, as to show views of fixtures that are more complicated. For instance, the views shown of the lavatory would be much more easily made than those of many of the fancy, high grade lavatories, and they would show the principles involved fully as well.

One very important fact to be remembered, is that no one mechanical view can show all sides of an object, or give all the information that is to be obtained. It is one of the greatest faults of those who are not conversant with the subject, to endeavor to make a certain view show facts concerning an object which cannot possibly be shown by that view. The result of such attempts is usually a distorted drawing which can only be understood after much study and surmising as to the meaning of the one who made it.

The drawings which the plumber will generally require are made up largely of piping, and experience shows that the plumber in making such drawings will have better results if he will draw single lines for his pipe, instead of double lines, such as are shown

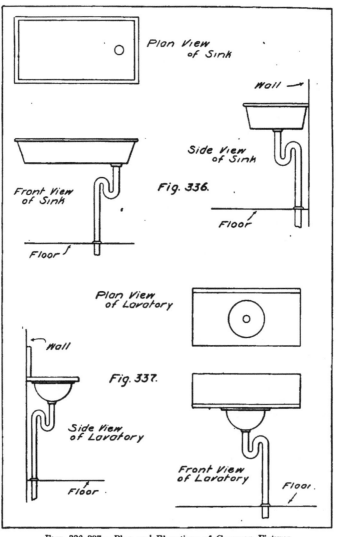

Plan View of Sink

Wall →

Side View of Sink

Front View of Sink

Fig. 336.

Floor

Floor

Plan View of Lavatory

Fig. 337.

Wall

Side View of Lavatory

Front View of Lavatory

Floor

Floor

Figs. 336–337.—Plan and Elevations of Common Fixtures.

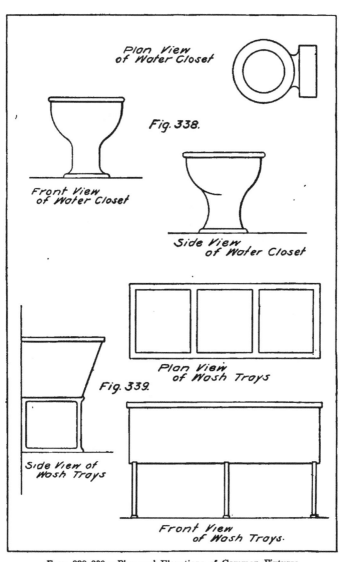

Plan View
of Water Closet

Fig. 338.

Front View
of Water Closet

Side View
of Water Closet

Plan View
of Wash Trays

Fig. 339.

Side View of
Wash Trays

Front View
of Wash Trays.

Figs. 338–339.—Plan and Elevations of Common Fixtures.

on all illustrations in this work, with the exception of several in this chapter.

Fig. 340 will serve as an illustration of the advice to use single lines, and when compared with many other illustrations in this work of similar nature, it will be seen that the labor in making the single line drawing is very much less, and in general shows the desired principles with equal clearness. The plumber, in making drawings, especially if he is only fair in his execution, should cut out all unnecessary detail. It is often full as well to omit drawing fixtures, simply showing traps and connections, and by proper lettering showing the location of the several fixtures. This feature also appears in Fig. 340. The sizes of pipes may be indicated by figures as in the same illustration, although it is often well to indicate the main lines of pipe by heavier lines than those used for the rest of the work.

If the drawing is in pencil, and it is desired to distinguish between the venting and the drainage, it may be done by the use of red and blue pencils, one color for the venting, and the other for the drainage. Different colored inks may be used in the same way on drawings made in ink.

Another method is the use of broken lines for the vent work, and full lines for the drainage. These same methods are often used also in drawings showing systems of hot water supply and systems of steam and hot water heating, broken lines or blue lines showing returns, and full lines or red lines showing supply pipes. It is often very desirable, and sometimes necessary, in making drawings which are to show changes and additions to the plumbing system, to use these same methods in distinguishing between the old and the new work. This idea is brought out in Fig. 341, and is often used on drawings submitted to boards of health or plumbing boards.

Before leaving the subject of drawing, the matter of scale drawings should be considered. This branch of the subject is of great importance to the plumber, inasmuch as all architects' drawings are of this nature. The plumber must understand scale drawings, in order to be able to figure lengths of piping, etc., from architects' plans.

It is obviously impossible to provide drawings of such a

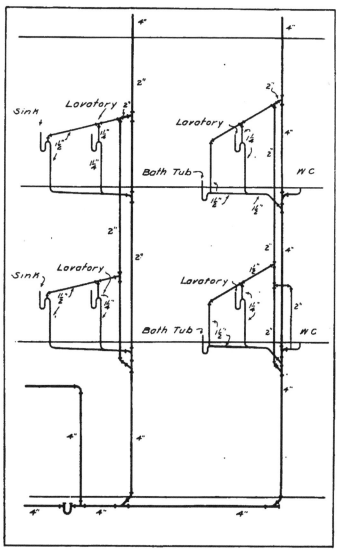

FIG. 340.—Single-Line Elevation of Plumbing System.

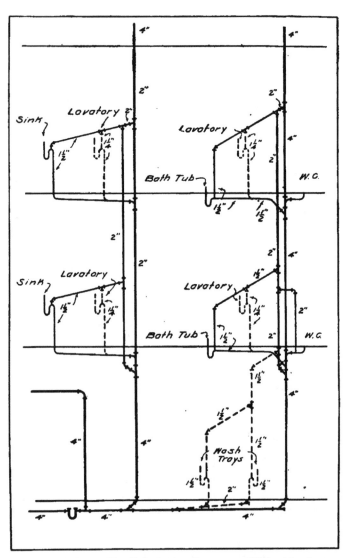

Fig. 341.—Single-Line Elevation Showing Changes on Old Plumbing System.

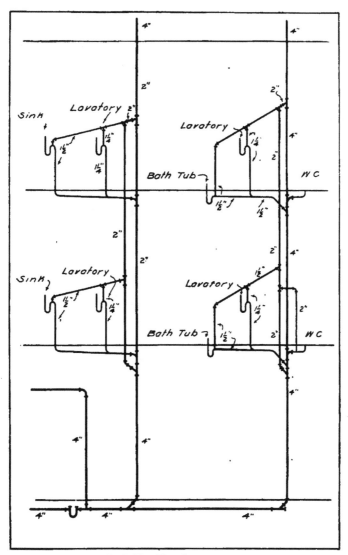

Fig. 340.—Single-Line Elevation of Plumbing System.

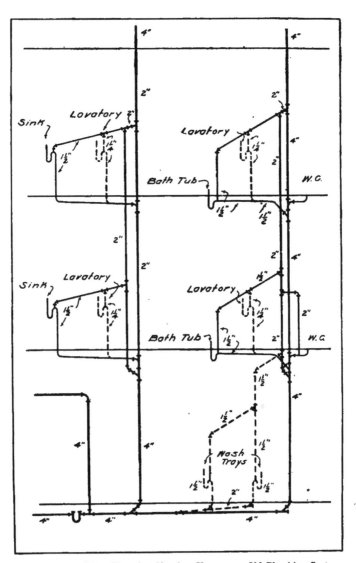

Fig. 341.—Single-Line Elevation Showing Changes on Old Plumbing System.

thing as a house, of full size. In order then to provide drawings of buildings, the architect reduces the size to such dimensions as will be desirable. Such reduced drawings are in the
actual proportions of the building itself, but on a very much
smaller scale. The most common architect's scale is $\frac{1}{4}$ inch to the
foot, although on large building plans, $\frac{1}{8}$ inch to the foot is often
used. The scale used is always named on each drawing of the set
of plans. If the scale is $\frac{1}{4}$ inch to the foot, a quarter inch measured
anywhere on the plan, means that the same measurement on the
building itself would give one foot.

In Figs. 342 and 343 are shown two cellar plans of the same
house and piping, the small one being just half the size of the
large one. Supposing that the upper plan is drawn at $\frac{1}{8}$ inch to
the foot, and the lower one at $\frac{1}{4}$ inch to the foot, an eight inch
measured on the upper represents one foot, and a quarter inch
measured on the lower represents one foot also. In referring
to building plans in figuring work, care should always be taken
before entering on the work, to ascertain the scale of the drawing.
The writer can recall instances that have come to his knowledge,
of plumbers figuring stock from plans drawn at one-eighth scale, as
if they were drawn at a quarter scale, the result being that only
one-half the straight pipe actually necessary for the work was
figured on.

The only special knowledge necessary to the plumber concerning scale drawings is the use of the scale, which is a very simple matter. It simply means that in figuring lengths of pipe,
whether vertical or horizontal, from the plans and elevation, as
many feet should be allowed for the pipe as the distances measure
in quarter or eighth inches, according to the scale of the drawings.
Thus, on a cellar plan drawn at $\frac{1}{4}$ inch to the foot, a line of pipe
measuring $5\frac{1}{4}$ inches would represent a length of pipe of 21 feet.

In Figs. 344 to 347 are shown the cellar and floor plans and
elevation of a two story house. The elevation will show the
vertical heights by the measurements of a, b, c, d and e.

A very important matter in many cases, is the offsetting of
vertical lines of pipe, shown by the location of risers on the cellar
and floor plans. If the estimator is careless in his work, he is
liable to estimate vertical lines of pipe without giving attention to

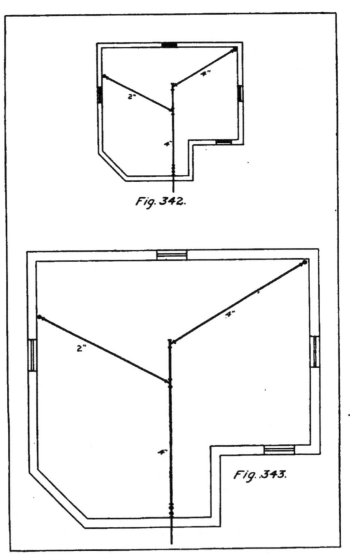

Fig. 342.

Fig. 343.

Figs. 342–343.—Scale Drawing.

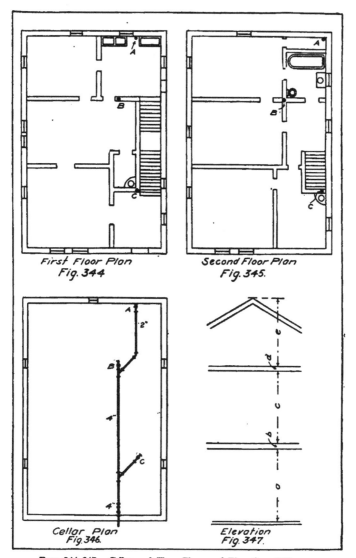

First Floor Plan
Fig. 344

Second Floor Plan
Fig. 345.

Cellar Plan
Fig. 346.

Elevation
Fig. 347.

Figs. 344–347.—Cellar and Floor Plans and Elevation of House.

offsets. This will cause him to leave out fittings from his estimate, and pipe also, in the case of long offsets.

Referring to Figs. 344-347, it will be seen from the location of stack A in the cellar and first floor plans, that it has no offset at these points, but has a straight rise. Its location on the second floor plan, however, shows that it does offset at the second floor, necessitating the estimating of two elbows, and a certain length of straight pipe.

The location of stack B in the three plans shows that this line of pipe rises through the roof without offsetting at any point.

In the case of stack C, the three locations of the riser show no offset at the first floor, but there is one at the second floor.

While the foregoing is by no means a complete treatise on this subject, the writer believes that those points which have special application to the plumber's requirements, have been touched upon, and that a careful study of the facts and suggestions given, will be of much assistance to any plumber who desires to perfect himself along these lines.

INDEX

1911

CATALOGUE

of

Practical Books

Published and for sale by

The Norman W. Henley Publishing Company

Publishers of Scientific and Practical Books

132 NASSAU STREET   NEW YORK, U.S.A.

All books in this Catalogue sent prepaid on receipt of price.

SUBJECT INDEX

INDEX BY AUTHORS

☞ANY BOOK ADVERTISED IN THIS CATALOGUE WILL BE SENT PROMPTLY TO ANY
ADDRESS IN THE WORLD, CHARGES PREPAID, UPON RECEIPT OF PRICE.

☞*How to Remit.*—Remit by Postal Money Order, Express Money Order, Bank Draft
or Registered Letter.

BALLOONS AND FLYING MACHINES

MODEL BALLOONS AND FLYING MACHINES. WITH A SHORT ACCOUNT OF THE PROGRESS OF AVIATION. By J. H. ALEXANDER.

This book has been written with a view to assist those who desire to construct a model airship or flying machine. It contains five folding plates of working drawings, each sheet containing a different sized machine. Much instruction and amusement can be obtained from the making and flying of these models.

A short account of the progress of aviation is included, which will render the book of greater interest. Several illustrations of full sized airship and flying machines of the latest types are scattered throughout the text. This practical work gives data, working drawings, and details which will assist materially those interested in the problems of flight. 127 pages, 45 illustrations, 5 folding plates. Price **$1.50**

BRAZING AND SOLDERING

BRAZING AND SOLDERING. By JAMES F. HOBART.

The only book that shows you just how to handle any job of brazing or soldering that comes along; tells you what mixture to use, how to make a furnace if you need one. Full of kinks. Fourth edition. . . . . **25 cents**

CHARTS

BOX CAR CHART.

A chart showing the anatomy of a box car, having every part of the car numbered and its proper name given in a reference list. . . . . **20 cents**

GONDOLA CAR CHART.

A chart showing the anatomy of a gondola car, having every part of the car numbered and its proper reference name given in a reference list. . . . . **20 cents**

PASSENGER CAR CHART.

A chart showing the anatomy of a passenger car, having every part of the car numbered and its proper name given in a reference list. . . . . **20 cents**

WESTINGHOUSE AIR-BRAKE CHARTS.

Chart I.—Shows (in colors) the most modern Westinghouse High Speed and Signal Equipment used on Passenger Engines, Passenger Engine Tenders, and Passenger Cars. Chart II.—Shows (in colors) the Standard Westinghouse Equipment for Freight and Switch Engines, Freight and Switch Engine Tenders, and Freight Cars. Price for the set . **50 cents**

TRACTIVE POWER CHART.

A chart whereby you can find the tractive power or drawbar pull of any locomotive, without making a figure. Shows what cylinders are equal, how driving wheels and steam pressure affect the power. What sized engine you need to exert a given drawbar pull or anything you desire in this line. . . . . **50 cents**

HORSE POWER CHART.

Shows the horse power of any stationary engine without calculation. No matter what the cylinder diameter of stroke; the steam pressure or cut-off; the revolutions, or whether condensing or non-condensing, it's all there. Easy to use, accurate, and saves time and calculations. Especially useful to engineers and designers. . . . . **50 cents**

BOILER ROOM CHART. By GEO. L. FOWLER.

A Chart—size 14 x 28 inches—showing in isometric perspective the mechanisms belonging in a modern boiler room. Water tube boilers, ordinary grates and mechanical stokers, feed water heaters and pumps comprise the equipment. The various parts are shown broken or removed, so that the internal construction is fully illustrated. Each part is given a reference number, and these, with the corresponding name, are given in a glossary printed at the sides. This chart is really a dictionary of the boiler room—the names of more than 200 parts being given. It is educational—worth many times its cost. . . . . **25 cents**

CIVIL ENGINEERING

HENLEY'S ENCYCLOPEDIA OF PRACTICAL ENGINEERING AND ALLIED TRADES.
Edited by JOSEPH G. HORNER, A.M.I., M.E.

This set of five volumes contains about 2,500 pages with thousands of illustrations, including diagrammatic and sectional drawings with full explanatory details. This work covers the entire practice of Civil and Mechanical Engineering. The best known experts in all branches of engineering have contributed to these volumes. The Cyclopedia is admirably well adapted to the needs of the beginner and the self-taught practical man, as well as the mechanical engineer, designer, draftsman, shop superintendent, foreman, and machinist. The work will be found a means of advancement to any progressive man. It is encyclopedic in scope, thorough and practical in its treatment of technical subjects, simple and clear in its descriptive matter, and without unnecessary technicalities or formulae. The articles are as brief as may be and yet give a reasonably clear and explicit statement of the subject, and are written by men who have had ample practical experience in the matters of which they write. It tells you all you want to know about engineering and tells it so simply, so clearly, so concisely, that one cannot help but understand. As a work of reference it is without a peer. $6.00 per volume. For complete set of five volumes, price **$25.00**

COKE

COKE—MODERN COKING PRACTICE; INCLUDING THE ANALYSIS OF MATERIALS AND PRODUCTS. By T. H. BYROM and J. E. CHRISTOPHER.

A handbook for those engaged in Coke manufacture and the recovery of By-products. Fully illustrated with folding plates. It has been the aim of the authors, in preparing this book, to produce one which shall be of use and benefit to those who are associated with, or interested in, the modern developments of the industry. **Contents:** I. Introductory. II. General Classification of Fuels. III. Coal Washing. IV. The Sampling and Valuation of Coal, Coke, etc. V. The Calorific Power of Coal and Coke. VI. Coke Ovens. VII. Coke Ovens, continued. VIII. Coke Ovens, continued. IX. Charging and Discharging of Coke Ovens, X. Cooling and Condensing Plant. XI. Gas Exhausters. XII. Composition and Analysis of Ammoniacal Liquor. XIII. Working-up of Ammoniacal Liquor. XIV. Treatment of Waste Gases from Sulphate Plants. XV. Valuation of Ammonium Sulphate. XVI. Direct Recovery of Ammonia from Coke Oven Gases. XVII. Surplus Gas from Coke Oven. Useful Tables. Very fully illustrated. Price . . . .**$3.50 net**

COMPRESSED AIR

COMPRESSED AIR IN ALL ITS APPLICATIONS. By GARDNER D. HISCOX.

This is the most complete book on the subject of Air that has even been issued, and its thirty-five chapters include about every phase of the subject one can think of. It may be called an encyclopedia of compressed air. It is written by an expert, who, in its 665 pages, has dealt with the subject in a comprehensive manner, no phase of it being omitted. Over 500 illustrations, 5th Edition, revised and enlarged. Cloth bound, $5.00: Half Morocco, price **$6.50**

CONCRETE

ORNAMENTAL CONCRETE WITHOUT MOLDS. By A. A. HOUGHTON.

The process for making ornamental concrete without molds, has long been held as a secret and now, for the first time, this process is given to the public. The book reveals the secret and is the only book published which explains a simple, practical method whereby the concrete worker is enabled, by employing wood and metal templates of different designs, to mold or model in concrete any Cornice, Archivolt, Column, Pedestal, Base Cap, Urn or Pier in a monolithic form—right upon the job. These may be molded in units or blocks, and then built up to suit the specifications demanded. This work is fully illustrated, with detailed engravings. Price **$2.00**

CONCRETE FROM SAND MOLDS. By A. A. HOUGHTON.

A Practical Work treating on a process, which has heretofore been held as a trade secret, by the few who possessed it, and which will successfully mold every and any class of ornamental concrete work. The process of molding concrete with sand molds is of the utmost practical value, possessing the manifold advantages of a low cost of molds, the ease and rapidity of operation, perfect details to all ornamental designs, density, and increased strength of the concrete, perfect curing of the work without attention and the easy removal of the molds regardless of any undercutting the design may have. 192 pages. Fully illustrated. Price **$2.00**

CONCRETE WALL FORMS. By A. A. HOUGHTON.

A new automatic wall clamp is illustrated with working drawings. Other types of wall forms, clamps, separators, etc., are also illustrated and explained. . . . . . . **50 cents**

CONCRETE FLOORS AND SIDEWALKS. By A. A. HOUGHTON.

The molds for molding squares, hexagonal and many other styles of mosaic floor and sidewalk blocks are fully illustrated and explained. . . . . **50 cents**

4

CONCRETE SILOS. By A. A. HOUGHTON.

Complete working drawings and specifications are given for several styles of concrete silos, with illustrations of molds for monolithic and block silos. The tables, data and information presented in this book are of the utmost value in planning and constructing all forms of concrete silos. . . . . 50 cents

CONCRETE CHIMNEYS, SLATE AND ROOF TILES. By A. A. HOUGHTON.

The manufacture of all types of concrete slate and roof tile is fully treated. Valuable data on all forms of reinforced concrete roofs are contained within its pages. The construction of concrete chimneys by block and monolithic systems is fully illustrated and described. A number of ornamental designs of chimney construction with molds are shown in this valuable treatise. . . . . 50 cents

MOLDING AND CURING ORNAMENTAL CONCRETE. By A. A. HOUGHTON.

The proper proportions of cement and aggregates for various finishes, also the methods of thoroughly mixing and placing in the molds, are fully treated. An exhaustive treatise on this subject that every concrete worker will find of daily use and value. . . . . . 50 cents

CONCRETE MONUMENTS, MAUSOLEUMS AND BURIAL VAULTS. By A. A. HOUGHTON.

The molding of concrete monuments to imitate the most expensive cut stone is explained in this treatise, with working drawings of easily built molds. .Cutting inscriptions and designs is also fully treated. . . . . 50 cents

CONCRETE BATH TUBS, AQUARIUMS AND NATATORIUMS. By A. A. HOUGHTON.

Simple molds and instruction are given for molding many styles of concrete bath tubs, swimming pools, etc. These molds are easily built and permit rapid and successful work. 50 cents

ARTISTIC CONCRETE BRIDGES. By A. A. HOUGHTON.

A number of ornamental concrete bridges with illustrations of molds are given. A collapsible center or core for bridges, culverts and sewers is fully illustrated with detailed instructions for building . . . . 50 cents

CONSTRUCTING CONCRETE PORCHES. By A. A. HOUGHTON.

A number of designs with working drawings of molds are fully explained so any one can easily construct different styles of ornamental concrete porches without the purchase of expensive molds. . . . . 50 cents

CONCRETE FLOWER POTS, BOXES AND JARDINIERES. By A. A. HOUGHTON.

The molds for producing many original designs of flower pots, urns, flower boxes, jardinières, etc., are fully illustrated and explained, so the worker can easily construct and operate same. 50 cents

CONCRETE FOUNTAINS AND LAWN ORNAMENTS. By A. A. HOUGHTON.

The molding of a number of designs of lawn seats, curbing, hitching posts, pergolas, sun dials and other forms of ornamental concrete for the ornamentation of lawns and gardens, is fully illustrated and described. 50 cents

CONCRETE FOR THE FARM AND SHOP. By A. A. HOUGHTON.

The molding of drain tile, tanks, cisterns, fence posts, stable floors, hog and poultry houses and all the purposes for which concrete is an invaluable aid to the farmer are numbered among the contents of this handy volume. . . . . 50 cents

POPULAR HANDBOOK FOR CEMENT AND CONCRETE USERS. By MYRON H. LEWIS.

This is a concise treatise of the principles and methods employed in the manufacture and use of cement in all classes of modern works. The author has brought together in this work, all the salient matter of interest to the user of concrete and its many diversified products. The matter is presented in logical and systematic order, clearly written, fully illustrated and free from involved mathematics. Everything of value to the concrete user is given including kinds of cement employed in construction, concrete architecture, inspection and testing, waterproofing, coloring and painting, rules, tables, working, and cost data. Price $2.50

DICTIONARIES

STANDARD ELECTRICAL DICTIONARY. By T. O'CONOR SLOANE.

An indispensable work to all interested in electrical science. Suitable alike for the student and professional. A practical hand-book of reference containing definitions of about 5,000 distinct words, terms and phrases. The definitions are terse and concise and include every term used in electrical science. Recently issued. An entirely new edition. Should be in the possession of all who desire to keep abreast with the progress of this branch of science. Complete, concise and convenient. 682 pages. 393 illustrations. Price. $3.00

DIES—METAL WORK

DIES, THEIR CONSTRUCTION AND USE FOR THE MODERN WORKING OF SHEET METALS. By J. V. WOODWORTH.

A most useful book, and one which should be in the hands of all engaged in the press working of metals; treating on the Designing, Constructing, and Use of Tools, Fixtures and Devices, together with the manner in which they should be used in the Power Press, for the cheap and rapid production of the great variety of sheet metal articles now in use. It is designed as a guide to the production of sheet metal parts at the minimum of cost with the maximum of output. The hardening and tempering of Press tools and the classes of work which may be produced to the best advantage by the use of dies in the power press are fully treated. Its 505 illustrations show dies, press fixtures and sheet metal working devices, the descriptions of which are so clear and practical that all metal-working mechanics will be able to understand how to design, construct and use them. Many of the dies and press fixtures treated were either constructed by the author or under his supervision. Others were built by skilful mechanics and are in use in large sheet metal establishments and machine shops. Price **$3.00**

PUNCHES, DIES AND TOOLS FOR MANUFACTURING IN PRESSES. By J. V. WOODWORTH.

This work is a companion volume to the author's elementary work entitled "Dies, Their Construction and Use." It does not go into the details of die making to the extent of the author's previous book, but gives a comprehensive review of the field of operations carried on by presses. A large part of the information given has been drawn from the author's personal experience. It might well be termed an Encyclopedia of Die Making, Punch Making, Die Sinking, Sheet Metal Working, and Making of Special Tools, Sub-presses, Devices and Mechanical Combinations for Punching, Cutting, Bending, Forming, Piercing, Drawing, Compressing and Assembling Sheet Metal Parts, and also Articles of other Materials in Machine Tools. Price **$4.00**

DROP FORGING, DIE SINKING AND MACHINE FORMING OF STEEL. By J. V. WOODWORTH.

This is a practical treatise on Modern Shop Practice, Processes, Methods, Machines, Tools and Details, treating on The Hot and Cold Machine-Forming of Steel and Iron into Finished Shapes; Together with Tools, Dies, and Machinery involved in the manufacture of Duplicate Forgings and Interchangeable Hot and Cold Pressed Parts from Bar and Sheet Metal. Fully illustrated by 300 detailed illustrations. Price. **$2.50**

DRAWING—SKETCHING PAPER

LINEAR PERSPECTIVE SELF-TAUGHT. By HERMAN T. C. KRAUS.

This work gives the theory and practice of linear perspective, as used in architectural, engineering, and mechanical drawings. Persons taking up the study of the subject by themselves will be able by the use of the instruction given to readily grasp the subject, and by reasonable practice become good perspective draftsmen. The arrangement of the book is good; the plate is on the left-hand, while the descriptive text follows on the opposite page, so as to be readily referred to. The drawings are on sufficiently large scale to show the work clearly and are plainly figured. The whole work makes a very complete course on perspective drawing, and will be found of great value to architects, civil and mechanical engineers, patent attorneys, art designers, engravers, and draftsmen. **$2.50**

PRACTICAL PERSPECTIVE. By RICHARDS and COLVIN.

Shows just how to make all kinds of mechanical drawings in the only practical perspective isometric. Makes everything plain so that any mechanic can understand a sketch or drawing in this way. Saves time in the drawing room, and mistakes in the shops. Contains practical examples of various classes of work. . . . . **50 cents**

SELF-TAUGHT MECHANICAL DRAWING AND ELEMENTARY MACHINE DESIGN. By F. L. SYLVESTER, M.E., Draftsman, with additions by ERIK OBERG, associate editor of "Machinery."

This is a practical treatise on Mechanical Drawing and Machine Design, comprising the first principles of geometric and mechanical drawing, workshop mathematics, mechanics, strength of materials and the calculations and design of machine details. Specially prepared for the practical mechanic and young draftsman. It is primarily intended for the man who must study without a teacher. It is clearly written, comprehensive, and carefully arranged. Price **$2.00**

A NEW SKETCHING PAPER.

A new specially ruled paper to enable you to make sketches or drawings in isometric perspective without any figuring or fussing. It is being used for shop details as well as for assembly drawings, as it makes one sketch do the work of three, and no workman can help seeing just what is wanted. Pads of 40 sheets, 6 x 9 inches, 25 cents. Pads of 40 sheets, 9 x 12 inches. **50 cents**

6

ELECTRICITY

ARITHMETIC OF ELECTRICITY. By Prof. T. O'Conor Sloane.

A practical treatise on electrical calculations of all kinds reduced to a series of rules, all of the simplest forms, and involving only ordinary arithmetic; each rule illustrated by one or more practical problems, with detailed solution of each one. This book is classed among the most useful works published on the science of electricity covering as it does the mathematics of electricity in a manner that will attract the attention of those who are not familiar with algebraical formulas. 160 pages. Price **$1.00**

COMMUTATOR CONSTRUCTION. By Wm. Baxter, Jr.

The business end of any dynamo or motor of the direct current type is the commutator. This book goes into the designing, building, and maintenance of commutators, shows how to locate troubles and how to remedy them; everyone who fusses with dynamos needs this. **25 cents**

DYNAMO BUILDING FOR AMATEURS, OR HOW TO CONSTRUCT A FIFTY-WATT DYNAMO. By Arthur J. Weed, Member of N. Y. Electrical Society.

This book is a practical treatise showing in detail the construction of a small dynamo or motor. the entire machine work of which can be done on a small foot lathe.
Dimensioned working drawings are given for each piece of machine work and each operation is clearly described.
This machine, when used as a dynamo, has an output of fifty watts; when used as a motor it will drive a small drill press or lathe. It can be used to drive a sewing machine on any and all ordinary work.
The book is illustrated with more than sixty original engravings showing the actual construction of the different parts. Price, paper, 50 cents. Cloth **$1.00**

ELECTRIC FURNACES AND THEIR INDUSTRIAL APPLICATIONS. By J. Wright.

This is a book which will prove of interest to many classes of people; the manufacturer who desires to know what product can be manufactured successfully in the electric furnace, the chemist who wishes to post himself on the electro-chemistry, and the student of science who merely looks into the subject from curiosity. The book is not so scientific as to be of use only to the technologist, nor so unscientific as to suit only the tyro in electro-chemistry; it is a practical treatise of what has been done, and of what is being done, both experimentally and commercially with the electric furnace.
In important processes not only are the chemical equations given, but complete thermal data are set forth and both the efficiency of the furnace and the cost of the product are worked out, thus giving the work a solid commercial value aside from its efficacy as a work of reference. The practical features of furnace building are given the space that the subject deserves. The forms and refractory materials used in the linings, the arrangement of the connections to the electrodes, and other important details are explained. 288 pages. New Revised Edition. Fully illustrated. Price **$3.00**

ELECTRIC LIGHTING AND HEATING POCKET BOOK. By Sydney F. Walker.

This book puts in convenient form useful information regarding the apparatus which is likely to be attached to the mains of an electrical company. Tables of units and equivalents are included and useful electrical laws and formulas are stated.
One section is devoted to dynamos, motors, transformers and accessory apparatus; another to accumulators, another to switchboards and related equipment, a fourth to a description of various systems of distribution, a fifth section to a discussion of instruments, both for portable use and switchboards; another section deals with electric lamps of various types and accessory appliances, and the concluding section is given up to electric heating apparatus. In each section a large number of commercial types are described, frequent tables of dimensions being included. A great deal of detail information of each line of apparatus is given and the illustrations shown give a good idea of the general appearance of the apparatus under discussion. The book also contains much valuable information for the central station engineer. 438 pages. 300 engravings. Bound in leather pocket book form. Price . **$3.00**

ELECTRIC TOY MAKING, DYNAMO BUILDING, AND ELECTRIC MOTOR CONSTRUCTION. By Prof. T. O'Conor Sloane.

This work treats of the making at home of electrical toys, electrical apparatus, motors, dynamos and instruments in general, and is designed to bring within the reach of young and old the manufacture of genuine and useful electrical appliances. The work is especially designed for amateurs and young folks.
Thousands of our young people are daily experimenting, and busily engaged in making electrical toys and apparatus of various kinds. The present work is just what is wanted to give the much needed information in a plain, practical manner, with illustrations to make easy the carrying out of the work. Price **$1.00**

ELECTRIC WIRING, DIAGRAMS AND SWITCHBOARDS. By Newton Harrison.

This is the only complete work issued showing and telling you what you should know about direct and alternating current wiring. It is a ready reference. The work is free from advanced technicalities and mathematics, arithmetic being used throughout. It is in every respect a handy, well-written, instructive, comprehensive volume on wiring for the wireman, foreman, contractor or electrician. 272 pages; 105 illustrations. Price. **$1.50**

ELECTRICIAN'S HANDY BOOK. By Prof. T. O'Conor Sloane.

This work of 768 pages is intended for the practical electrician who has to make things go. The entire field of electricity is covered within its pages. Among some of the subjects treated are: The Theory of the Electric Current and Circuit, Electro-Chemistry, Primary Batteries, Storage Batteries, Generation and Utilization of Electric Powers, Alternating Current, Armature Winding, Dynamos and Motors, Motor Generators, Operation of the Central Station Switchboards, Safety Appliances, Distribution of Electric Light and Power, Street Mains, Transformers, Arc and Incandescent Lighting, Electric Measurements, Photometry, Electric Railways, Telephony, Bell-Wiring, Electro-Plating, Electric Heating, Wireless Telegraphy, etc. It contains no useless theory; everything is to the point. It teaches you just what you want to know about electricity. It is the standard work published on the subject. Forty-one chapters, 610 engravings, handsomely bound in red leather with title and edges in gold. Price: **$3.50**

ELECTRICITY IN FACTORIES AND WORKSHOPS, ITS COST AND CONVENIENCE. By Arthur P. Haslam.

A practical book for power producers and power users showing what a convenience the electric motor, in its various forms, has become to the modern manufacturer. It also deals with the conditions which determine the cost of electric driving, and compares this with other methods of producing and utilizing power.

Among the chapters contained in the book are: The Direct Current Motor; The Alternating Current Motor; The Starting and Speed Regulation of Electric Motors; The Rating and Efficiency of Electric Motors; The Cost of Energy as Affected by Conditions of Working. The Question for the Small Power User; Independent Generating Plants; Oil and Gas Engine Plants; Steam Plants; Power Station Tariffs; The Use of Electric Power in Textile Factories; Electric Power in Printing Works; The Use of Electric Power in Engineering Workshops Miscellaneous Application of Electric Power; The Installation of Electric Motors; The Lighting of Industrial Establishments. 312 pages. Very fully illustrated. Price. **2.50**

ELECTRICITY SIMPLIFIED. By Prof. T. O'Conor Sloane.

The object of "Electricity Simplified" is to make the subject as plain as possible and to show what the modern conception of electricity is; to show how two plates of different metals immersed in acid can send a message around the globe; to explain how a bundle of copper wire rotated by a steam engine can be the agent in lighting our streets, to tell what the volt, ohm and ampere are, and what high and low tension mean; and to answer the questions that perpetually arise in the mind in this age of electricity. 172 pages. Illustrated. Price **$1.00**

HOW TO BECOME A SUCCESSFUL ELECTRICIAN. By Prof. T. O'Conor Sloane.

Every young man who wishes to become a successful electrician should read this book. It tells in simple language the surest and easiest way to become a successful electrician. The studies to be followed, methods of work, field of operation and the requirements of the successful electrician are pointed out and fully explained. Every young engineer will find this an excellent stepping-stone to more advanced works on electricity which he must master before success can be attained. Many young men become discouraged at the very outstart by attempting to read and study books that are far beyond their comprehension. This book serves as the connecting link between the rudiments taught in the public schools and the real study of electricity. It is interesting from cover to cover. Twelfth edition. 202 pages. Illustrated. Price **$1.00**

MANAGEMENT OF DYNAMOS. By Lummis-Paterson.

A handbook of theory and practice. This work is arranged in three parts. The first part covers the elementary theory of the dynamo. The second part, the construction and action of the different classes of dynamos in common use are described; while the third part relates to such matters as affect the practical management and working of dynamos and motors. The following chapters are contained in the book: Electrical Units; Magnetic Principles; Theory of the Dynamo; Armature; Armature in Practice; Field Magnets; Field Magnets in Practice; Regulating Dynamos; Coupling Dynamos; Installation, Running, and Maintenance of Dynamos; Faults in Dynamos; Faults in Armatures; Motors. 292 pages. 117 illustrations. Price **$1.50**

STANDARD ELECTRICAL DICTIONARY. By T. O'Conor Sloane.

An indispensable work to all interested in electrical science. Suitable alike for the student and professional. A practical hand-book of reference containing definitions of about 5,000 distinct words, terms and phrases. The definitions are terse and concise and include every term used in electrical science. Recently issued. An entirely new edition. Should be in the possession of all who desire to keep abreast with the progress of this branch of science. Complete, concise, and convenient. 682 pages. 393 illustrations. Price **$3.00**

SWITCHBOARDS. By William Baxter, Jr.

This book appeals to every engineer and electrician who wants to know the practical side of things. It takes up all sorts and conditions of dynamos, connections and circuits and shows by diagram and illustration just how the switchboard should be connected. Includes direct and alternating current boards, also those for arc lighting, incandescent, and power circuits. Special treatment on high voltage boards for power transmission. 190 pages. Illustrated. Price **$1.50**

TELEPHONE CONSTRUCTION, INSTALLATION, WIRING, OPERATION AND MAINTENANCE. By W. H. RADCLIFFE and H. C. CUSHING.

This book gives the principles of construction and operation of both the Bell and Independent instruments; approved methods of installing and wiring them; the means of protecting them from lightning and abnormal currents; their connection together for operation as series or bridging stations; and rules for their inspection and maintenance. Line wiring and the wiring and operation of special telephone systems are also treated.
Intricate mathematics are avoided, and all apparatus, circuits and systems are thoroughly described. The appendix contains definitions of units and terms used in the text. Selected wiring tables, which are very helpful, are also included. 100 pages, 125 illustrations. $1.00

WIRING A HOUSE. By HERBERT PRATT.

Shows a house already built; tells just how to start about wiring it; where to begin; what wire to use; how to run it according to Insurance Rules; in fact just the information you need. Directions apply equally to a shop. Fourth edition. . . . . 25 cents

WIRELESS TELEPHONES AND HOW THEY WORK. By JAMES ERSKINE-MURRAY.

This work is free from elaborate details and aims at giving a clear survey of the way in which Wireless Telephones work. It is intended for amateur workers and for those whose knowledge of electricity is slight. Chapters contained: How We Hear; Historical; The Conversion of Sound into Electric Waves; Wireless Transmission; The Production of Alternating Currents of High Frequency; How the Electric Waves are Radiated and Received; The Receiving Instruments; Detectors; Achievements and Expectations; Glossary of Technical Work. Cloth. Price. $1.00

FACTORY MANAGEMENT, ETC.

MODERN MACHINE SHOP CONSTRUCTION, EQUIPMENT AND MANAGEMENT. By O. E. PERRIGO, M.E.

The only work published that describes the modern machine shop or manufacturing plant from the time the grass is growing on the site intended for it until the finished product is shipped. By a careful study of its thirty-two chapters the practical man may economically build, efficiently equip, and successfully manage the modern machine shop or manufacturing establishment. Just the book needed by those contemplating the erection of modern shop buildings, the re-building and re-organization of old ones, or the introduction of modern shop methods, time and cost system. It is a book written and illustrated by a practical shop man for practical shop men who are too busy to read *theories* and want *facts*. It is the most complete all around book of its kind ever published. It is a practical book for practical men, from the apprentice in the shop to the president in the office. It minutely describes and illustrates the most simple and yet the most efficient time and cost system yet devised. Price $5.00

FUEL

COMBUSTION OF COAL AND THE PREVENTION OF SMOKE. By WM. M. BARR.

This book has been prepared with special reference to the generation of heat by the combustion of the common fuels found in the United States, and deals particularly with the conditions necessary to the economic and smokeless combustion of bituminous coals in Stationary and Locomotive Steam Boilers.
The presentation of this important subject is systematic and progressive. The arrangement of the book is in a series of practical questions to which are appended accurate answers, which describe in language, free from technicalities, the several processes involved in the furnace combustion of American fuels; it clearly states the essential requisites for perfect combustion, and points out the best methods of furnace construction for obtaining the greatest quantity of heat from any given quality of coal. Nearly 350 pages, fully illustrated. . . . $1.00

SMOKE PREVENTION AND FUEL ECONOMY. By BOOTH and KERSHAW.

A complete treatise for all interested in smoke prevention and combustion, being based on the German work of Ernst Schmatolla, but it is more than a mere translation of the German treatise, much being added. The authors show as briefly as possible the principles of fuel combustion, the methods which have been and are at present in use, as well as the proper scientific methods for obtaining all the energy in the coal and burning it without smoke. Considerable space is also given to the examination of the waste gases, and several of the representative English and American mechanical stoker and similar appliances are described. The losses carried away in the waste gases are thoroughly analyzed and discussed in the Appendix, and abstracts are also here given of various patents on combustion apparatus. The book is complete and contains much of value to all who have charge of large plants. 194 pages. Illustrated. Price $2.50

9

GAS ENGINES AND GAS

CHEMISTRY OF GAS MANUFACTURE. By H. M. ROYLES.

This book covers points likely to arise in the ordinary course of the duties of the engineer or manager of a gas works not large enough to necessitate the employment of a separate chemical staff. It treats of the testing of the raw materials employed in the manufacture of illuminating coal gas, and of the gas produced. The preparation of standard solutions is given as well as the chemical and physical examination of gas coal including among its contents—Preparations of Standard Solutions, Coal, Furnaces, Testing and Regulation. Products of Carbonization. Analysis of Crude Coal Gas. Analysis of Lime. Ammonia. Analysis of Oxide of Iron. Naphthalene. Analysis of Fire-Bricks and Fire-Clay. Weldom and Spent Oxide. Photometry and Gas Testing. Carburetted Water Gas. Metropolis Gas. Miscellaneous Extracts. Useful Tables. **$4.50**

AGRICULTURAL GAS ENGINES. By XENO W. PUTNAM.

The gas engine within the past few years is being so much used on the farm to simplify work, that the publication of this practical treatise will prove of greatest value. The author takes up first, and treats in detail the working of the engine, then the transmission mediums are treated, as well as traction engines and their application. Price **$1.50**

GAS ENGINE CONSTRUCTION, OR HOW TO BUILD A HALF-HORSE-POWER GAS ENGINE. By PARSELL and WEED.

A practical treatise of 300 pages describing the theory and principles of the action of Gas Engines of various types and the design and construction of a half-horse power Gas Engine, with illustrations of the work in actual progress, together with the dimensioned working drawings giving clearly the sizes of the various details; for the student, the scientific investigator and the amateur mechanic.

This book treats of the subject more from the standpoint of practice than that of theory. The principles of operation of Gas Engines are clearly and simply described and then the actual construction of a half-horse power engine is taken up, step by step, showing in detail the making of the Gas Engine. 300 pages. Price **$2.50**

GAS, GASOLINE, AND OIL ENGINES. By GARDNER D. HISCOX.

Just issued, 18th revised and enlarged edition. Every user of a gas engine needs this book. Simple, instructive, and right up-to-date. The only complete work on the subject. Tells all about the running and management of gas, gasoline and oil engines, as designed and manufactured in the United States. Explosive motors for stationary, marine and vehicle power are fully treated, together with illustrations of their parts and tabulated sizes, also their care and running are included. Electric ignition by induction coil and jump spark are fully explained and illustrated, including valuable information on the testing for economy and power and the erection of power plants.

The rules and regulations of the Board of Fire Underwriters in regard to the installation and management of gasoline motors is given in full, suggesting the safe installation of explosive motor power. A list of United States Patents issued on gas, gasoline, and oil engines and their adjuncts from 1875 to date is included. 484 pages. 410 engravings Price . . **$2.50 net**

MODERN GAS ENGINES AND PRODUCER GAS PLANTS. By R. E. MATHOT, M.E.

A guide for the gas engine designer, user, and engineer in the construction, selection, purchase, installation, operation, and maintenance of gas engines. More than one book on gas engines has been written, but not one has thus far even encroached on the field covered by this book. Above all Mr. Mathot's work is a practical guide. Recognizing the need of a volume that would assist the gas engine user in understanding thoroughly the motor upon which he depends for power, the author has discussed his subject without the help of any mathematics and without elaborate theoretical explanations. Every part of the gas engine is described in detail, tersely, clearly, with a thorough understanding of the requirements of the mechanic. Helpful suggestions as to the purchase of an engine, its installation, care, and operation form a most valuable feature of the work. 320 pages. 175 detailed illustrations. Price . . . **$2.50**

GEARING AND CAMS

BEVEL GEAR TABLES. By D. AG. ENGSTROM.

A book that will at once commend itself to mechanics and draftsmen. Does away with all the trigonometry and fancy figuring on bevel gears and makes it easy for anyone to lay them out or make them just right. There are 36 full-page tables that show every necessary dimension for all sizes or combinations you're apt to need. No puzzling figuring or guessing. Gives placing distance, all the angles (including cutting angles), and the correct cutter to use. A copy of this prepares you for anything in the bevel gear line. 66 pages. . **$1.00**

CHANGE GEAR DEVICES. By OSCAR E. PERRIGO.

A practical book for every designer, draftsman, and mechanic interested in the invention and development of the devices for feed changes on the different machines requiring such mechanism. All the necessary information on this subject is taken up, analyzed, classified, sifted, and concentrated for the use of busy men who have not the time to go through the masses of irrelevant matter with which such a subject is usually encumbered and select such information as will be useful to them.

It shows just what has been done, how it has been done, when it was done, and who did it. It saves time in hunting up patent records and re-inventing old ideas. 88 pages. $1.00

DRAFTING OF CAMS. By LOUIS ROUILLION.

The laying out of cams is a serious problem unless you know how to go at it right. This puts you on the right road for practically any kind of cam you are likely to run up against. 25 cents

HYDRAULICS

HYDRAULIC ENGINEERING. By GARDNER D. HISCOX.

A treatise on the properties, power, and resources of water for all purposes. Including the measurement of streams; the flow of water in pipes or conduits; the horse-power of falling water; turbine and impact water-wheels; wave-motors, centrifugal, reciprocating, and air-lift pumps. With 300 figures and diagrams and 36 practical tables.

All who are interested in water-works development will find this book a useful one, because it is an entirely practical treatise upon a subject of present importance, and cannot fail in having a far-reaching influence, and for this reason should have a place in the working library of every engineer. 320 pages. Price $4.00

ICE AND REFRIGERATION

POCKET BOOK OF REFRIGERATION AND ICE MAKING. By A. J. WALLIS-TAYLOR.

This is one of the latest and most comprehensive reference books published on the subject of refrigeration and cold storage. It explains the properties and refrigerating effect of the different fluids in use, the management of refrigerating machinery and the construction and insulation of cold rooms with their required pipe surface for different degrees of cold; freezing mixtures and non-freezing brines, temperatures of cold rooms for all kinds of provisions, cold storage charges for all classes of goods, ice making and storage of ice, data and memoranda for constant reference by refrigerating engineers, with nearly one hundred tables containing valuable references to every fact and condition required in the installment and operation of a refrigerating plant. Price $1.50

INVENTIONS—PATENTS

INVENTOR'S MANUAL, HOW TO MAKE A PATENT PAY.

This is a book designed as a guide to inventors in perfecting their inventions, taking out their patents and disposing of them. It is not in any sense a Patent Solicitor's Circular, nor a Patent Broker's Advertisement. No advertisements of any description appear in the work. It is a book containing a quarter of a century's experience of a successful inventor, together with notes based upon the experience of many other inventors. Price $1.00

LATHE WORK

MODERN AMERICAN LATHE PRACTICE. By OSCAR E. PERRIGO.

This is a new book from cover to cover, and the only complete American work on the subject written by a man who knows not only how work ought to be done but who also knows how to do it, and how to convey this knowledge to others. It is strictly up-to-date in its descriptions and illustrations, which represent the very latest practice in lathe and boring mill operations as well as the construction of and latest developments in the manufacture of these important classes of machine tools. 424 pages. 314 illustrations. Price $2.50

PRACTICAL METAL TURNING. By JOSEPH G. HORNER.

This important and practical subject is treated in a full and exhaustive manner and nothing of importance is omitted. The principles and practice and all the different branches of Turning are considered and well illustrated. All the different kinds of Chucks of usual forms, as well as some unusual kinds, are shown. A feature of the book is the important section devoted to modern Turret practice; Boring is another subject which is treated fully; and the chapter on Tool Holders illustrates a large number of representative types. Thread Cutting is treated at reasonable length; and the last chapter contains a good deal of information relating to the High-Speed Steels and their work. The numerous tools used by machinists are illustrated, and also the adjuncts of the lathe. In fact, the entire subject is treated in such a thorough manner as to make this book the standard one on the subject. It is indispensable to the manager, engineer, and machinist as well as to the student, amateur, and experimental man who desires to keep up-to-date. 400 pages, fully illustrated. Price $3.50

TURNING AND BORING TAPERS. By FRED H. COLVIN.

There are two ways to turn tapers; the right way and one other. This treatise has to do with the right way; it tells you how to start the work properly, how to set the lathe, what tools to use and how to use them, and forty and one other little things that you should know. Fourth edition. . . . . 25 cents

LIQUID AIR

LIQUID AIR AND THE LIQUEFACTION OF GASES. By T. O'CONOR SLOANE.

This book gives the history of the theory, discovery, and manufacture of Liquid Air, and contains an illustrated description of all the experiments that have excited the wonder of audiences all over the country. It shows how liquid air, like water, is carried hundreds of miles and is handled in open buckets. It tells what may be expected from it in the near future.

A book that renders simple one of the most perplexing chemical problems of the century. Startling developments illustrated by actual experiments.

It is not only a work of scientific interest and authority, but is intended for the general reader, being written in a popular style—easily understood by every one. Second edition. 365 pages. Price $2.00

LOCOMOTIVE ENGINEERING

AIR-BRAKE CATECHISM. By ROBERT H. BLACKALL.

This book is a standard text book. It covers the Westinghouse Air-Brake Equipment, including the No. 5 and the No. 6 E. T Locomotive Brake Equipment; the K (Quick-Service) Triple Valve for Freight Service; and the Cross-Compound Pump. The operation of all parts of the apparatus is explained in detail, and a practical way of finding their peculiarities and defects, with a proper remedy, is given. It contains 2,000 questions with their answers, which will enable any railroad man to pass any examination on the subject of Air Brakes. Endorsed and used by air-brake instructors and examiners on nearly every railroad in the United States. 23d Edition. 380 pages, fully illustrated with folding plates and diagrams. $2.00

AMERICAN COMPOUND LOCOMOTIVES. By FRED. H. COLVIN.

The only book on compounds for the engineman or shopman that shows in a plain, practical way the various features of compound locomotives in use. Shows how they are made, what to do when they break down or balk. Contains sections as follows:—A Bit of History. Theory of Compounding Steam Cylinders. Baldwin Two-Cylinder Compound. Pittsburg Two-Cylinder Compound. Rhode Island Compound. Richmond Compound. Rogers Compound. Schenectady Two-Cylinder Compound. Vauclain Compound. Tandem Compounds. Baldwin Tandem. The Colvin-Wightman Tandem. Schenectady Tandem. Balanced Locomotives. Baldwin Balanced Compound. Plans for Balancing. Locating Blows. Breakdowns. Reducing Valves. Drifting. Valve Motion. Disconnecting. Power of Compound Locomotives. Practical Notes.

Fully illustrated and containing ten special "Duotone" inserts on heavy Plate Paper, showing different types of Compounds. 142 pages. Price $1.00

APPLICATION OF HIGHLY SUPERHEATED STEAM TO LOCOMOTIVES. By ROBERT GARBE.

A practical book. Contains special chapters on Generation of Highly Superheated Steam; Superheated Steam and the Two-Cylinder Simple Engine; Compounding and Superheating; Designs of Locomotive Superheaters; Constructive Details of Locomotives using Highly Superheated Steam; Experimental and Working Results. Illustrated with folding plates and tables. Price $2.50

COMBUSTION OF COAL AND THE PREVENTION OF SMOKE. By WM. M. BARR.

This book has been prepared with special reference to the generation of heat by the combustion of the common fuels found in the United States, and deals particularly with the conditions necessary to the economic and smokeless combustion of bituminous coals in Stationary and Locomotive Steam Boilers.

The presentation of this important subject is systematic and progressive. The arrangement of the book is in a series of practical questions to which are appended accurate answers, which describe in language, free from technicalities, the several processes involved in the furnace combustion of American fuels; it clearly states the essential requisites for perfect combustion, and points out the best methods of furnace construction for obtaining the greatest quantity of heat from any given quality of coal. Nearly 350 pages, fully illustrated. . . . $1.00

LINK MOTIONS, VALVES AND VALVE SETTING. By FRED H. COLVIN, Associate Editor of "American Machinist."

A handy book for the engineer or machinist that clears up the mysteries of valve setting. Shows the different valve gears in use, how they work, and why. Piston and slide valves of different types are illustrated and explained. A book that every railroad man in the motive power department ought to have. Contains chapters on Locomotive Link Motion, Valve Movements, Setting Slide Valves, Analysis by Diagrams, Modern Practice, Slip of Block, Slide Valves, Piston Valves, Setting Piston Valves, Joy-Allen Valve Gear, Walschaert Valve Gear, Gooch Valve Gear, Alfree-Hubbell Valve Gear, etc., etc. Fully illustrated. Price. . . . . **50 cents**

LOCOMOTIVE BOILER CONSTRUCTION. By FRANK A. KLEINHANS.

The construction of boilers in general are treated, and following this, the locomotive boiler is taken up in the order in which its various parts go through the shop. Shows all types of boilers used; gives details of construction; practical facts, such as life of riveting, punches and dies; work done per day, allowance for bending and flanging sheets, and other data. Locomotive boilers present more difficulty in laying out and building than any other type, and for this reason the author uses them as examples. Anyone who can handle them can tackle anything.
Contains chapters on Laying Out Work; Flanging and Forging; Punching; Shearing; Plate Planing; General Tables; Finishing Parts; Bending; Machinery Parts; Riveting; Boiler Details; Smoke Box Details; Assembling and Calking; Boiler Shop Machinery, etc., etc.
There isn't a man who has anything to do with boiler work, either new or repair work, who doesn't need this book. The manufacturer, superintendent, foreman, and boiler worker—all need it. No matter what the type of boiler, you'll find a mint of information that you wouldn't be without. Over 400 pages, five large folding plates. Price **$3.00**

LOCOMOTIVE BREAKDOWNS AND THEIR REMEDIES. By GEO. L. FOWLER. Revised by WM. W. WOOD, Air-Brake Instructor. Just issued. Revised pocket edition.

It is out of the question to try and tell you about every subject that is covered in this pocket edition of Locomotive Breakdowns. Just imagine all the common troubles that an engineer may expect to happen some time, and then add all of the unexpected ones, troubles that could occur, but that you had never thought about, and you will find that they are all treated with the very best methods of repair. Walschaert Locomotive Valve Gear Troubles, Electric Headlight Troubles, as well as Questions and Answers on the Air Brake are all included. 294 pages. Fully illustrated. **$1.00**

LOCOMOTIVE CATECHISM. By ROBERT GRIMSHAW.

The revised edition of "Locomotive Catechism," by Robert Grimshaw, is a New Book from Cover to Cover. It contains twice as many pages and double the number of illustrations of previous editions. Includes the greatest amount of practical information ever published on the construction and management of modern locomotives. Specially Prepared Chapters on the Walschaert Locomotive Valve Gear, the Air Brake Equipment and the Electric Head Light are given.
It commends itself at once to every Engineer and Fireman, and to all who are going in for examination or promotion. In plain language, with full complete answers, not only all the questions asked by the examining engineer are given, but those which the young and less experienced would ask the veteran, and which old hands ask as "stickers." It is a veritable Encyclopedia of the Locomotive, is entirely free from mathematics, easily understood and thoroughly up-to-date. Contains over 4,000 Examination Questions with their Answers. 825 pages, 437 illustrations and three folding plates. **$2.50**

NEW YORK AIR-BRAKE CATECHISM. By ROBERT H. BLACKALL.

This is a complete treatise on the New York Air-Brake and Air-Signalling Apparatus, giving a detailed description of all the parts, their operation, troubles, and the methods of locating and remedying the same. 200 pages, fully illustrated. **$1.00**

POCKET RAILROAD DICTIONARY AND VADE MECUM. By FRED H. COLVIN, Associate Editor "American Machinist."

The Railroad Pocket Book is of value to every man on the road, as it contains valuable Railroad Data, Master Car Builders' Standards, Tests, Proportions of Locomotives and Boilers and various other Rules and Tables.
As a record of recent practice in all sections of railway work it stands alone, giving facts and figures from actual experience on such matters as Acetylene Lighting, Air Brakes, Axles, Bearings, Boilers, Cars, Costs of repairs and other items, Counterbalancing, Curves, Driving Wheels, Equalizers, Flues, Grades, Grates, Heating surfaces, Injectors, Locomotives, Maintenance of way, Oils, Power of Locomotives, Rails, Rods, Shops, Speed, Tires, Turntables, Valve Motions, Water, etc., etc. Second Edition. Price **$1.00**

TRAIN RULES AND DESPATCHING. By H. A. DALBY.

Every railroad man, no matter what department he's in, needs a copy of this book. It gives the standard rules for both single and double track, shows all the signals, with colors wherever necessary, and has a list of towns where time changes, with a map showing the whole country. The rules are explained wherever there is any doubt about their meaning or where they are modified by different railroads. It's the only practical book on train rules in print. Over 220 pages. Leather cover. Price **$1.50**

WALSCHAERT LOCOMOTIVE VALVE GEAR. By WM. W. WOOD.

If you would thoroughly understand the Walschaert Valve Gear you should possess a copy of this book, as the author takes the plainest form of a steam engine—a stationary engine in the rough, that will only turn its crank in one direction—and from it builds up—with the reader's help—a modern locomotive equipped with the Walschaert Valve Gear, complete. The points discussed are clearly illustrated: two large folding plates that show the positions of the valves of both inside or outside admission type, as well as the links and other parts of the gear when the crank is at nine different points in its revolution, are especially valuable in making the movement clear. These employ sliding cardboard models which are contained in a pocket in the cover.
The book is divided into four general divisions, as follows: I. Analysis of the gear. II. Designing and erecting the gear. III. Advantages of the gear. IV. Questions and answers relating to the Walschaert Valve Gear.
This last division contains sixty pertinent questions with full answers on all the features of this type of valve gear, which will be especially valuable to firemen and engineers in preparing for an examination for promotion. Nearly 200 pages. Price **$1.50**

WESTINGHOUSE E—T AIR-BRAKE INSTRUCTION POCKET CATECHISM. By WM. W. WOOD, Air-Brake Instructor.

Here is a book for the railroad man, and the man who aims to be one. It is without doubt the only complete work published on the Westinghouse E-T Locomotive Brake Equipment. Written by an Air Brake Instructor who knows just what is needed. It covers the subject thoroughly. Everything about the New Westinghouse Engine and Tender Brake Equipment, including the Standard No. 5 and the Perfected No. 6 Style of brake, is treated in detail. Written in plain English and profusely illustrated with Colored Plates, which enable one to trace the flow of pressures throughout the entire equipment. The best book ever published on the Air Brake. Equally good for the beginner and the advanced engineer. Will pass any one through any examination. It informs and enlightens you on every point. Indispensable to every engineman and trainman.
Contains examination questions and answers on the E-T equipment. Covering what the E-T Brake is. How it should be operated. What to do when defective. Not a question can be asked of the engineman up for promotion on either the No. 5 or the No. 6 E-T equipment that is not asked and answered in the book. If you want to thoroughly understand the E-T equipment get a copy of this book. It covers every detail. Makes Air Brake troubles and examinations easy. Price **$1.50**

MACHINE SHOP PRACTICE

AMERICAN TOOL MAKING AND INTERCHANGEABLE MANUFACTURING. By J. V. WOODWORTH.

A "shoppy" book, containing no theorizing, no problematical or experimental devices, there are no badly proportioned and impossible diagrams, no catalogue cuts, but a valuable collection of drawings and descriptions of devices, the rich fruits of the author's own experience. In its 500-odd pages the one subject only, Tool Making, and whatever relates thereto, is dealt with. The work stands without a rival. It is a complete practical treatise on the art of American Tool Making and system of interchangeable manufacturing as carried on to-day in the United States. In it are described and illustrated all of the different types and classes of small tools, fixtures, devices, and special appliances which are in general use in all machine manufacturing and metal working establishments where economy, capacity and interchangeability in the production of machined metal parts are imperative. The science of jig making is exhaustively discussed, and particular attention is paid to drill jigs, boring, profiling and milling fixtures and other devices in which the parts to be machined are located and fastened within the contrivances. All of the tools, fixtures, and devices illustrated and described have been or are used for the actual production of work, such as parts of drill presses, lathes, patented machinery, typewriters, electrical apparatus, mechanical appliances, brass goods, composition parts, mould products, sheet metal articles, drop forgings, jewelry, watches, medals, coins, etc. 531 pages. Price **$4.00**

HENLEY'S ENCYCLOPEDIA OF PRACTICAL ENGINEERING AND ALLIED TRADES. Edited by JOSEPH G. HORNER, A. M. I., M. E.

This set of five volumes contains about 2,500 pages with thousands of illustrations, including diagrammatic and sectional drawings with full explanatory details. This work covers the entire practice of Civil and Mechanical Engineering. The best known experts in all branches of engineering have contributed to these volumes. The Cyclopedia is admirably well adapted to the needs of the beginner and the self-taught practical man, as well as the mechanical engineer, designer, draftsman, shop superintendent, foreman, and machinist. The work will be found a means of advancement to any progressive man. It is encyclopedic in scope, thorough and practical in its treatment of technical subjects, simple and clear in its descriptive matter, and without unnecessary technicalities or formulae. The articles are as brief as may be and yet give a reasonably clear and explicit statement of the subject, and are written by men who have had ample practical experience in the matters of which they write. It tells you all you want to know about engineering and tells it so simply, so clearly, so concisely, that one cannot help but understand. As a work of reference it is without a peer. $6.00 per single volume. For complete set of five volumes. Price **$25.00**

MACHINE SHOP ARITHMETIC. By COLVIN-CHENEY.

This is an arithmetic of the things you have to do with daily. It tells you plainly about: how to find areas of figures; how to find surface or volume of balls or spheres; handy ways for calculating; about compound gearing; cutting screw threads on any lathe; drilling for taps; speeds of drills, taps, emery wheels, grindstones, milling cutters, etc.; all about the Metric system with conversion tables; properties of metals; strength of bolts and nuts; decimal equivalent of an inch. All sorts of machine shop figuring and 1,001 other things, any one of which ought to be worth more than the price of this book to you, and it saves you the trouble of bothering the boss. 131 pages. Price . . . . **50 cents**

MECHANICAL MOVEMENTS, POWERS, AND DEVICES. By GARDNER D. HISCOX.

This is a collection of 1,890 engravings of different mechanical motions and appliances, accompanied by appropriate text, making it a book of great value to the inventor, the draftsman, and to all readers with mechanical tastes. The book is divided into eighteen sections or chapters in which the subject matter is classified under the following heads: Mechanical Powers; Transmission of Power; Measurement of Power, Steam Power; Air Power Appliances; Electric Power and Construction, Navigation and Roads; Gearing; Motion and Devices; Controlling Motion; Horological; Mining; Mill and Factory Appliances; Construction and Devices; Drafting Devices; Miscellaneous Devices, etc. 11th edition. 400 octavo pages. Price **$2.50**

MECHANICAL APPLIANCES, MECHANICAL MOVEMENTS AND NOVELTIES OF CONSTRUCTION. By GARDNER D. HISCOX.

This is a supplementary volume to the one upon mechanical movements. Unlike the first volume, which is more elementary in character, this volume contains illustrations and descriptions of many combinations of motions and of mechanical devices and appliances found in different lines of machinery. Each device being shown by a line drawing with a description showing its working parts and the method of operation. From the multitude of devices described, and illustrated, might be mentioned, in passing, such items as conveyors and elevators, Prony brakes, thermometers, various types of boilers, solar engines, oil-fuel burners, condensers, evaporators, Corliss and other value gears, governors, gas engines, water motors of various descriptions, air ships, motors and dynamos, automobile and motor bicycles, railway block signals, car coupes, link and gear motions, ball bearings, breech block mechanism for heavy guns, and a large accumulation of others of equal importance. 1,000 specially made engravings. 396 octavo pages. Price **$2.50**

MODERN MACHINE SHOP CONSTRUCTION, EQUIPMENT AND MANAGEMENT. By OSCAR E. PERRIGO.

The only work published that describes the Modern Machine Shop or Manufacturing Plant from the time the grass is growing on the site intended for it until the finished product is shipped Just the book needed by those contemplating the erection of modern shop buildings, the rebuilding and reorganization of old ones, or the introduction of Modern Shop Methods, time and cost systems. It is a book written and illustrated by a practical shop man for practical shop men who are too busy to read theories and want facts. It is the most complete all-around book of its kind ever published. 400 large quarto pages. 225 original and specially-made illustrations. Price **$5.00**

MACHINE SHOP TOOLS AND SHOP PRACTICE. By W. H. VANDERVOORT.

A work of 555 pages and 673 illustrations, describing in every detail the construction, operation, and manipulation of both hand and machine tools. Includes chapters on filing, fitting, and scraping surfaces; on drills, reamers, taps, and dies; the lathe and its tools; planers, shapers, and their tools; milling machines and cutters; gear cutters and gear cutting; drilling machines and drill work; grinding machines and their work; hardening and tempering; gearing, belting and transmission machinery; useful data and tables. 5th edition. Price **$3.00**

THE MODERN MACHINIST. By JOHN T. USHER.

This is a book showing, by plain description and by profuse engravings, made expressly for the work, all that is best, most advanced, and of the highest efficiency in modern machine shop practice, tools, and implements, showing the way by which and through which, as Mr. Maxim says, "American machinists have become and are the finest mechanics in the world." Indicating as it does, in every line, the familiarity of the author with every detail of daily experience in the shop, it cannot fail to be of service to any man practically connected with the shaping or finishing of metals.

There is nothing experimental or visionary about the book, all devices being in actual use and giving good results. It might be called a compendium of shop methods, showing a variety of special tools and appliances which will give new ideas to many mechanics, from the superintendent down to the man at the bench. It will be found a valuable addition to any machinist's library, and should be consulted whenever a new or difficult job is to be done, whether it is boring, milling, turning, or planing, as they are all treated in a practical manner. Fifth Edition. 320 pages. 250 illustrations. Price. **$2.50**

MODERN MILLING MACHINES: THEIR DESIGN, CONSTRUCTION AND OPERA-TION. By JOSEPH G. HORNER.

This book describes and illustrates the Milling Machine and its work in such a plain, clear, and forceful manner, and illustrates the subject so clearly and completely, that the up-to-date machinist, student, or mechanical engineer cannot afford to do without the valuable information which it contains. It describes not only the early machines of this class, but notes their gradual development into the splendid machines of the present day, giving the design and construction of the various types, forms, and special features produced by prominent manufacturers, American and foreign.

Milling cutters in all their development and modernized forms are illustrated and described, and the operations they are capable of producing upon different classes of work are carefully described in detail, and the speeds and feeds necessary are discussed, and valuable and useful data given for determining these usually perplexing problems. The book is the most comprehensive work published on the subject. 304 pages. 300 illustrations. Price . . **$4.00**

MODERN MECHANISM. Edited by PARK BENJAMIN.

A practical treatise on machines, motors and the transmission of power, being a complete work and a supplementary volume to Appleton's Cyclopedia of Applied Mechanics. Deals solely with the principal and most useful advances of the past few years. 959 pages containing over 1,000 illustrations; bound in half morocco. **$4.00**

"SHOP KINKS." By ROBERT GRIMSHAW.

A book of 400 pages and 222 illustrations, being entirely different from any other book on machine shop practice. Departing from conventional style, the author avoids universal or common shop usage and limits his work to showing special ways of doing things better, more cheaply and more rapidly than usual. As a result the advanced methods of representative establishments of the world are placed at the disposal of the reader. This book shows the proprietor where large savings are possible, and how products may be improved. To the employee it holds out suggestions that, properly applied, will hasten his advancement. No shop can afford to be without it. It bristles with valuable wrinkles and helpful suggestions. It will benefit all, from apprentice to proprietor. Every machinist, at any age, should study its pages. Fifth Edition. Price **$2.50**

THREADS AND THREAD CUTTING. By COLVIN and STABEL.

This clears up many of the mysteries of thread-cutting, such as double and triple threads, internal threads, catching threads, use of hobs, etc. Contains a lot of useful hints and several tables. Price . . . . **25 cents**

TOOLS FOR MACHINISTS AND WOOD WORKERS, INCLUDING INSTRUMENTS OF MEASUREMENT. By JOSEPH G. HORNER.

The principles upon which cutting tools for wood, metal, and other substances are made are identical, whether used by the machinist, the carpenter, or by any other skilled mechanic in their daily work, and the object of this book is to give a correct and practical description of these tools as they are commonly designed, constructed, and used. 340 pages, fully illustrated. Price **$3.50**

MANUAL TRAINING

ECONOMICS OF MANUAL TRAINING. By LOUIS ROUILLION.

The only book published that gives just the information needed by all interested in Manual Training, regarding Buildings, Equipment, and Supplies. Shows exactly what is needed for all grades of the work from the Kindergarten to the High and Normal School. Gives itemized lists of everything used in Manual Training Work and tells just what it ought to cost. Also shows where to buy supplies, etc. Contains 174 pages, and is fully illustrated. Price **$1.50**

MARINE ENGINEERING

MARINE ENGINES AND BOILERS, THEIR DESIGN AND CONSTRUCTION. By DR. G. BAUER, LESLIE S. ROBERTSON, and S. BRYAN DONKIN.

In the words of Dr. Bauer, the present work owes its origin to an oft felt want of a Condensed Treatise, embodying the Theoretical and Practical Rules used in Designing Marine Engines and Boilers. The need for such a work has been felt by most engineers engaged in the construction and working of Marine Engines, not only by the younger men, but also by those of greater experience. The fact that the original German work was written by the chief engineer of the famous Vulcan Works, Stettin, is in itself a guarantee that this book is in all respects thoroughly up-to-date, and that it embodies all the information which is necessary for the design and construction of the highest types of marine engines and boilers. It may be said, that the motive power which Dr. Bauer has placed in the fast German liners that have been turned out of late years from the Stettin Works, represent the very best practice in marine engineering of the present day.

This work is clearly written, thoroughly systematic, theoretically sound; while the character of its plans, drawings, tables, and statistics is without reproach. The illustrations are careful reproductions from actual working drawings, with some well-executed photographic views of completed engines and boilers. 722 pages. 550 illustrations. . . . **$9.00 net**

MINING

ORE DEPOSITS, WITH A CHAPTER ON HINTS TO PROSPECTORS. By J. P. JOHNSON.

This book gives a condensed account of the ore-deposits at present known in South Africa. It is also intended as a guide to the prospector. Only an elementary knowledge of geology and some mining experience are necessary in order to understand this work. With these qualifications, it will materially assist one in his search for metalliferous mineral occurrences and, so far as simple ores are concerned, should enable one to form some idea of the possibilities of any they may find.
Among the chapters given are: Titaniferous and Chromiferous Iron Oxides—Nickel—Copper—Cobalt—Tin—Molybdenum—Tungsten—Lead—Mercury—Antimony—Iron—Hints to Prospectors. **$2.00**

PRACTICAL COAL MINING. By T. H. COCKIN.

An important work, containing 428 pages and 213 illustrations, complete with practical details, which will intuitively impart to the reader, not only a general knowledge of the principles of coal mining, but also considerable insight into allied subjects. The treatise is positively up to date in every instance, and should be in the hands of every colliery engineer, geologist, mine operator, superintendent, foreman, and all others who are interested in or connected with the industry. **$2.50**

PHYSICS AND CHEMISTRY OF MINING. By T. H. BYROM.

A practical work for the use of all preparing for examinations in mining or qualifying for colliery managers' certificates. The aim of the author in this excellent book is to place clearly before the reader useful and authoritative data which will render him valuable assistance in his studies. The only work of its kind published. The information incorporated in it will prove of the greatest practical utility to students, mining engineers, colliery managers, and all others who are specially interested in the present-day treatment of mining problems. Among its contents are chapters on: The Atmosphere; Laws Relating to the Behavior of Gases; The Diffusion of Gases; Composition of the Atmosphere; Sundry Constituents of the Atmosphere; Water; Carbon; Fire-Damp; Combustion; Coal Dust and Its Action; Explosives; Composition of Various Coals and Fuels; Methods of Analysis of Coal; Strata Adjoining the Coal Measures; Magnetism and Electricity; Appendix; Useful Tables, etc.; Miscellaneous Questions. 160 pages. Illustrated. **$2.00**

PATTERN MAKING

PRACTICAL PATTERN MAKING. By F. W. BARROWS.

This is a very complete and entirely practical treatise on the subject of pattern making, illustrating pattern work in wood and metal. From its pages you are taught just what you should know about pattern making. It contains a detailed description of the materials used by pattern makers, also the tools, both those for hand use, and the more interesting machine tools; having complete chapters on the band saw, The Buzz Saw, and the Lathe. Individual patterns of many different kinds are fully illustrated and described, and the mounting of metal patterns on plates for molding machines is included. Price **$2.00**

PERFUMERY

HENLEY'S TWENTIETH CENTURY BOOK OF RECEIPTS, FORMULAS AND PROCESSES Edited by G. D. HISCOX.

The most valuable Techno-chemical Receipt Book published. Contains over 10,000 practical receipts, many of which will prove of special value to the perfumer, a mine of information, up-to-date in every respect. Price, Cloth, $3.00; half morocco **$4.00**

PERFUMES AND THEIR PREPARATION. By G. W. ASKINSON, Perfumer.

A comprehensive treatise, in which there has been nothing omitted that could be of value to the Perfumer. Complete directions for making handkerchief perfumes, smelling-salts, sachets, fumigating pastilles; preparations for the care of the skin, the mouth, the hair, cosmetics, hair dyes and other toilet articles are given, also a detailed description of aromatic substances; their nature, tests of purity, and wholesale manufacture. A book of general, as well as professional interest, meeting the wants not only of the druggist and perfume manufacturer, but also of the general public. Third edition. 312 pages. Illustrated. . **$3.00**

PLUMBING

MECHANICAL DRAWING FOR PLUMBERS. By R. M. Starbuck.

A concise, comprehensive and practical treatise on the subject of mechanical drawing in its various modern applications to the work of all who are in any way connected with the plumbing trade. Nothing will so help the plumber in estimating and in explaining work to customers and workmen as a knowledge of drawing, and to the workman it is of inestimable value if he is to rise above his position to positions of greater responsibility. 150 illustrations. Price **$1.50**

MODERN PLUMBING ILLUSTRATED. By R. M. Starbuck.

This book represents the highest standard of plumbing work. It has been adopted and used as a reference book by the United States Government, in its sanitary work in Cuba, Porto Rico, and the Philippines, and by the principal Boards of Health of the United States and Canada.

It gives connections, sizes and working data for all fixtures and groups of fixtures. It is helpful to the master plumber in demonstrating to his customers and in figuring work. It gives the mechanic and student quick and easy access to the best modern plumbing practice. Suggestions for estimating plumbing construction are contained in its pages. This book represents, in a word, the latest and best up-to-date practice, and should be in the hands of every architect, sanitary engineer and plumber who wishes to keep himself up to the minute on this important feature of construction. 400 octavo pages, fully illustrated by 55 full-page engravings. Price **$4.00**

STANDARD PRACTICAL PLUMBING. By R. M. Starbuck.

A complete practical treatise of 450 pages covering the subject of Modern Plumbing in all its Branches, a large amount of space being devoted to a very complete and practical treatment of the subject of Hot Water Supply and Circulation and Range Boiler Work. Its thirty chapters include about every phase of the subject, one can think of, making it an indispensable work to the master plumber, the journeyman plumber, and the apprentice plumber. Fully illustrated by 347 engravings. Price **$3.00**

RECEIPT BOOK

HENLEY'S TWENTIETH CENTURY BOOK OF RECEIPTS, FORMULAS AND PROCESSES.
Edited by Gardner D. Hiscox.

The most valuable Techno-chemical Receipt Book published, including over 10,000 selected scientific, chemical, technological, and practical receipts and processes.

This is the most complete Book of Receipts ever published, giving thousands of receipts for the manufacture of valuable articles for everyday use. Hints, Helps, Practical Ideas, and Secret Processes are revealed within its pages. It covers every branch of the useful arts and tells thousands of ways of making money and is just the book everyone should have at his command. 800 pages. Price **$3.00**

RUBBER

RUBBER HAND STAMPS AND THE MANIPULATION OF INDIA RUBBER. By T. O'Conor Sloane.

This book gives full details on all points, treating in a concise and simple manner the elements of nearly everything it is necessary to understand for a commencement in any branch of the India Rubber Manufacture. The making of all kinds of Rubber Hand Stamps, Small Articles of India Rubber, U. S. Government Composition, Dating Hand Stamps, the Manipulation of Sheet Rubber, Toy Balloons, India Rubber Solutions, Cements, Blackings, Renovating Varnish, and Treatment for India Rubber Shoes, etc.; the Hektograph Stamp Inks, and Miscellaneous Notes, with a Short Account of the Discovery, Collection, and Manufacture of India Rubber are set forth in a manner designed to be readily understood, the explanations being plain and simple. Second edition. 144 pages. Illustrated. **$1.00**

SAWS

SAW FILINGS AND MANAGEMENT OF SAWS. By Robert Grimshaw.

A practical hand book on filing, gumming, swaging, hammering, and the brazing of band saws, the speed, work, and power to run circular saws, etc. A handy book for those who have charge of saws, or for those mechanics who do their own filing, as it deals with the proper shape and pitches of saw teeth of all kinds and gives many useful hints and rules for gumming, setting, and filing, and is a practical aid to those who use saws for any purpose. New edition, revised and enlarged. Illsutrated. Price **$1.00**

STEAM ENGINEERING

AMERICAN STATIONARY ENGINEERING. By W. E. CRANE.

This book begins at the boiler room and takes in the whole power plant. A plain talk on every-day work about engines, boilers, and their accessories. It is not intended to be scientific or mathematical. All formulas are in simple form so that any one understanding plain arithmetic can readily understand any of them. The author has made this the most practical book in print; has given the results of his years of experience, and has included about all that has to do with an engine room or a power plant. You are not left to guess at a single point. You are shown clearly what to expect under the various conditions; how to secure the best results; ways of preventing "shut downs" and repairs; in short, all that goes to make up the requirements of a good engineer, capable of taking charge of a plant. It's plain enough for practical men and yet of value to those high in the profession. Has a complete examination for a license. **$2.00**

EMINENT ENGINEERS. By DWIGHT GODDARD.

Everyone who appreciates the effect of such great inventions as the Steam Engine, Steamboat, Locomotive, Sewing Machine, Steel Working, and other fundamental discoveries, is interested in knowing a little about the men who made them and their achievements.
Mr. Goddard has selected thirty-two of the world's engineers who have contributed most largely to the advancement of our civilization by mechanical means, giving only such facts as are of general interest and in a way which appeals to all, whether mechanics or not. 280 pages. 35 illustrations. Price **$1.50**

ENGINE RUNNER'S CATECHISM. By ROBERT GRIMSHAW.

A practical treatise for the stationary engineer, telling how to erect, adjust and run the principal steam engines in use in the United States. Describing the principal features of various special and well-known makes of engines: Temper Cut-off, Shipping and Receiving Foundations, Erecting and Starting, Valve Setting, Care and Use, Emergencies, Erecting and Adjusting Special Engines.
The questions asked throughout the catechism are plain and to the point, and the answers are given in such simple language as to be readily understood by anyone. All the instructions given are complete and up-to-date; and they are written in a popular style, without any technicalities or mathematical formulæ. The work is of a handy size for the pocket, clearly and well printed, nicely bound, and profusely illustrated. To young engineers this catechism will be of great value, especially to those who may be preparing to go forward to be examined for certificates of competency; and to engineers generally it will be of no little service, as they will find in this volume more really practical and useful information than is to be found anywhere else within a like compass. 387 pages. Seventh edition. Price. **$2.00**

ENGINE TESTS AND BOILER EFFICIENCIES. By J. BUCHETTI.

This work fully describes and illustrates the method of testing the power of steam engines, turbines and explosive motors. The properties of steam and the evaporative power of fuels. Combustion of fuel and chimney draft; with formulas explained or practically computed. 255 pages, 179 illustrations. **$3.00**

HORSE POWER CHART.

Shows the horse power of any stationary engine without calculation. No matter what the cylinder diameter of stroke; the steam pressure or cut-off; the revolutions, or whether condensing or non-condensing, it's all there. Easy to use, accurate, and saves time and calculations. Especially useful to engineers and designers. . . . . **50 cents**

MODERN STEAM ENGINEERING IN THEORY AND PRACTICE. By GARDNER D. HISCOX

This is a complete and practical work issued for Stationary Engineers and firemen dealing with the care and management of boilers, engines, pumps, superheated steam, refrigerating machinery, dynamos, motors, elevators, air compressors, and all other branches with which the modern engineer must be familiar. Nearly 200 questions with their answers on steam and electrical engineering, likely to be asked by the Examining Board, are included. 487 pages. 405 engravings. Price **$3.00**

STEAM ENGINE CATECHISM. By ROBERT GRIMSHAW.

This unique volume of 413 pages is not only a catechism on the question and answer principle; but it contains formulas and worked-out answers for all the Steam problems that appertain to the operation and management of the Steam Engine. Illustrations of various valves and valve gear with their principles of operation are given. Thirty-four Tables that are indispensable to every engineer and fireman that wishes to be progressive and is ambitious to become master of his calling are within its pages. It is a most valuable instructor in the service of Steam Engineering. Leading engineers have recommended it as a valuable educator for the beginner as well as a reference book for the engineer. It is thoroughly indexed for every detail. Every essential question on the Steam Engine with its answer is contained in this valuable work. Sixteenth edition. Price **$2.00**

STEAM ENGINEER'S ARITHMETIC. By COLVIN-CHENEY.

A practical pocket book for the steam engineer. Shows how to work the problems of the engine room and shows "why." Tells how to figure horse-power of engines and boilers; area of boilers; has tables of areas and circumferences; steam tables; has a dictionary of engineering terms. Puts you on to all all of the little kinks in figuring whatever there is to figure around a power plant. Tells you about the heat unit; absolute zero; adiabatic expansion; duty of engines; factor of safety; and 1,001 other things; and everything is plain and simple—not the hardest way to figure, but the easiest. . . . . **50 cents**

STEAM HEATING AND VENTILATION

PRACTICAL STEAM, HOT-WATER HEATING AND VENTILATION. By A. G. KING.

This book is the standard and latest work published on the subject and has been prepared for the use of all engaged in the business of steam, hot water heating, and ventilation. It is an original and exhaustive work. Tells how to get heating contracts, how to install heating and ventilating apparatus, the best business methods to be used, with "Tricks of the Trade" for shop use. Rules and data for estimating radiation and cost and such tables and information as make it an indispensable work for everyone interested in steam, hot water heating, and ventilation. It describes all the principal systems of steam, hot water, vacuum, vapor, and vacuum-vapor heating, together with the new accelerated systems of hot water circulation, including chapters on up-to-date methods of ventilation and the fan or blower system of heating and ventilation. 367 pages. 300 detailed engravings. Price **$3.00**

STEAM PIPES

STEAM PIPES: THEIR DESIGN AND CONSTRUCTION. By WM. H. BOOTH.

This book fills in a deep gap in scientific literature, as there has been very little written on the practical side of steam pipe construction. Steam piping to-day is such a costly item, and the successful operation of a large plant depends so much upon it, that the problem of minimum cost and maximum efficiency becomes very important. The work is well illustrated in regard to pipe joints, expansion offsets, flexible joints, and self-contained sliding joints for taking up the expansion of long pipes. In fact, the chapters on the flow of steam and expansion of pipes are most valuable to all steam fitters and users. The pressure strength of pipes and method of hanging them is well treated and illustrated. Valves and by-passes are fully illustrated and described, as are also flange joints and their proper proportions, exhaust heads and separators. One of the most valuable chapters is that on superheated steam and the saving of steam by insulation with the various kinds of felting and other materials with comparison tables of the loss of heat in thermal units from naked and felted steam pipes. Contains 187 pages. Price **$2.00**

STEEL

AMERICAN STEEL WORKER. By E. R. MARKHAM.

This book tells how to select, and how to work, temper, harden, and anneal steel for everything on earth. It doesn't tell how to temper one class of tools and then leave the treatment of another kind of tool to your imagination and judgment, but it gives careful instructions for every detail of every tool, whether it be a tap, a reamer or just a screw-driver. It tells about the tempering of small watch springs, the hardening of cutlery, and the annealing of dies. In fact there isn't a thing that a steel worker would want to know that isn't included. Price **$2.50**

HARDENING, TEMPERING, ANNEALING, AND FORGING OF STEEL. By J. V. WOODWORTH.

A new work treating in a clear, concise manner all modern processes for the heating, annealing, forging, welding, hardening, and tempering of steel, making it a book of great practical value to the metal-working mechanic in general, with special directions for the successful hardening and tempering of all steel tools used in the arts, including milling cutters, taps, thread dies, reamers, both solid and shell, hollow mills, punches and dies, and all kinds of sheet metal working tools, shear blades, saws, fine cutlery, and metal cutting tools of all description, as well as for all implements of steel both large and small. In this work the simplest and most satisfactory hardening and tempering processes are given.

The uses to which the leading brands of steel may be adapted are concisely presented, and their treatment for working under different conditions explained, also the special methods for the hardening and tempering of special brands.

A chapter devoted to the different processes for case-hardening is also included, and special reference made to the adoption of machinery steel for tools of various kinds. Price . **$2.50**

WATCH MAKING

WATCHMAKER'S HANDBOOK. By CLAUDIUS SAUNIER.

This famous work has now reached its seventh edition and there is no work issued that can compare to it for clearness and completeness. It contains 498 pages and is intended as a workshop companion for those engaged in Watch-making and allied Mechanical Arts. Nearly 250 engravings and fourteen plates are included. Price **$3.00**

CPSIA information can be obtained
at www.ICGtesting.com
Printed in the USA
BVHW041155290321
603646BV00016B/69